Asylum, Welfare and the Cosmopolitan Ideal

Asylum, Welfare and the Cosmopolitan Ideal: A Sociology of Rights puts forward the argument that rights must be understood as part of a social process: a terrain for strategies of inclusion and exclusion but also of contestation and negotiation. Engaging debate about how 'cosmopolitan' principles and practices may be transforming national sovereignty, Lydia Morris explores this premise through a case study of legal activism, civil society mobilisation, and judicial decision-making. The book documents government attempts to use destitution as a deterrent to control asylum numbers, and examines a series of legal challenges to this policy, spanning a period both before and after the introduction of the Human Rights Act. Lydia Morris shows how human rights can be used as a tool for radical change, and in so doing proposes a multi-layered 'model' for understanding rights. This incorporates political background, policy content, civil society mobilisation, judicial decision-making, and their public impact, and advances a dynamic understanding of rights as part of the recurrent encounter between principles and politics. Rights are therefore seen as both a social product and a social force.

Lydia Morris is a Professor of Sociology at the University of Essex and a member of the Human Rights Centre.

Asylum, Welfare and the Cosmopolitan Ideal

A Sociology of Rights

Lydia Morris

Routledge
Taylor & Francis Group

a GlassHouse book

First published 2010 by Routledge
2 Park Square, Milton Park, Abingdon, Oxon, OX14 4RN

Simultaneously published in the USA and Canada
by Routledge
270 Madison Avenue, New York, NY 10016

A GlassHouse book
Routledge is an imprint of the Taylor & Francis Group, an informa business

© 2010 Lydia Morris

Typeset in Sabon by T&F Books
Printed and bound in Great Britain by CPI Antony Rowe, Chippenham,
Wiltshire

British Library Cataloguing in Publication Data
A catalogue record for this book is available from the British Library

Library of Congress Cataloguing in Publication Data
Morris, Lydia, 1949-
Asylum, welfare and the cosmopolitan ideal a sociology of rights / Lydia
Morris.
   p. cm.
"A GlassHouse book."
1. Asylum, Right of–Social aspects. 2. Human rights. 3. Asylum, Right of–Great
Britain. I. Title.
K3268.3.M67 2010
342.08′3–dc22
2009038245

ISBN 10: 0-415-49773-6 (hbk)
ISBN 13: 978-0-415-49773-2 (hbk)

ISBN 10: 0-203-85528-0 (ebk)
ISBN 13: 978-0-203-85528-7 (ebk)

Contents

Abbreviations   vi
Acknowledgements   viii

1 The right to have rights: fond illusion or credo for our times?   1

2 Asylum immigration and the art of government   23

3 Welfare asylum and the politics of judgement   45

4 Civil society and civil repair   68

5 An emergent cosmopolitan paradigm?   89

6 Civic stratification and the cosmopolitan ideal   107

7 Cosmopolitanism, human rights and judgement   125

8 Conclusion: a sociology of rights   145

Bibliography   158
Index   166

Abbreviations

ASRP	As soon as reasonably practicable
CA	Court of Appeal
CSR	Convention on the Status of Refugees
DL	Discretionary Leave
ECHR	European Convention on Human Rights
EEA	European Economic Area
ELR	Exceptional Leave to Remain
EU	European Union
EWCA	England and Wales Court of Appeal
EWHC	England and Wales High Court
HB	Housing Benefit
HC	High Court
HIG	Housing and Immigration Group
HO	Home Office
HoL	House of Lords
HP	Humanitarian protection
HRA	Human Rights Act
IAP	Inter-agency Partnership
IDT	Inhuman and degrading treatment
ILPA	Immigration Law Practitioners Association
J	Justice
JCHR	Joint Committee on Human Rights
JCWI	Joint Council for the Welfare of Immigrants
JR	Judicial Review
KWNS	Keynesian Welfare National State
LJ	Lord Justice
NAA	National Assistance Act
NASS	National Asylum Support System
NGO	Non-government organisation
NL	New Labour
QBD	Queens Bench Division
RC	Refugee Council

S55	Section 55 (of the 2002 Nationality Asylum and Immigration Act)
SSAC	Social Security Advisory Committee
SSHD	Secretary of State for the Home Department
SSSS	Secretary of State for Social Security
SWPR	Schumpterian Workfare Postnational Regime
UDHR	Universal Declaration of Human Rights
UK	United Kingdom
UKHL	United Kingdom House of Lords
UNHCR	United Nations High Commission for Refugees

Acknowledgements

I would like to take this opportunity to thank the barristers, solicitors and non-governmental organisation workers who shared their time and expertise with extraordinary generosity. I hope this account of the history they helped to make in some way repays their effort. I must also record my thanks to the British Academy/Leverhulme Trust, for the award of a Senior Research Fellowship. This freed me from departmental duties for a year during which I was able to write up the core chapters of this book. Finally, I would like to thank Robert Fine, with whom I discussed many aspects of this work, for his interest and encouragement.

Four chapters of this work are based on articles published in the course of writing up my material, and I would like to acknowledge the journals concerned, as follows:

'Asylum welfare and the politics of judgment', *Journal of Social Policy*, 2010, 39:1–20, which provides the basis for Chapter 3.

'Welfare, asylum and civil society: a case study in civil repair', *Citizenship Studies*, 2009, 13:365–79, which provides the basis for Chapter 4.

'An emergent cosmopolitan paradigm? – asylum, welfare and human rights', *British Journal of Sociology*, 2009, 60:215–315, which provides the basis for Chapter 5.

'Civic stratification and the cosmopolitan ideal: the case of welfare and asylum', *European Societies*, 2009, 11:603–24, which provides the basis for Chapter 6.

Chapter 2 draws partially on the following previously published work:

'Governing at a distance', *International Migration Review*, 1998, 32:949–73.
'New Labour's Community of Rights', *Journal of Social Policy*, 2007, 36:39–57.

Chapter 1

The right to have rights

Fond illusion or credo for our times?

> We became aware of the existence of a right to have rights and a right to belong to some kind of organised community only when millions of people had emerged who had lost and could not regain those rights.
>
> (Arendt, 1979:297)

Hannah Arendt was writing of the stateless persons generated by the breakup of four[1] multinational empires in the aftermath of the First World War. However, her comments were prompted by a dilemma which is still apparent in contemporary society and which stems from the problematic relationship between citizenship and human rights, as illuminated by the position of cross-border migrants and more especially asylum seekers. This book examines the extent to which human rights can be evoked to support the rights of asylum seekers denied access to the necessities of life while their claim is being assessed. In so doing, it also considers a much broader question; the role of rights in drawing the moral boundaries of the community we live in, and in securing dignity and respect for the vulnerable. This first chapter therefore begins by considering the problem of rights in the light of the historical relationship between citizenship and human rights: Arendt's paradox. It then goes on to examine a variety of sociological approaches to the practice of rights as a contested terrain in which the role of judgement is increasingly significant. When large numbers of people live outside of their national country of origin, determining decisions on the contours and content of rights provides a barometer by which we can measure practical commitment to the notion of a shared humanity and the cosmopolitan ideal.

Arendt's paradox

The idea of universal rights, possessed by people as a direct result of their humanity, grew out of a tradition of natural law which was given expression at the end of the eighteenth century in the Declaration of the Rights of Man and Citizen. This declaration acted in large part as a guarantee of protection for the individual against the sovereign actions of the state (Arendt, 1979:291). However, the pairing of man and citizen is curious and as Agamben (1998:126) has noted, begs questions about the nature and purpose of the distinction, which appears to subsume 'citizen' under the broader category of 'man'. For Arendt, writing in 1948, the distinction acquired a different meaning when the appearance of stateless persons on a large scale demonstrated that people without full membership of a national polity *via* citizenship had no institutionalised means of claiming their 'inalienable' human rights. This is what I here term 'Arendt's paradox'.

The rights associated with the Rights of Man and Citizen were addressed to claims arising in the context of a given political community, rather than to trans-national movements emerging from the breakup of empires. Hence, within the nation-states of inter-war Europe it seemed that only people of the appropriate national origin could enjoy access to those rights, to the extent that even naturalised citizens were commonly assimilated into the status of alien (Arendt, 1979:285). Although Arendt herself embraced the idea of rights to be guaranteed by virtue of humanity alone, a lingering concern was captured in her fear that: 'It is by no means certain whether this is possible' (p. 298). Her writing on this matter, in the context of her work on the origins of totalitarianism, is particularly striking when read against one of the foundational documents of modern cosmopolitan thought, Kant's 'To Perpetual Peace' (1994). In this philosophical sketch the sole cosmopolitan right identified is a right to hospitality:

> the right of an alien not to be treated as an enemy upon his arrival in another's country. *If it can be done without destroying him*, he can be turned away; but as long as he behaves peaceably he cannot be treated as an enemy.
>
> (Kant, 1994: para 358)

This is, in effect, a right to refuge.

Arendt's reflections coincided with the formulation of the Universal Declaration of Human Rights (UDHR) in 1948, which was followed by a variety of more specialised instruments made available for ratification. These included the European Convention for the Protection of Human Rights and Fundamental Freedoms (ECHR), in force since 1953, and the Convention on the Status of Refugees (CSR), in force since 1954. The non-binding UDHR includes the right to seek and enjoy asylum but places no obligation on countries to offer asylum, and while the CSR requires of signatory countries a commitment to *non-refoulement*,[2] this first assumes access to a national territory. The ECHR provides a raft of basic rights, and though some may be subject to qualification there are a small number which are absolute in nature, and thus aspire to be truly universal. Such instruments do not necessarily challenge the nation-state framework that Arendt remarks upon, insofar as they require voluntary adherence or ratification by individual nations. However, they have gone some considerable way towards institutionalising human rights within an enforceable legal framework. Nevertheless, Arendt's comments have a haunting quality and retain some salience in contemporary society, where the refugee still stands as the principal subject and true test of cosmopolitan right.

Benhabib (2004) links Arendt's paradox to a dilemma at the heart of liberal democracy; the tension between sovereign self-determination and adherence to universal human rights. In Benhabib's account, the rights of the citizen rest upon the rights of man, such that the two are co-implicated (p. 43); modern democracies embrace universal principles, but apply them within the context of a bounded civil and political community. Accordingly, her analysis of 'a right to have rights' illuminates a problem. The first instance of the word 'right' in this phrase implies membership in a community of consociates to whom the right is addressed, while the second instance of the term refers to the rights that follow from this membership. Thus the right to have rights rests upon a status of belonging within some form of rights-granting community which then has a duty to honour the claim to a variety of contingent rights. Without such membership the right to have rights had no force and this led Arendt to conclude that, in the absence of any juridico-political community to adjudicate *universal* claims, the loss of citizenship was tantamount to a loss of human rights altogether. As Michelman (1996:203) puts it:

> As matters have developed ... the having of rights depends on receipt of a special sort of social recognition and acceptance – that is, of one's juridical status within some particular concrete community.

In Agamben's (1998) nihilistic account, which draws heavily on Arendt's analysis, a category of 'bare life' excluded from the polis will always exist, for however the lines are drawn, the rights of the insider are defined against a category of outsider, such that the two are co-dependent.

Arendt was by no means so fatalistic, but clearly saw that identification of the Rights of Man with nationally sovereign states contained problems which only came to light when significant numbers of people lacked their own political community and therefore the status of membership. She fully appreciated the irony of a situation in which human rights acquired a new connotation as little more than a right of exception (p. 293); a protection for the underprivileged and for those with nothing else to fall back on. Any attempt to claim these rights broke down when states were confronted with 'the abstract nakedness of being human' (p. 299). Hence:

> The paradox involved in the loss of human rights is that such loss coincides with the instant when a person becomes a human being in general ... and different in general, representing nothing but his own absolutely unique individuality ...
>
> (p. 302)

Arendt saw that then, as now, the sphere of international law operated in terms of reciprocal agreements and treaties between sovereign states, that a sphere above nations did not exist, and that every new republic necessarily drew lines of inclusion and exclusion. Yet while she was conscious of the tensions inherent in the nation-state system, she was also deeply suspicious of the idea of a world government, especially given the crimes against humanity which had emerged as 'a speciality of totalitarian regimes' (p. 298). Thus, in her view, a benign universalism would by no means be the guaranteed outcome of any system of global governance.

The situation today is somewhat changed, in that a plethora of treaties and conventions now exists and can be called into play to assert the rights of non-citizens, and in some cases be tested in international and/or national courts. However, access to these rights is commonly administered by the nation-state, which remains the principal unit of membership.[3] Although the treatment of those on national territory is by no means unchecked, and the nation-states of Europe are legally bound by a variety of trans-national instruments, the right of control over entry and stay is still a fiercely protected sovereign privilege. While 'free movement' within the European Union (EU) stands as an exception to this rule, it is hedged with caution; the external borders of the EU are ever more tightly policed, and there has been a simultaneous increase in internal controls (see Morris, 2002). For those seeking to claim asylum, Kant's original cosmopolitan right, an application will normally first require presence within the territory of the receiving country, and a variety of devices are in play which make arrival prohibitively difficult (Cruz, 1995; Morris, 2002). This aptly captures Benhabib's liberal democratic dilemma, described by Habermas as the Janus-faced nature of the nation-state. Thus:

> The tension between the universalism of an egalitarian legal community and the particularism of a community united by historical destiny is built into the very concept of the national state.
>
> (Habermas, 1998:115)

Cosmopolitanism and communitarianism are therefore locked in a struggle which has yet to be resolved.

In an era of high levels of immigration and asylum seeking, a tension exists between the demand for universal rights and protections, and the practices of nation-states operating on the basis of exclusive rights of membership. Yet while membership of the nation-state is determined by citizenship status, presence on the national territory is not. Indeed:

> There has never been perfect overlap between the circle of those who stand under the law's authority and the full members of the demos.
>
> (Benhabib, 2004:20)

The issue of who has what claim to which rights is not, therefore, determined once and for all by the question of membership, but is revisited in the context of a global competition for skilled labour, of family members wishing to rejoin their migrant kin, and of civil wars and oppressive regimes generating large numbers of asylum seekers. While modern democracies in contemporary society have undertaken commitments which govern these and other situations, through the ratification and implementation of a wide variety of transnational instruments, the actual content and delivery of many of the rights at issue remain subject to qualification, limitation and interpretation. Rights may be reciprocal and therefore limited to citizens of co-signatory states, they may apply only to those legally present on the territory, or they may have a variety of other conditions attached. Some of the so-called universal human rights can be qualified, with reference to national security, public safety or the economic well-being of the country, while even those rights which are absolute raise difficult questions of interpretation and application. The practice and language of human rights therefore opens up an uncertain terrain of claims making, deliberation and negotiation, and one specific example is detailed in the chapters to follow. The present introduction, however, is cast more broadly and will examine sociological approaches to the understanding and analysis of rights in practice, with a view to elaborating the contemporary resonance of a 'right to have rights'.

Membership and equal status

Marshall's (1950) famous essay 'Citizenship and Social Class' is in fact an essay about rights; their historical development, their mutual interdependence, and their importance in confirming equal social standing or status. As such, it is an interesting precursor of more recent work linking rights to recognition (Taylor, 1994; Honneth, 1995), an important theme of the present study. In viewing citizenship as a status of inclusion, Marshall explicitly addresses only one aspect of Arendt's paradox, but his work offers a number of insights of more general significance which have direct relevance for an understanding of the practice of rights. The essay is well known as an account of the gradual development of civil, political and social rights in Britain, each right being associated with a different century, and each underpinned by different institutional supports. Marshall's argument is that the rights associated with the equal status of citizenship were extracted from the status dimension of social class, robbing class inequality of much of its force and acting as a source of social stability. Hence:

> There is a basic human equality associated with the concept of full membership of a community ... [such that] the inequality of the social class system may be acceptable provided equality of citizenship is recognised.
>
> (Marshall, 1950:6)

His focus on stability should not blind us to the recognition in his work of a series of status struggles – against serfdom in the case of civil rights; against economic privilege in the case of political rights; and against social ostracism in the case of social rights. In this connection, Marshall also recognised the indivisibility of rights, seeing the significance of civil rights in the fight for political and social rights, and the importance of social rights for the full enjoyment of all other rights. With respect to the latter, he provides what might be construed as a definition of social inclusion, which encompasses a range of factors:

> from the right to a modicum of economic welfare and security to the right to share to the full in the social heritage and to live the life of a civilised being according to the standards prevailing in society.
>
> (Marshall, 1950:8)

Conversely, he was aware of the force of class prejudice and economic inequality as a bar to the full realisation of rights which were formally held, hence invoking two contrasting dimensions of status – formal status determining legal entitlement, and informal status attaching to wealth and power.

While Marshall's interest in these issues was in relation to the development and functioning of a system of full social inclusion through citizenship, we can derive from his work an analytical framework which associates rights with status and recognition, and sees in rights a foundation on which social relations are built. In this respect, one of the idealised functions of an inclusive model of citizenship lies in breaking down status distinctions within society, leading to Marshall's conclusion that the basic human equality associated with full membership compensates for other forms of inequality. In his view:

> Inequalities can be tolerated within a fundamentally egalitarian society provided they are not dynamic, that is to say that they do not create incentives which spring from dissatisfaction ...
>
> (Marshall, 1950:44)

However, 'dissatisfaction' in relation to entitlements has driven a variety of civil society movements in the quest for a fuller realisation of rights and the recognition which accompanies them.

As noted, Marshall's work addresses only one side of Arendt's paradox, the guaranteed inclusion associated with citizenship, and seems blinkered against the associated exclusion which denies rights to those who do not possess full membership. This has, of course, been one common criticism. However, if we read the essay less as a treatise on citizenship and more as a sociological treatment of rights, then we find some insights which may help to address the other side of the paradox. Marshall recognised, for example, that rights themselves can function as a source of inequality, through differentiated entitlement, access and implementation. He was also aware of the role of rights in conferring social status, thus providing a form of recognition, raising expectations of legitimate treatment, and illuminating remaining inequalities and injustice. Indeed, the basic human equality he describes was also thought to make other inequalities more open to challenge, and to encourage an associated aim of removing all those inequalities which could not be regarded as legitimate.

Thus, while Marshall has been criticised for his implicit evolutionary approach to the unfolding of rights, his account is by no means blind to struggle (Bottomore, 1992:55–56) and such struggle has often been apparent in the case of migrants and asylum seekers. Commentators have sometimes argued that we are now on the brink of a fourth stage of rights (eg Bottomore, 1992; Turner, 1993; Soysal, 1994; Habermas, 2001) in the form of claims to membership and inclusion beyond the status of national citizenship, and framed in terms of universal human rights or cosmopolitan citizenship. To avoid the charge of an assumed evolutionary development often aimed at Marshall, however, these speculations must be paired with an awareness that rights can contract as well as expand.

Criticisms of Marshall derive in part from the fact that (despite writing at more or less the same time as Arendt) his essay is not attuned to the problems of our times, which have brought to the fore the exclusions created by citizenship. One mode of criticism attacks from the outside, focusing on this taken-for-granted view of the nation-state and Marsall's failure to deal with national closure and the position of non-citizens. The other attacks from the inside, and addresses the false universals underpinning traditional conceptions of citizenship and their accompanying blindness to particularity. In fact, Marshall's essay itself provides some tools which can help to advance both positions.

Citizenship from the outside and the inside

The fact that citizenship creates categories of insiders and outsiders is clear from Arendt's work, and her concern that exclusion from the formal status of membership meant an exclusion from all rights. One optimistic response to this exclusionary aspect of citizenship has been to argue (Soysal, 1994) that with growing trans-national migration and the expansion of trans-national agreements we have entered a period of 'post-nationalism' in which citizenship has been superseded by residence, and in which non-citizens have access to rights by virtue of universal personhood. While these claims are not entirely without foundation, they seem to overstate the case and to simplify a complex and constantly changing picture. A corresponding literature has therefore grown up with a view to demonstrating the limits of the post-national position. This literature paints a picture in which formal entitlements are granted selectively, informal impediments to the realisation of formally held entitlement are rife, and the contours of rights are constantly shifting (Joppke, 1998; Bloch and Schuster, 2002; Morris, 2002).

A third body of literature has now emerged with the capacity to embrace both the optimism of the post-national position and the scepticism of its critics, under the banner of cosmopolitanism. This literature takes its bearings from Kant's (1994) model for perpetual peace in which the rights of individuals are guaranteed by the republican constitution of every nation. The nation then enters into a contract dedicated to the maintenance and security of each nation's freedom, in which a cosmopolitan right of hospitality is extended to strangers in peril. In its current guise cosmopolitan scholarship has three dimensions (Beck, 2006): a normative element seeks to advance the values given expression by the principles of universal human rights; a methodological element contests the reification of society as a national space; and an empirical element documents manifestations of cosmopolitanism in the contemporary world. There is no assumption that a cosmopolitan condition has now been achieved, but rather an awareness of and sensitivity to social and political change which may move us in that direction.

The transformative aim of this movement is to 'denature and decentre' conceptions of the nation-state, and in so doing to 'emancipate social science from its bounded national presuppositions', and social theory from a 'container' approach to society (Fine, 2007:5–7). Among its empirical referents are trans-national migration and asylum seeking, the consolidation and expansion of international instruments for the protection of human rights, and the gradual emergence of a multi-layered global order. The hope is that these features will combine at the national level to produce a constitutional patriotism wedded to the principles of universal human rights (Habermas, 1998). Such a movement would relativise national ways of life, grant strangers the same rights as citizens, and enlarge tolerance and respect for others (Fine, 2007). At the trans-national level the aim is to produce forms of political community which transcend the nation-state, and an adherence to principles which can underpin the emergence of a global form of citizenship (Habermas, 2001).

A strength of the cosmopolitan perspective is that it can also inform a critical approach to the inclusive guarantees of citizenship status. One aspect of cosmopolitan writing therefore addresses different modes of dealing with difference, and directs our attention to the varied manifestations of cosmopolitanism in everyday life, asking how people deal with difference and borders under conditions of global interdependence (Beck, 2006). Claims to cultural recognition have come to contest an exclusionary aspect of citizenship, which in this case is operated from within, and are captured by the notion of a right to be different. A universalism based on respect for others as equals is argued by Beck (2006) to neglect the importance of difference for identity, and to contain no requirement of respect for difference. In this context, Taylor (1994) has argued for the collective cultural rights of minorities as a form of recognition which is a necessary basis for their self-respect and sense of identity. However,

Beck (2006) has a further concern, that while diversity should be accorded intrinsic value, cultural recognition may foster a relativism allied with notions of incommensurability which is inimical to the cosmopolitan project.

Failure to address cultural difference and cultural rights has been one source of criticism levelled at Marshall's approach to citizenship, linked to his neglect of inequalities which can operate inside the ostensibly 'universal' guarantees of citizenship. Beck (2006) sees in this issue a challenge for cosmopolitan thinking and argues for a contextualised universalism which accepts cultural inter-mingling as a historical reality and rejects the either/or opposition of universalism and relativism. He therefore seeks a means of combining sameness and difference through a contextualised universalism, which implies different cultural routes to shared universal values, echoing Parekh's (2006) minimal universalism. In taking this position, Beck rejects what he terms an essentialising approach to identity, which views individuals as epiphenomena of their cultures, and instead valorises hybridity, diaspora, rootlessness, and 'living between'.

In the course of setting out these arguments, Beck touches on a more concrete problem, which emerges when self-consciousness of difference and awareness of entitlement combine with experiences of disadvantage and discrimination. The matter at issue here is not the accommodation of cultural difference per se, but that of informal impediments to the realisation of formally held entitlement. Though Marshall foresaw the possibility that discriminatory factors such as prestige, wealth and power could distort the ideal of a universal status of citizenship, it has fallen to more contemporary writers to fully develop the implications of this insight. One example can be found in the feminist critique of Marshall (Philips, 1992; Lister, 2003), which addresses his neglect of the gendered assumptions shaping citizenship. This critique challenges the public/private divisions informing conceptions of rights and the 'false universals' which underpin the traditional guarantees of citizen-ship. A similar argument could be made with respect to the neglect of cultural difference, and the ethno-centric nature of the functioning of many rights. Both positions can in turn be linked to an emphasis on the embodiment of rights and the lived experience of difference, which of course applies not just to gender or culture but to race, ethnicity, sexuality, disability and age. Such dynamics are writ large in the application and interpretation of universal human rights.

Differentiated rights

While Beck touches on the issue of inequality with respect to rights his account is focused on the dilemmas posed by cultural difference, yet cosmopolitanism also needs to address the constructed inequalities which accompany difference. As noted above, these may be informal in nature, as in many cases of ethnic, gender, or age discriminations, but can also take the form of differentiated legal entitlement. There is therefore a growing interest in empirical study of both the dynamic unfolding of rights and of what might be termed rights in practice (Morris, 2006), which takes in all matters pertaining to their allocation, contestation and delivery. The formal allocation of rights first requires the creation of an appropriate legal status, as in 'the right to have rights', or as Habermas (2001:114) puts this:

> A legal community has a spatio-temporal location and protects its members only insofar as they acquire the artificial status of bearers of individual rights.

The word 'artificial' here presumably refers to the fact that rights are a social product, and rest on constructed categories of legal persons, so a first step in assessing moves towards a more cosmopolitan society would be to consider what categories carry which formal entitlements. In taking this step it soon becomes clear that rights are not simply a means of conferring recognition and asserting equality, but are also a means of constructing inequality.

Despite Marshall's account of citizenship as a status which guarantees equal respect and full social inclusion, he was aware that the practice often fell short of this ideal. Lockwood (1996) translates this insight into a mode of analysis by outlining a system of civic stratification, that is, a pattern of inequality which exists by virtue of the rights that are granted or denied by the state. In addressing the extent to which citizenship fulfils its promise of securing social integration, Lockwood uncovers a variety of ways in which the practice of citizenship generates inequalities in terms of both the formal possession of entitlement and the informal disadvantages and discriminations which may prevent full enjoyment of a right. While he is principally concerned with inequalities generated within the status of citizenship itself, the approach readily lends itself to the analysis of a variety of positions which fall outside of citizenship. This is the main thrust of Brubaker's (1989) work, which measures the nation-state ideal against varied practices of partial membership. In his account of the idealised model of membership, citizenship is egalitarian, sacred, national, democratic and unique; that is pertaining to a sole nation, which commands dedication, and permits democratic participation. Correspondingly, the nation-state is therefore doubly bounded, by both territory and membership, but Brubaker's real interest lies with empirical departures from this ideal.

Brubaker recognises a tendency for long-term residents to be accorded most of the rights of citizens, though rarely core political rights, and he sees in this a devaluation of citizenship. However, it might rather be argued that citizenship is not so much being devalued as disaggregated (Benhabib, 2004) such that the various rights which are conferred by full membership now attach to differing degrees and in different combinations to a variety of lesser statuses. Brubaker therefore analyses the different goods which attach to a variety of positions of partial membership, while Morris (2002) shows how such a system of differentiated entitlement has acted as a means to attract or repel different categories of migrant. So, for example, global competition for skilled workers has led some countries to offer preferential terms of access to the labour market and ease of transition to secure residence. Conversely, as we see in later chapters, the erosion of welfare rights for some categories of asylum seeker has been used to deter arrival. The finessing of such a system of stratified rights has been a key feature in the development of systems of managed migration and illustrates the way in which rights become implicated in systems of control. Thus, states not only police entry to their territory but also exert control over the distribution of collective goods, whose conditions of access provide a basis for the monitoring and surveillance of holders of a variety of immigration statuses (Morris, 1998).

A harnessing of rights in the quest for control may usefully be viewed in Foucauldian terms as part of a process of 'governmentality', outlined by Foucault (1991:102) in his lectures on Security, Territory and Population. Focusing as it does on the management of resources and the government of a population in the context of territorial sovereignty, the concept has a particular salience for the study of migration and the management of 'outsider' groups. Though this topic was not addressed by Foucault himself, he describes the process of governmentality in terms of:

> The ensemble formed by the institutions, procedures, analyses and reflections, the calculations and tactics that allow the exercise of this very specific albeit complex form of power.
>
> (Foucault, 1991:102)

There are two dimensions to this process (see Rose and Miller, 1992): the political rationality or epistemology underlying government action and the technologies of government, or strategies, techniques and procedures by which it is pursued. These two dimensions of governmentality combine in the practice of 'governing at a distance' (Rose and Miller, 1992:181). The object of study thus becomes the proliferation of practices which permeate the structures and institutions of civil society. What emerges is a picture of regulation which cross-cuts conventional distinctions between the political and non-political, operating through the 'delegation of regulatory oversight (and power) to the micro-level' (Gordon, 1991:26). Gordon also notes a related process of the 'disciplinarization of the state' (p. 27) in which the state's disciplinary technique is focused on the organisation of its own staffs and apparatuses.

We can therefore see how the elaboration of a system of differentiated rights, or 'civic stratification' might function as part of the process of governmentality. This process rests on the classification of different population groups into a variety of citizenship or immigration statuses with different associated forms of entitlement (Morris, 2004). Where conditions attach to the realisation of a right, as, for example, the UK rule of 'no recourse to public funds' for statuses outside of secure residence (JCWI, 1997), monitoring and surveillance will be a necessary aspect of their administration. With some conditions, such as the prohibition on paid employment, the monitoring process extends beyond state personnel to implicate employers in the policing of immigration (see Migrant Rights Network, 2008). In other instances, the very mode of provision has monitoring and control built in, as in various regimes of housing and maintenance for asylum seekers (eg Dwyer, 2005), such that denial of support can mean a consequent loss of this monitoring capacity. More generally, such measures can fall short of their justificatory rationale in a number of ways, including effects on non-targeted groups, unwieldy and costly administration, and constraints flowing from judicial oversight. Indeed, the functioning of a system of differentiated rights is a constantly shifting process as the strategies and objectives of both migrants and government change, and as the system itself meets active resistance.

Recognition and the shifting contours of rights

One approach to differential entitlement might involve a mapping of the varied citizenship/immigration statuses in play, and their associated bundles of rights. This however, begs the question of how such a classification of persons comes into being, and once established, how far it is amenable to change. In other words, it raises questions about the social construction of rights. Fine (2007:58) implicitly raises this issue in his discussion of cosmopolitanism, noting a tendency on the part of Habermas (2006) to depict political and intellectual choice as a law of nature, and to turn the constitutionalisation of rights into a form of natural law. This is argued to underestimate the role of political judgement in determining the balance between the social norms of an immediate national community and those of a more distant world community (Fine, 2007:127). In fact, a number of writers, Habermas included, have looked to the input of civil society as a key factor in shaping the outcome of such deliberation, and hence the contours of rights themselves (Habermas, 1996; Alexander, 2006; Fine, 2007). In addressing this process Donnelly (2003:36) notes that:

> The struggle of dispossessed groups has typically been a struggle for full legal and political recognition by the state and thus inclusion among those whose rights are protected by the state.

He speaks of a moral claim which precedes the process of legal conferral while Plummer (2006) envisages a sequence which begins with the 'imagining' of a right, followed by a quest for public recognition and legitimacy. Levy and Sznaider (2006) capture a similar dynamic when they speak of 'norm entrepreneurs'. All require the framing of an issue such that it engages public interest and sympathy as a first step towards formal institutionalisation.

Honneth (1995) has developed a framework for thinking about rights as a form of recognition, such that an individual's self-realisation depends on the positive social judgements of their fellows, which take place within the value nexus of a specific political community. Drawing on Hegel, Honneth seeks to break with atomistic conceptions of rights to see the community in terms of an ethical unity in which mores and customs offer a value framework within which individual subjects have their being. Society's ethical relations therefore present a form of practical inter-subjectivity which contains the potential for moral tension and conflict over the quest for recognition. The construction of the social world can therefore be seen as emerging via various stages of struggle driven by demands for reciprocal recognition, which Honneth suggests may be fuelled by experiences of social disrespect.

Applying this insight to Marshall's work, Honneth sees a decoupling of rights claims from the ascription of social status, the former being rooted in general principles of equality and best understood as the outcome of social struggles. However, he observes that while modern law offers a medium of recognition based on universal qualities, *social* worth is measured by the degree to which individuals can contribute to the realisation of specific societal goals. The mutual recognition embodied in citizenship is therefore tied to the presupposition that membership means a shared conception of these goals, thus forming the basis of a functioning ethical community. However, he sees in this nexus a culturally pre-given value order in which social groups will tend to deny access for non-members, while this underprivileging will in turn produce a sense of personal shame.

Honneth's central interest lies in the question of how far individuals can be liberated from social shame by active movements of protest and resistance (Honneth, 1995:121). He argues that in the historical unfolding of rights, collective confrontations which sought to establish new values led to legal relations which incorporated social esteem through the concept of universal human dignity. The cultural framework for assessing individuals was thus reduced to social honour or prestige, expressed in terms of the social recognition earned by contributing to societal goals. However, Honneth sees a tension built into this modern organisation of esteem which leaves it permanently subject to social conflict, such that an absence of recognition or active disrespect can provide the motivation for political resistance. This will occur wherever the experience of disrespect or mis-recognition finds a means of articulation through the mobilisation of social movements, and is thus transformed into a collective struggle for recognition.

This connection between rights, recognition and social honour is found in rather different but nonetheless comparable form in Lockwood's (1996) account of civic stratification, which ties full enjoyment of a right to the moral and/or material resources of the individual. Again a linkage is made to the scope for collective expressions of discontent in response to a variety of forms of what Honneth would term disrespect. Lockwood starts from the assumption that citizenship establishes a common legal status, whereby:

> All that remains of hierarchical status is the weaker form of social inclusion and exclusion, (and) of deference and derogation.
>
> (Lockwood, 1996:533)

However, there are imperfections in the functioning of citizenship, and these are argued to be most glaring when identifiable social categories are denied full rights, either *de jure*, as in the case of some migrant workers, or *de facto*, as in the case of the 'civic disabilities' attaching to race, gender or ethnicity. Lockwood speaks of 'civic exclusion' where there is formal denial of a right and of 'civic deficit' where lack of resources prevents the exercise of a right, or where exercise of the right is in itself stigmatising. So, for example, the value of self-responsibility may translate into demerit in the case of state dependants, a group increasingly singled out as lacking civic virtue and which therefore has no 'moral leverage'. Lockwood also notes corresponding cases of 'civic gain' where moral or material resources enhance enjoyment of a right, and 'civic expansion' where they underpin aspirations to an enlargement of rights.

Like Honneth, Lockwood is interested in the potential for collective action contained in these differing aspects of civic stratification, posing the question:

> Which forms of civic stratification ... are more or less likely to give rise to widespread and legitimable discontent.
>
> (Lockwood, 1996:543)

He notes that while civic exclusion generated intense and widespread dis-affection in the past, once civil and political rights had been won this was unlikely to be a continuing source of significant social conflict. However, he makes one sole exception, that of a civic deficit which verges on exclusion as a result of personal and institutional discrimination against guestworkers and ethnic minorities, to which we can add asylum seekers. Lockwood then poses the question of why protest has not taken a more widespread political form, and one reason given is the differing degrees of integration and achievement within the groups affected. Another is the fear that action 'outside the rules' would fuel further prejudice and discrimination. However, Lockwood does see scope for political movements of civic activism, which draw from members of the privileged strata in promoting new and otherwise neglected causes. Campaigns on behalf of the human rights of those otherwise suffering civic exclusion or deficit would be good examples, as in the case history outlined in the chapters to follow. Civic deficit alone, however, is considered unlikely to fuel strong social movements. That based on stigma (or disrespect in Honneth's terms) tends to affect those whose material and moral resources are weak to begin with, while the treatment they receive is likely to confirm existing feelings of inadequacy, producing an incapacity to undertake an effective challenge.

Cosmopolitanism, civil society and the national interest

Both Honneth and Lockwood see some scope for civic action on the basis of a denial or deficit in the realm of rights, though there is some question as to how far the associated social shame or stigma will either be a focus for mobilisation or will itself become disabling. Both writers, however, recognise that exclusions from the full status of citizenship are a likely source of disaffection, and a link can be made to recent writing on cosmopolitanism which looks to the scope for creating a world citizenship (in terms of entitlement) and a world citizenry (in terms of value commitment):

> Cosmopolitanism imagines a global order in which the idea of human rights is an operative principle of justice and mechanisms of global governance are established specifically for the protection of human rights.
>
> (Fine, 2009:8)

As a contemporary intellectual movement cosmopolitanism seeks both to document and advance changes in the nature of society such that it is no longer conceived of as synonymous with the nation-state (see Beck and Sznaider, 2006). Both human rights and international migration are seen as key elements in the empirical manifestation of cosmopolitanism, but the plight of the less privileged migrants, and particularly of asylum seekers, poses questions about quite how far the cosmopolitan ideal has advanced in practice. Indeed, Beck (2006) recognises that nationalisms will react with conscious resistance against threats to the local life form, but that these nationalisms themselves presuppose the actual everyday experience of globalisation. Cosmopolitanism is therefore both a set of norms and a process which is underway but far from complete, the latter being termed 'cosmopolitanisation' (Beck, 2006).

Cosmopolitanisation is conceived by Beck as globalisation from within, and one objective he sets for social science is to illuminate the trans-nationality that is arising within the nation-state. While the presence of trans-national migrants is one example, the actual circumstances of non-citizens with respect to rights is better portrayed by the contours of civic stratification than the idea of a world citizenship. However, one aspect of cosmopolitanism has been the imagining and promotion of a political community at national level which is more in keeping with cosmopolitan values (Fine, 2009). In this respect, human rights function as both an instance of change, as with their incorporation into domestic law, and a force for change, as with the pursuit of their fuller realisation by civil society movements. Once established in principle, human rights norms provide what Levy and Sznaider (2006:659) term a globally available foundation for grounding legitimate claims making. For Douzinas (2000) human rights exist even when they have not been legislated, and their institutional consolidation can be brought about by a performative declaration, which 'creates the ground on which it stands' (p. 343).

This awareness of the transformative capacity of claims making, together with work which looks to the area of rights as a likely focus for political action, inevitably turns attention to the role of civil society. Writing of the prospects for a cosmopolitan solidarity, Habermas (2001:55–56) argues:

> This change in perspective to a world domestic policy cannot be expected from ruling elites until the population itself, on the basis of its own understanding of its own best interests, rewards them for it.

This seems to place a strong weight on civil society as the potential driving force for change, as well as showing considerable faith in the likely outcome. The role of civil society in Habermas's understanding of rights is to provide a conduit between the political system and a public sphere rooted in the lifeworld; a function which cannot be performed by aggregations of passive voters. For Habermas, a vital civil society can promote topics of general public interest as well as acting as advocates for neglected issues and under-represented groups. A test of its dynamism is a willingness:

> To go beyond self defence and take a universalist stand against the open or concealed exclusion of minorities or marginal groups.
>
> (Habermas, 1996:376)

Alexander (2006) too is interested in the solidaristic potentialities of civil society as a 'civil sphere' of social criticism and democratic integration, with aspirations to universalism and the capacity to initiate repairs that aim to 'mend the social fabric' (p. 34).

Both writers, however, are speaking only of potentialities and Habermas recognises that the public sphere at rest will be infiltrated by administrative and social power, and dominated by the mass media. Alexander in turn notes the contradictory and fragmented nature of 'real' civil societies, and the role of law not only in protecting rights, but in dividing and excluding. An optimistic approach to the role of civil society in securing a solidaristic universalism must therefore reckon with the narrowly defined national interest which Beck sees as a likely response to the 'banal cosmopolitanism' of everyday life. Compelling examples of this response are found in state actions to limit the reach of universal recognition, to harness rights in the quest for control, to shape public opinion through the positive or negative constructions of key target groups (Schneider and Ingram, 1993), and to guide public sentiment through a process of 'social steering' (Rodger, 2003). Examples can be readily found in the state's management of migration by means of the differential allocation and delivery of rights, sometimes resulting in a clash between national interests and cosmopolitan principles, or between immigration control and human rights.

Human rights sovereignty and judgement

While the principles of human rights have for some served as a 'repertoire for claims making' (Levy and Sznaider, 2006) and the basis of 'rights talk' (Plummer, 2006) in the generation and/or expansion of entitlements, human rights do have a concrete existence in the form of established legal instruments. Some have seen the institutionalisation of human rights as representing the denationalisation of legitimacy, contributing to a possible reconfiguring of sovereignty (Levy and Sznaider, 2006), or underpinning a universal personhood which supersedes the status of citizenship (Soysal, 1994). Levy and Sznaider see the result as a form of 'cosmopolitanised sovereignty' in which the state's treatment of its population is governed by supranational bodies or international legal norms, shifting attention away from the protection of borders and territoriality to the more juridical dimensions of the state. The result of these developments is not necessarily an expansion of rights, however, and the policing of borders has been augmented by internal control and surveillance in the realm of rights (eg Morris, 1998). In the process, we find that many of the impediments to an equitable functioning of citizenship rights reappear in relation to the implementation of universal human rights.

We have already noted that despite their 'universal' quality human rights instruments themselves contain a legitimate hierarchy of absolute, limited, and qualified rights. There may also be informal deficit, in the manner outlined earlier, whereby moral or material resources favour some and disadvantage others in the realisation of their formally held entitlements. Absolute rights come the closest to what we can think of as truly universal rights, and are in that sense the best approximation of 'natural law' in practice, but these rights are limited in number and are themselves amenable to differing interpretations. Nevertheless, the codification of human rights norms in trans-national instruments does make them available as legal tools, amenable to judicial deliberation over their meaning and application. The incorporation of such instruments into domestic law is of particular significance for the process of cosmopolitanisation, as it allows such deliberation to take place in national courts under the authority of a national judiciary.

For some the codification of human rights goes against their essential spirit, and Douzinas (2000) sees a gap between the notion of humanity and the content and application of legal rights, or between 'the utopian moment in human rights and law' (p. 344). This means that their 'redemptive urge' has not subsided and is to be found, for Douzinas, in the ethics of alterity which exists outside of any law and creates an obligation to respond to the suffering of others. Thus:

> Morality is not synonymous therefore with human rights and does not derive from them. Ethical responsibility precedes rights, gives them their force and legitimacy and becomes the judge of their and state action.
>
> (Douzinas, 2000:353)

In other words, our ethical obligation to others is not a result of human rights law, but is the driving force behind it. Drawing on Arendt, Douzinas sees the figure of the refugee as the ultimate test for human rights; a test which in Arendt's account they failed. Thus, if morality stands outside the law this means that the law can itself be judged and found wanting in ethical terms. For Douzinas, human rights cannot be reduced to legal 'categorisation and classification', and there is an undecidable element in the functioning of human rights which we should not seek to foreclose.

In fact, much legal theory can accommodate this point, and the claims of legal positivism as to the fixity of legal rules have been the object of a sceptical scrutiny for several decades. Even absolute human rights leave considerable scope for interpretive debate, but while indeterminacy is a strength in Douzinas's account, for many legal theorists it is a problem to be resolved. This problem has been variously addressed through the search for integrity in the whole system of law (Dworkin, 1986), or in the argument that legal judgements inescapably turn on political interest (Unger, 1986). Habermas (1996), however, seeks certainty in procedure rather than content and offers a discourse theory of law as his preferred characterisation of legal indeterminacy. Recognising that rights are a social construction he sees argumentation about their precise content and application as part of a deliberative process which is conducted through the courts. In this account the legal order is always provisional and part of an unending process of debate and dispute (p. 227), with particular emphasis placed on contextualised interpretation.

This model depends on a well-functioning system of legal deliberation which gives due weight to participant perspectives. In Alexander's approach to the civil sphere, law offers both symbolic constructions and normative judgements in the name of the civil community, though exclusions and inclusions can battle for dominance, posing the question of why justice should ever prevail. Nevertheless, he argues that aspirations to universalism have often initiated a process of 'civil repair', giving meaning to the idea of a broader society which exists outside of group particularity, even to the point of contesting the dominance of the state. In this context the law becomes a vehicle of demands for more symmetry between the ostensibly equal legal standing of marginalised groups and their lesser status in other spheres. It provides a medium for civil repair which may challenge the exclusions that the law elsewhere creates, and this is especially the case in relation to immigration, when conflicts over distribution and inequality also become struggles for identity and social recognition. Universal human rights can therefore stand as the ideal against which marginal groups measure their inclusions and exclusions, but it is interpretive judgement which determines their concrete meaning and application.

Outline of the book

This book provides a case study which tests the limits of human rights in the context of Arendt's (1979:297) notion of the 'abstract nakedness of being nothing but human'. The basis for this study is a series of 14 judgements on the withdrawal of welfare support from asylum seekers who do not declare themselves on entry to the country. These judgements have been supplemented by interviews with solicitors, barristers, and voluntary sector organisations. Chapter 2 provides a review of recent UK government policy in this area, against a background of theorising with respect to asylum. It sketches two theoretical positions that serve as reference points in much of the relevant literature – communitarian particularism, which emphasises resource constraints and citizens rights; and cosmopolitan universalism, which emphasises the obligation to others implied by a common humanity. However, much of this literature points to the conclusion that neither position can do justice to the actual practice of Western states, in that even states wishing to limit the claims of non-citizens have a continuing interest in maintaining their liberal democratic credentials. It is therefore suggested that state action in the field of asylum cannot be fully understood in terms of principles alone, but also requires an analysis of the practice of compromise. This compromise is considered within a 'governmentality' framework, which explores how states go about managing the tensions involved in honouring obligations in principle but limiting access in practice. This turns in part on the way the very conception of the refugee has been constructed in the West, linked to civil and political freedoms, and based on evidence of individualised persecution, as opposed to *en bloc* response to humanitarian crises. In outlining these arguments, the chapter traces the devices deployed by UK governments from the 1980s onwards in their attempt to limit numbers while retaining the claim to support those genuinely fleeing persecution.

Chapter 3 then examines the case history as it unfolded, through a sequence of judgements compelled to grapple with Arendt's paradox in addressing a policy of deterrence which raises questions about the rights owed to non-citizens. A challenge to the denial of support for late claimers in effect opens up deliberation about the boundary of our social and moral community, and highlights the determining role of legal judgement in this matter. The chapter therefore looks to the decisive moment of judgement in each of our 14 cases – what was at issue, what general principles were in play, and in what ways did they shape the outcome. However, the history implicitly raises a broader issue – the role of judgement as part of political exchange, and we therefore consider the formulation and delivery of the judgements with respect both to their explicit political content and their practical policy impact. Taken as a whole, the case study provides a positive instance of the force of rights in challenging policy interests, played out through a sometimes conflictual dialogue between judges and at times containing a direct message to government. It therefore presents a picture of the judiciary as active participants in a process of social and political change, and sees judgement as a critical component in determining the boundary of rights.

Chapter 4 addresses the role of civil society groups in mounting a challenge to the policy in question. It illuminates a set of issues which arise from attempts to incorporate sociology into legal studies, and elaborates the scope for 'civil repair' in the case of a group outside of citizenship and rendered marginal by the law. It shows how the actions of a small network of national non-governmental organisations and activist lawyers working through domestic legal institutions were able to forge a link between everyday politics and 'cosmopolitan' virtues. In this endeavour, civil society groups play a key role for deliberative politics, with voluntary associations potentially shaping public opinion and acting as advocates for neglected issues and under-represented groups. If parliament is an increasingly imperfect vehicle for participatory representation (Fredman, 2000), then the process of litigation can itself provide an opportunity for participation by means of argument before the court on the nature and scope of rights. The chapter therefore explores the role played by civil society groups in prompting litigation, in furnishing evidence and in offering interventions which inform judgement. Their actions are considered here in the light of Habermas's (1996) model of deliberative judgement and Alexander's (2006) concept of civil repair.

Chapter 5 goes further in combining legal and social theory, using the case history to address sociological debate about an emergent cosmopolitan society. Beck (2006) has argued that key features in building a cosmopolitan outlook have been the scale of trans-national migration and the assertion of universal human rights. However, the cases examined here document the process of legal determination when the two come into conflict. The chapter again draws on Habermas (1996) and his argument for a proceduralist understanding of the law built on regulated competition between paradigms. Close analysis of judgements in the present history reveal two competing perspectives: a) a 'cosmopolitan' orientation, characterised by reference to the standards of civilised society and to human dignity; and b) a 'national' orientation, emphasising policy objectives and the need to strike a balance between the individual and society. The argument developed shows how these paradigms aid analysis of the current case history, though there is potential deliberative stalemate when the two perspectives conflict. This conflict serves to highlight what may be termed the private moment in judgement, turning in the present history on a reflexive exercise of imaginative identification with the claimants. Based on accounts of the experience and suffering of disentitled asylum seekers the concluding judgement yields a final ruling on the concrete requirements of the ideal of human dignity, and an ultimate validation of the cosmopolitan paradigm.

Chapter 6 sets the study in a broader political context and against Beck's (2006) claims of a 'blurring' of distinctions with respect to rights, examines rather the *expansion* of distinctions, through a complex system of civic stratification (Lockwood, 1996; Morris, 2002). The construction of particular social groups as targets for policy initiatives provides a dynamic illustration of some aspects of the civic stratification argument, and holds considerable potential for the understanding of social change. The chapter documents this process with respect to late claimers for asylum and considers the connection between the formal aspects of entitlement and the informal public standing of a particular social group. The potential impact of the judgements in the case history – which finds the enforced destitution of asylum seekers to be inhuman and degrading – is considered in this light. The judgements deal principally with formal rights, notably to fair treatment and to protection from inhuman and degrading treatment. However, each of these rights also asserts the basic worth of the individual in a way which approximates Honneth's notion of recognition, and thus offers some degree of reparation for the informal status denial contained within the policy and heightened by its mode of administration. The judgements therefore counter the construction by the government of a specific target group, whose rights had been eroded and whose moral worth had been impugned.

Chapter 7 reflects on the foregoing chapters, reviewing the conclusions to be drawn from an encounter between cosmopolitan ideals and exclusionary policies of control, to sketch the outline of a distinctively sociological approach to judgement. It pursues the theme of an encounter between the normative and empirical manifestations of cosmopolitanism and shows how the consolidation of human rights guarantees in legal instruments represents one step in bringing the two together. However, we also note the uncertain content of this developing area of law, and the pivotal role of interpretation in its application. It is this underlying indeterminacy that opens the way for a sociological approach to judgement, placing legal decisions in their broader social and political context and seeing the content of judgement as a part of deliberative debate over the contours of society and the boundary of rights. The chapter (and the book as a whole) therefore presents a layered approach to judgement which moves from the construction of a problem and the framing of a policy, to its contested application and the mobilisation of a civil society challenge. This whole process then yields the emergence of two different paradigms, given expression through deliberation in the courts, and resolved in this instance through the eventual dominance of the cosmopolitan orientation.

The concluding chapter considers the import of this study for a sociology of rights.

Notes

1 Czarist Russia, the Austro-Hungarian Empire, the Ottoman Empire, and the Kaiserreich.
2 The return of an asylum seeker to a situation in which their life or freedom might be under threat.
3 Though an exception may exist in the European Union (EU), EU citizenship is a derivative status which cannot be acquired other than by citizenship of one of the member-states.

Chapter 2

Asylum immigration and the art of government

Widely perceived as an unprecedented crisis, the number of refugees originating in the developing world since the 1970s has generated urgent concern throughout the West. Such concern is an ambiguous mixture of compassion for the plight of the unfortunates who have been cast adrift and of fear that they will come pouring in.

(Zolberg et al., 1989:v)

Comparing banishment from one's own country to the 'social death' associated with slavery, Zolberg et al. (1989:7) provide a mirror image of Walzer's (1983:31) assertion that: 'the primary good that we distribute to one another is membership in some human community', otherwise expressed as Arendt's 'right to have rights'. For asylum seekers, the social death of exile and the quest for access to the foundational right of membership in some human community is mediated by the process of status determination and by formal definition of the 'refugee'. This process is therefore located at the heart of a dilemma for liberal democracy – how to accommodate both sovereign self-determination and adherence to universal human rights (Benhabib, 2004:45).

Benhabib (2004:5) has argued that even when other aspects of sovereignty may have been undermined, the nation-state retains its monopoly power over immigration and citizenship policy. For states which are signatories to the Convention Relating to the Status of Refugees (CSR, otherwise known as the Geneva Convention) asylum seems to stand as an exception to this claim, by virtue of the commitment to *non-refoulement*. This agreement not to return an asylum seeker to a country where their life or freedom would be threatened in effect means they must either be transferred to a safe third country, or given admission to the territory of the country of arrival, at least until their claim has been resolved. This does not, however, mean that control has been entirely relinquished, but rather that states respond pragmatically to the problem of how to blend the moral and the ethical, or the universal and the particular.

The problem is expressed by Benhabib (2004:19) as:

> An irresolvable contradiction ... between the expansive and inclusionary principles of moral and political universalism, as anchored in universal human rights, and exclusionary conceptions of democratic closure.

In fact, this opposition has motivated much of the theorising around the phenomenon of asylum, which tends to weigh the principles of cosmopolitan universalism against those of communitarian particularism (see Schuster, 2003; Gibney, 2004; Tazreiter, 2004). According to Zolberg et al. (1989:12) Arendt seeks the roots of this opposition in the corruption of the traditional Western doctrine of human rights, which gave way to that of nationally guaranteed rights, extending the full protection of legal institutions only to citizens, and relegating non-citizens to some law of exception. For liberal democratic states, that law of exception finds expression in the CSR, which defines a refugee as a person who is outside their country of nationality, who is unable or unwilling to seek protection from their own government, and who has a well-founded fear of persecution on grounds of race, religion, nationality, political opinion or membership of a social group.

Hathaway (1990) argues that the greatest factor shaping international legal responses to refugees since the Second World War has been the pursuit by states of their own well-being. Yet while in Britain there is almost daily evidence of government scepticism over asylum seekers, as well as legislation crafted with a view to deterrence, the institution of asylum survives. The communitarian/cosmopolitan opposition, however, presents two contrasting normative approaches each of which leads to a different conclusion regarding our commitment to asylum seekers. Thus Gibney (2004) outlines the partialist (communitarian) perspective that sees states as cultural entities prioritising the needs and interests of citizens over those of refugees. He then sets this against an impartialist (cosmopolitan) view that sees states as moral agents, taking equal account of both citizens and refugees. Similarly, Tazreiter (2004) identifies the communitarian commitment to the particularities of the national community and the cosmopolitan commitment to trans-national justice as two polar positions in debate.

The communitarian/cosmopolitan opposition

The communitarian or particularist orientation has both a cultural and resource dimension. The former is expressed by the argument that membership of a cultural collectivity is an important dimension of identity, which is necessarily derived from the individual's experience of a constitutive social matrix (Gibney, 2004). The associated bonds of attachment thus formed are then argued to dictate the level and nature of material support afforded to those in need, according to their proximity, so making up the resource dimension of membership and affiliation. This latter view is best represented by Walzer's (1983) argument that the ideal political order is one based on citizenship, and that state sovereignty both demarcates and facilitates 'communities of character' (p. 42). Policies of admission and exclusion can therefore be a vital aspect of this collective identity, and will tend to privilege the interests of members over obligations to others, both in terms of cultural unity and economic well-being (Hathaway, 1990).

The converse position is adopted by a cosmopolitan or universalist orientation which in recognising the relatedness of all humanity emphasises transnational obligations and the force of universal norms. These are increasingly expressed in terms of a 'world culture', and Meyer et al. (1997) point to a strong consensus among states which endorses principles of citizenship, justice, human rights, etc. and for which they claim universal applicability. Similarly, Jacobson (1996) argues that there have been related institutional changes, turning people into trans-national actors whose claim to rights no longer depends on citizenship but is grounded in universal principles. In other words, the 'right to have rights' is argued to have superseded the constraints of the nation-state order to find legitimacy in the principles of universal human rights, and effectiveness in the expanding reach of international law.

Any attempt to apply these differing perspectives in practice immediately raises problems; hence Tazreiter (2004:9) notes that the idea of universal rights will provoke ambivalence because of the problem of 'situating obligations' and giving them practical meaning. Such ambivalence is also a product of national self-defence or protectionism in the face of complexity and uncertainty. In fact, despite a polarisation in terms of principle, adherents of each position concede ground when addressing practical applications, in a manner which perhaps suggests scope for convergence (see Schuster, 2003). For example, while Walzer (1983) sees a community of citizens as the ideal political order, he recognises the need to move beyond a particularist framework when considering responsibility towards refugees. Where numbers are small this responsibility goes unquestioned, but where they are large then issues of ideological or ethnic affinity will affect choice. Nevertheless, he states: 'at the extreme, the claim of asylum is virtually undeniable' (Walzer, 1983:51). Compare this position with that of Carens (1992), who though an adherent of the cosmopolitan perspective, recognises that states are not obliged to admit overwhelming numbers and thus introduces pragmatic constraint to the application of universal principles.

To express this in terms of the liberal dilemma, sovereign nation-states which are founded on principles of equal human worth and dignity must extend minimum standards of treatment to those in need, whether citizens or not (Tazreiter, 2004). Hence, despite Benhabib's recognition of the states' monopoly power over immigration and citizenship, she also argues that territoriality has become anachronistic, and cites the CSR as one instance of international human rights norms which call sovereignty into question. However, she recognises some limitation, the CSR being binding on signatory countries only, and being inter-statal in nature rather than truly cosmopolitan, or supra-statal. Tazreiter identifies the same uneasy balance whereby obligations towards asylum seekers exist, but less unambiguously than the rights of citizens. She sees asylum seekers caught up in a zero-sum game whereby – in the view of receiver societies, conferring rights on the former will detract from the rights of the latter.

In Gibney's (2004) view, acceptance of the full logic of the cosmopolitan position would undermine the conditions for communal self-determination and the provision of public goods in the host society. However, an extreme communitarian approach would legitimate states in paying scant regard to many in great need, hence:

> The knowledge that a convincing ideal must attend both to partial and impartial claims should at least make us very sceptical of global liberal [cosmopolitan] and utilitarian communitarian accounts.
>
> (Gibney, 2004:83)

Goodwin-Gill (2001) has expressed a similar sentiment in his reference to three common assumptions: that the CSR is out of date; that the refusal of a majority of claims is evidence of abuse; and (nevertheless) that the protection of refugees is still an ideal to be protected. Hence his view that:

> Human rights and refugee protection is necessarily a matter of tensions: between government and applicants; judiciary and appellants; government and judiciary; past and present; present and future. Resolving these tensions is an integral part of the dynamic of any civil society founded upon values such as individual worth and integrity, and on the rule of law.
>
> (Goodwin-Gill, 2001:8)

He also argues that there is a cost attached to any principle once it moves from the abstract terrain of theory into practical application.

Managing the liberal dilemma

As we have seen, a number of writers observe that state sovereignty is expressed through control over the entry and stay of non-citizens, such that:

> There are few areas of national sovereignty which states are less willing to surrender to international control than the entry of aliens.
>
> (Coles, cited by Hathaway, 1990:172)

With respect to refugees, therefore:

> [States] have insisted on defining very precisely the persons who are eligible for such status and reserving the right to make determinations of that status.
>
> (Coles, cited by Hathaway, 1990:172)

The refugee problem is in effect a product of the nation-state system itself (Arendt, 1979; Zolberg et al., 1989), but while it is inconceivable that states will give up the right to exercise control over their borders, a complete abnegation of human rights obligations is equally difficult to imagine. Liberal democratic states are political-cultural entities that embrace universalistic constitutional ideals (Habermas, 2001; Schuster, 2003; Benhabib, 2004), and this means in Hollifield's (1992) terms that the actions of nation-states are constrained by embedded liberalism. The accommodation of asylum seekers and refugees is therefore at once an expression of these ideals and a threat to sovereign control.

The result, Tazreiter (2004) argues, is that the principles of human worth and dignity imply minimal expectations with respect to the treatment of marginalised groups and non-citizens. For Hathaway (1990:174) this suggests that:

> International refugee law is currently a means of reconciling the prerogative of states to control immigration with the reality of forced migrations of people at risk.

It is therefore the management of this tension which is central to a sociological understanding of the treatment of asylum seekers and refugees, a tension which cannot be resolved purely at the level of principle, but which requires the study of quite how national governments, legal institutions, and civil society actors negotiate an outcome. The problem raises a number of interesting issues about the indeterminacy of rights and the social processes by which this indeterminacy is negotiated.

Hathaway has documented the emergence of international refugee law in terms of three key periods. The first, from 1920 to 1935, is characterised by 'humanitarian exception to the protectionist norm' (1990:137) in response to an unstoppable flow of involuntary migrants across European borders. In the early stages there was no attempt to prevent or to control the flows, but eventually the absence of restrictions gave way to an endeavour to hold humanitarian exception more closely to existing immigration norms. Thus, in the period that followed (1935–1950), under the authority of the International Committee of Refugees (1938), it was no longer sufficient for someone to be a displaced person, and assistance was limited to those forced to flee as a result of their political opinion, religious belief, or racial origin. This shift in orientation is represented as a move from *en bloc* humanitarian protection of groups to a more individuated conception of the refugee. The dominant concern was with civil and political rights, and thus coincided with the liberal ideology of Western states. The following period, 1951 and beyond, is therefore characterised as one of self-interested control which protects the West from the bulk of third world asylum seekers, and sees the transfer under the Geneva Convention of administrative authority to signatory states.

As Schuster (2003) records, the Convention was drawn up without contributions from the USSR, who had opted out of deliberations, and was consequently biased in favour of the protection of civil and political rights rather than social and economic rights. Protection was also confined to those fleeing as a result of pre-1951 events within Europe, and only 16 years later did the New York protocol (1967) extend the geographical reach of the Convention to all countries. Hathaway (1990:166) notes four significant features of the outcome:

1. International law does not address the necessary features of status determination.
2. The definition adopted is sufficiently flexible to tailor protection to national interests.
3. States are explicitly authorised to exclude those deemed undesirable or unworthy of assistance.
4. There is no requirement to offer asylum, but only a commitment to *non-refoulement*.

Asylum as self-interested action

Schuster (2003) argues that the grant of asylum has commonly been used as a tool of foreign policy, and that only rarely has it been purely altruistic. The readiness to grant refugee status to those fleeing communist controlled regimes is a key example, with the politicisation of refugees a common ploy in the assertion of national interests and identity (Tazreiter, 2004). More recently, however, source countries have multiplied and diversified, such that in 2000 the top 10 source countries for asylum seekers in the UK were Iraq, Sri Lanka, former Yugoslavia, Iran, Afghanistan, Somalia, former USSR, China, Turkey and Pakistan. The combined success rate that year was 30% (including refugee status and Exceptional Leave to Remain), though the average for 1985–2000 was 40%. Over that period the number of applicants rose from 4,389 to 80,315 to peak at 84,130 in 2002 (Home Office, 2002a) – the year of the legislation at issue in the following chapters.

Yet despite continuing expressions of concern about border control and comment on the outdated nature of the Geneva Convention (eg Straw, 2000; Cm 4018) the official position of the UK Government in 2005 was a reassertion of their commitment. Thus, in a policy document published that year, we find the statement:

> The 1951 Convention is part of the legal and ethical framework that enshrines basic principles of human decency. We reject the idea of a fixed quota on refugee numbers or pulling out of the Convention as unworkable, unjust and counter-productive.
>
> (Cm 6472:17)

On the ECHR, the principle basis for subsidiary protection, David Blunkett (2003)[1] as Home Secretary has stated that withdrawal from the Convention was a move not to be contemplated lightly because of the 'acrimony' and 'disdain' of the international community which would follow. Thus, political debate commonly cites asylum as the hallmark of a civilised and liberal state, while Skinner (1978) has argued that a country could not abolish asylum and still plausibly retain the claim to be a liberal democratic state. Goodwin-Gill accepts a necessary tension surrounding state responses to asylum seekers, and notes:

> Resolving these tensions is an integral part of the dynamic of any civil society founded upon values such as individual worth and integrity, and on the rule of law.
>
> (Goodwin-Gill, 2001:8)

The end result is often a rhetoric of moral obligation and a practice of pragmatism, such that what we owe to non-citizens is the object of constant negotiation (Morris, 1997). In fact, the very framing of the Geneva Convention turns on a compromise in granting the right 'to seek and enjoy asylum' without establishing any duty on states to admit refugees, or any adequate international monitoring system. So Tazreiter (2004:23) writes:

> The appeal which human rights have as moral concepts which cut across borders, cultures, political and social systems ... gains substance only when this right is able to be lodged as a claim.

Furthermore, states are actively engaged in limiting the access of asylum seekers while also adopting various means of deterrence. Hence:

> While continuing formally to proclaim their commitment to the sheltering of all refugees, industrialised states are busily building upon the Convention's guarantee of domestic procedural control in order to construct a maze of visa controls, 'direct flight' rules, screening mechanisms, and unfair determination systems.
>
> (Hathaway, 1990:183)

So, as Hailbronner notes (1990) a commitment to *non-refoulement* does not stand in the way of a variety of devices of control and deterrence. Furthermore, by debating asylum in terms of immigration, and presenting asylum seekers as economic migrants, states can distance themselves from their humanitarian obligation, a move often associated with the claim that a majority of asylum seekers are 'bogus' (see Chapter 6). We therefore find a number of pragmatic moves which allow states to discredit asylum seekers and limit their numbers while retaining their claim to function as liberal democracies committed to the rule of law and the protection of fundamental rights. This pragmatism is not adequately addressed by the opposing philosophies of communitarianism and cosmopolitanism. It requires a rather different frame for investigation and analysis which looks instead at the macro and micro system of governance deployed as a means of living with the liberal dilemma.

The art of government

Zolberg (1989:405) has argued that:

> One important theoretical development of the past quarter of a century is recognition that it is precisely the control which states exercise over borders that defines international migration as a distinctive social process.

However, this control is not confined to operations at the border; states not only police access to entry but also exert control over the distribution of collective goods within the territory, while both of these functions are shaped to some degree by international obligations. Together they constitute the terrain for a pragmatic approach to immigration and asylum and invite attention to the principles and practices of governance in this field, a focus which evokes what Foucault (1991:89) has termed 'the art of government' (see Burchell et al., 1991; Rose and Miller, 1992). The elaboration of this 'art', otherwise referred to as 'governmental rationality' or 'governmentality' (Foucault 1991:102), is documented in Foucault's related course of lectures on 'Security, Territory and Population', and centres on the management of resources and the government of a population in the context of territorial sovereignty. Hence, it is the interplay of the three components of his title which is placed at the heart of 'governmentality'.

Foucault's particular interest was in the state's strong reliance on surveillance and control, and the means by which it could be achieved; less through a concentration of government per se than through a complex of institutions and practices shaping the daily conduct of governance. The process rests upon 'the many and varied alliances between political and other authorities that seek to govern economic activity, social life and individual conduct' (Rose and Miller, 1992:173). Foucault's lecture in large part concerns the technical manoeuvres through which a state can exert its authority over the 'disposition of things' in relation to a territory and its inhabitants (Foucault, 1991:94). Nowhere, however, does it address the terms of access to the territory, techniques of inclusion and exclusion, and the question of the management and rights of outsider groups. These issues are important for the stated problematic in a number of ways, having resource implications and introducing into the population non-citizens from outside the national territory, who are nevertheless bearers of universal rights.

Britain has traditionally relied on 'external controls', that is, those which operate either before arrival or at the point of entry to a country, and represent the most direct and overt approach to policing asylum and immigration. However, despite the strength of this system, Britain in the late 1980s and early 1990s saw a rise in the numbers claiming asylum and an expansion of source countries from the third world. This meant that growing numbers of asylum applicants became a focus for political concern (IND, 1995, Table 5.2). A series of legislative changes at this time, during a period of Conservative rule, simultaneously addressed both resource protection and *internal* controls, through a set of concerns which broadly correspond to Foucault's title 'Security, Territory and Population'. This opens up the possibility that a governmentality perspective could usefully be applied to an analysis of the management of asylum and immigration, encompassing both the terms of access to a territory and the delimitation and policing of non-citizens' rights. Such an approach would serve to highlight the 'range of multiform tactics' (Foucault, 1991:95) marshalled by the state in responding to trans-national migration, and the 'rationality' driving these tactics.

Developments over this period demonstrate a tactical use of rules, procedures and legislation which operate indirectly, together with a transfer of political responsibility to non-political agencies. Their combined effect has been to limit access to asylum without the assumption of any overt position of denial, thus allowing the UK government to retain its claim to respect for fundamental rights, without having fully to confront the material consequences. So for example, asylum seeking is affected by the operation of the visa system which requires entry clearance to be given before travel, and which for Britain in recent years has operated with a refusal rate of around 20%.[2] Britain had been generally increasing its use of visas since the early 1980s, with the requirement often following signs that a country was likely to be generating significant numbers of asylum seekers (Shutter, 1995; Glidewell Panel, 1996). A request for asylum is not a valid reason for granting a visa, and asylum requests can only be made from inside the territory of the prospective 'host' country. For this reason, the impact of the visa system is most strongly felt, and can only be fully understood, in combination with carriers' liability.

Since the 1971 Immigration Act, carriers have been responsible for the detention and removal costs of passengers who are refused entry. Further legislation was introduced in Britain in 1987 and 1999 (and at various times in other European countries (Cruz, 1995)), aimed at the reduction of passengers who arrive without the necessary documentation (IND, 1995). Carriers are liable to a fine, currently of up to £2,000, for any such passenger they carry, and this erects a barrier against undocumented travellers which operates through financial penalties on carriers, and is administered by their routine personnel. Although the 1951 Geneva Convention asserts that 'illegal' entry into a country (for example, through the use of forged documents) in order to seek asylum should not be treated as a crime, the impact of the ruling will be strongly felt by asylum seekers. It is they who are most likely to have difficulty securing legitimate travel documents, and who may thus find their flight from persecution blocked, or that they are driven to use the services of traffickers. While there is no formal denial of Britain's human rights obligations, pursuit of those rights has been made more difficult for individuals by this orchestration of legislative and administrative tactics, and the incorporation of private organisations in the act of surveillance; all defining features of 'governmentality'.

Civic stratification

A key device for imposing terms and conditions on the presence of non-citizens once they have gained entry is what I have here termed civic stratification (Lockwood, 1996; Morris, 2002), which operates through a series of differentiated legal statuses with different rights attached. Broadly speaking, these statuses include: the professional elite of technical and administrative experts; other highly skilled workers; the family members of settled persons; those granted refugee status, humanitarian leave or discretionary leave; asylum seekers awaiting a final decision on their case; temporary workers allowed entry for a time-limited period; undocumented economic migrants; and failed asylum seekers. The key variable rights are the right to remain on the territory, the right to seek and to take employment, and the right to social support. Under the Conservative government of the 1980s and 1990s, the delivery of social support became central to certain developments in relation to immigration control. At that time, settled migrants and people granted refugee status or subsidiary protection had full entitlement to health and welfare provisions. Migrants whose stay was time limited (which includes all non-EU workers in their initial period of stay) were admitted on the condition of no recourse to public funds. People seeking asylum were granted temporary admission to the country and traditionally had been granted support until a final decision on their case had been made.

This basic system of civic stratification was made more complex by Britain's entry into the European Union (EU). During a period in which external controls on immigration had been tightened there was a simultaneous opening up to movement into Britain from continental Europe. Thus, against the pattern of restrictions on entry from third world countries came Britain's entry into the European Community, and with it an acceptance of the principle of the single market. This meant, as of 1992, the granting of rights to work and reside to all citizens of EU member-states,[3] rights not fully extended to *third country nationals* (non-EU citizens resident in the territory of the Union). There were also implications for asylum seekers when the EU launched the Dublin Convention, signed in 1990 and first implemented in 1997. This convention was designed to determine the country responsible for considering an asylum claim, whose decision would stand for all member-states. The intention was to prevent the circulation of asylum seekers throughout Europe – or 'asylum shopping' as it has sometimes been called.

One effect of growing complexity in the system of civic stratification was an increased interest in internal controls. However, an early response to debate about a 'frontier free Europe' was its use by Britain as an opportunity to define and defend its island traditions. Hence:

> The Government ... remains determined to maintain necessary controls at ports and airports to detect traffic in illegal goods ... to control immigration of non-Community nationals, and to detect and deter illegal immigration.
>
> (Select Committee on European Legislation, 1992)

Similarly:

> As an island, it makes sense for the UK to have the main focus of immigration controls at its frontiers. Countries on mainland Europe are in a different position and their traditional focus on internal control reflects this.
>
> (Select Committee on European Legislation, 1995)

It was additionally argued that for a lifting of border controls within the EU 'it would be necessary to establish a comprehensive system of internal controls, to compensate'.

When in 1994 an EU Joint Action (Council Document 12336/94)[4] was proposed to the effect that all 'foreigners be subject to a check on their immigration status whenever they came into contact with authority', the British response was cautious. The Home Office[5] pointed out that parts of the proposal 'appear to assume the existence of a system of residence permits for legally resident foreign nationals of each member state', while:

> A consequence of the UK's emphasis on frontier-based immigration controls has. ... been that powers to verify the status of foreign nationals within the UK are less extensive than those exercised by many other Member States.

However, the Home Office response also made reference to 'a scrutiny of inter-agency co-operation' which was actively considering aspects of internal control. Thus, while the discourse in Europe stressed national sovereignty, strong borders and internal freedoms, domestic debate had meanwhile been considering the possible development of internal controls through what may be seen as a further exercise in 'governmentality'. The 'political rationality' informing this exercise has focused on the increasingly complex system of legal statuses governing entry into Britain and access to resources, in which the granting and delivery of welfare assumed a growing significance.

Freeman (1986:52) has argued that:

> The welfare state requires boundaries because it establishes a principle of distributive justice that departs from the distributive principles of the free market.

Hence, the group of people protected by welfare must be delimited and entitlement for support will rest on decisions about both material need and moral desert, invoking judgements of merit and demerit (cf Lockwood, 1996). As a result, social rights under the modern welfare state involve both the 'rational' administration of national resources and the moral identification of a 'legitimate' claim. Thus, Geddes (2003) has argued the question is less how migration drives changes in the welfare state, but rather how the organisational and ideological aspects of welfare are deployed in the management of migration, highlighting the relationship between policy and governance (Daly, 2003).

In terms of implementation, there are two points at issue; one concerns the question of legal presence and the conditions of entry into the national territory, the other is bound up with access to various social provisions after entry. Correspondingly, there are two different systems of control, and in fact immigration conditions had not traditionally been enforced in regulations governing the administration of welfare. From 1985 to 1996 there was a gradual process of alignment between these two systems, alongside both a developing discourse of resource protection and an extension of the devices and techniques of control. Access to Supplementary Benefit (and subsequently Income Support), the principal means tested benefit, had always been affected by immigration status, at first on a discretionary basis (see Gordon and Newnham, 1985:8) but as of 1980 by excluding from eligibility those defined as 'persons from abroad' (SSAC, 1994a:7; Storey, 1994:19). Thereafter, any potential claimant who entered the country on the understanding that they would not have recourse to public funds was denied entitlement to these benefits. Exceptions were made under urgent cases provision, which covered asylum seekers. However, the move was a precursor to other changes which directly affected the position of many within this group.

There had for some time been an established practice of consultation with the Home Office in relation to the immigration status of particular clients (Social Security Committee, 1996:4), and at least the possibility of passing on doubts about the legality of their presence (see Gordon and Newnham, 1985:28). In October 1993 the Home Secretary set up a 'scrutiny' study of inter-agency co-operation on the enforcement of immigration laws in which access to welfare support was crucial. This study represented an exercise in both 'political rationality' and 'governmental technology', explicating the principal of resource protection and elaborating the mechanisms for its implementation. It was intended:

to examine ways in which the Government as a whole could work more effectively to strengthen immigration control and to prevent those temporarily or illegally in this country from receiving state benefits to which they should not be entitled

(HC Hansard, written answers, 18 July 1995, col 1027)[6]

It was reported that:

The scrutiny demonstrated that, in many cases, either the rules governing eligibility for benefit or the procedures for granting it were insufficiently rigorous to prevent abuse. It also showed that too often illegal immigrants were able to escape detection because procedures for identifying them were unclear.

(HC Hansard, written answers, 18 July 1995, col 1027)

The awareness that income-related benefits were not always operating in harmony with the immigration rules had become an issue even before the inter-agency study had reported. Among several steps taken to address this matter was an expansion of civic stratification by virtue of the denial of benefit rights for asylum seekers who did not claim on entry to the country – on the assumption that the availability of benefits was what attracted them to Britain (Social Security Committee, 1996). There had been a rapid growth in asylum seekers worldwide in the course of the 1980s and 1990s, and the dominant political response has been to argue that a majority of asylum seekers were 'bogus'; that is, that they were not genuinely fleeing persecution and were in fact 'economic migrants' (HC81, session 1995–96; for discussion see Gillespie, 1996). The Secretary of State for Social Security therefore argued:

The trouble is, our system almost invites people to claim asylum, to gain British benefits. Most people who claim asylum don't arrive here as refugees. They come as visitors, tourists or students. And they accept that they should support themselves. The problem is that if they later claim asylum, they can automatically claim benefits. That can't be right. And we're going to stop it.

(Social Security Committee, 1996)

At the time of the above statement 70% of asylum applications were made after entry and 30% were at port applications (SSAC, 1996:34). The recognition rate was marginally higher for the first group (4.9% as compared with 4.7% (Glidewell Panel, 1996:34)), and the reasons for the pattern are well known, with many asylum seekers wishing to gain entry and seek advice before declaring themselves (Glidewell Panel, 1995:34). Nevertheless, there followed a change in benefit rules such that those seeking asylum on entry to the country continued to qualify, while those whose entry was on other grounds, but who later made an asylum claim, did not.[7] The emphasis therefore shifted from using benefit agencies as a means of checking immigration status to the denial of entitlement as a means of deterrence.

The policy was initially implemented by a change in the Income Support regulations, but when these regulations were ruled *ultra vires* (*JCWI*, 4 AUER 385) key elements were enshrined in primary legislation through the 1996 Asylum and Immigration Act. This act also included a new power to impose fines of up to £5,000 on employers of people who were not in possession of the relevant leave. The situation was further compounded by subsequent events; local authorities already carried a responsibility under the Children Act (1989) and the NHS and Community Care Act (1990)[8] for some asylum seekers ineligible for income support. A judicial review concerning four single asylum seekers who fell outside of all provision massively expanded that responsibility (*M*, 1 CCLR 85 CA). The ultimate judgement was that these people were destitute and vulnerable within the meaning of the 1948 National Assistance Act (NAA) and that it fell to local authorities to make provision for them. These and other judgements are discussed in detail in the chapters to follow.

At this point the political rationality driving the benefit changes seemed to unravel. One argument had been that the elaboration of controls and restrictions was anyway disproportionate to the numbers involved (SSAC, 1994b:9; Bolderson and Roberts, 1995; Feria, 1996). More specifically, the London boroughs of Westminster, Hammersmith and Fulham challenged the government in court on the grounds of *irrationality*. The justification for changes in access to benefits had been estimated savings for the public purse amounting to £2 million, but this calculation had not taken account of costs to local authorities. The action was halted when the government agreed to partial financial compensation for local authorities to offset the costs of supporting asylum seekers. Thus, instead of limiting rights the changes in practice activated a previously neglected source of support, the 1948 NAA – upheld with considerable moral force by the judiciary. This was the situation inherited by the incoming New Labour (NL) government.

New Labour

The Conservatives lost power in 1997, to be replaced by an NL government which in 1999 reinstated maintenance rights to all asylum seekers via the National Asylum Support System (NASS). However, this removed asylum seekers from any provision through the standard Income Support system, and responsibility for their welfare moved to the Home Office, eliminating the need for complex inter-agency exchanges. Furthermore, in the Asylum and Immigration Act of 2002, NL introduced a measure which bore a striking similarity to the 1996 exclusions from support for in-country claimants. Under this new measure (Section 55(1)) asylum seekers who did not claim 'as soon as reasonably practicable' were to be denied benefit.

This policy and its implications are discussed in detail in later chapters, but it might be useful here to consider NL's more general orientation to rights, which can be characterised by a particular vision of their inter-relations with responsibility, opportunity and community (see Morris, 1997). The resulting 'communitarian' matrix emphasises the conditional nature of most rights, rather than a view of rights as inherent in individuals, and implies an associated balancing of 'community needs' against individual entitlements. This then provides a justification for treating rights as a tool of governance, and enhances the role of formal distinctions in an already stratified field, such that the increased elaboration of claimant groups becomes a basis for governance through heightened but variable conditionality. While Schuster and Solomos (2004) have convincingly argued that NL's immigration policy is a continuation of pre-existing concern with control, over-ridden only in the case of skilled workers, the detail of policy and practice warrants attention.

According to Jessop (1999) changes in the governance of welfare are inseparable from broader challenges to the Keynesian Welfare National State (KWNS) model. These challenges have reduced the viability of state-led, demand-side management of national economies, and its linkage to the delivery of economic and social rights. Governments must now secure insertion into a changing global division of labour, and the governance of welfare has a key role to play, as in the 'creeping conditionality' identified in the treatment of welfare claimants (Dwyer, 2004). Hence, Jessop documents a shift towards a Schumpterian Workfare Postnational Regime (SWPR) of permanent innovation, flexibility and competitiveness. In a related argument, Duvell and Jordan (2002) see an altered orientation towards labour migration as part of such a shift, noting EU recognition of 'urgent needs for both skilled and unskilled workers' (p. 499), despite continuing unemployment. They also note related changes both in the recruitment of migrant labour and in practices of national welfare delivery 'to increase labour market flexibility, improve work incentives, control costs and activate claimants' (p. 502). However, they recognise that secondary migration in the form of asylum seeking does not comfortably fit this model.

In relation to migration and asylum there have been three key policy documents under NL, published, respectively, in 1998, 2002 and 2005. The first document, *Fairer Faster and Firmer*, begins with a gesture of recognition to the contribution of immigrants, though what follows is cast in more negative terms:

> [Economic migrants] cannot normally satisfy the immigration rules and seek entry through another status. ... [they] will exploit whatever offers the best chance'
>
> (CM 5387:7)

It might be assumed from this document that economic immigration to Britain in the late 1990s was predominantly clandestine and unwanted, and yet the Immigration Statistics show a tripling of legal entry and settlement for labour migrants between 1997 and 2003 (Cm 6363: Tables 4.1 and 5.4). In fact, by the publication of *Secure Borders Safe Haven* (2002) there had been a radical shift in the presentation of economic migration, with a strong assertion of its value. This was echoed by the Home Secretary (Blunkett, 2003):

> Migrants make a disproportionate contribution to the wealth of the UK, accounting for 8% of the population but 10% of our gross domestic product – and are 20% more likely to be self-employed.

We learn of the value of this contribution in the context of an ageing population, and the absence of competition with the settled population. In this context, the removal of a concession which allowed asylum seekers the possibility of working after six months is significant in undermining both their capacity to be self-maintaining and as a result their social standing. In Honneth's terms, any prospect of earning recognition and inclusion is undermined.

In contrast, the enhanced status of highly skilled migrants was pre-figured by Immigration Minister Barbara Roche (2000), to emphasise the importance of access to new global markets for skilled labour. Shortly thereafter the newly named 'Work Permits UK' revised its procedures to become both more efficient and accessible (Flynn, 2003:6–7), with decision-making up from 70% within one week to 90% within one day (CM 5387). Economic migrants were no longer portrayed as the abusers of the system, illicitly seeking to further their own interests, but as dynamic, highly skilled, widely sought after workers in the global economy. Highly skilled migrants were even granted admission for a period to seek work. The *Five Year Strategy for Immigration and Asylum* (2005) was in some respects more cautious; the need for skilled labour was reasserted, and the proposed four- (now five-: Guardian, 2006) tier system of entry for work was largely an elaboration of arrangements put in place in 2002, but a number of more restrictive measures were outlined.

The most notable aspects of the associated system of civic stratification are the restriction of possibilities of settlement for non-European Economic Area (EEA) workers to 'certain skilled workers', the proposed extension of the qualifying period for settlement from four years to five, and the planned phasing out of schemes for low-skilled temporary labour. It is entirely consistent with this differentiated approach to economic migration that workers from new EU accession states were allowed entry only on terms that denied access to benefit rights for the first 12 months, in sharp contrast with the usual terms of free movement. All categories of non-EEA workers are denied recourse to public funds until securing permanency, so the extension of the qualifying period for settlement also delays the point of entitlement to welfare rights. Their early presence in the country is therefore conditional, sustaining an approach to rights based on a language of contract, opportunity and responsibility, paired with increasing control and selectivity in terms of skill levels and labour market needs.

This contractual communitarian approach to immigration is in many ways compatible with thinking behind other aspects of welfare reform (Morris, 2007), which treats the granting or withholding of social rights as a means of micro managing both population and economy. However, the underpinning shifts in government positioning raise interesting questions about the relationship between the formal treatment of particular groups and their informal standing in society. See, for example, Rodger's (2003) comments on the public impact of this kind of 'social steering', while Dean (1998) similarly speaks of 'moral repertoires'. In this context, the stronger language of the Five Year Plan, stating that our 'traditional tolerance is under threat … from those … breaking our rules and abusing our hospitality' (p. 5) seems ill judged. The overall picture sketched out in relation to migration is tighter immigration control, selective entry for desirable labour, fuller integration for those who achieve settlement,[9] and a clearer boundary between those on track for full membership and those who are denied the possibility of earning permanent residence, or even legal presence.

New Labour's safe haven

The contractual foundation for entry and residence embraced by NL is closely linked to market demand, and cannot accommodate the position of asylum seekers, who are activating an absolute right based on membership of the community of humanity. Furthermore, in this heightened atmosphere, asylum seekers represented a threat to the managed migration project, being a group whose presence could be neither fully predicted nor completely controlled. However, the treatment of asylum seekers over the last decade also offers several examples of the harnessing of rights as a means of governance. This has operated in part through an elaboration of different statuses of protection with different rights attached, but also through the construction of subsidiary systems of support, with built-in surveillance and control. The approach has raised interesting questions about the degree of support necessary for pursuit of an asylum claim, the deterrent effect of eroding provision, and their possible impact on public perceptions of desert, especially when the 2002 Nationality Immigration and Asylum Act again withdrew support from asylum seekers not claiming 'as soon as reasonably practicable'.

As we have seen, the basic rights of asylum seekers derive from the 1951 Geneva Convention and its 1967 protocol, defining contracting states obligations not to return a refugee to persecution. They draw on absolute rights, which are not therefore open to qualification, though as Jack Straw (2000) has noted with respect to the Geneva Convention:

> The Convention gives us the obligation to consider any claims made within our territory … but no obligation to facilitate the arrival on our territory of those who wish to make a claim.

The same applies to subsidiary protection.[10] As we have seen, this absence has been exploited through the joint effect of visa requirements (Glidewell Panel, 1996), and carrier sanctions (Cruz, 1995), thus introducing a *deficit* to the implied right to seek asylum. However, despite these established devices of control, the incoming NL government inherited a huge backlog of applications awaiting a decision, and a support system in chaos. Decision-making has since accelerated, but with signs of some deterioration in quality; successful appeals increased from 6% in 1997 to 17% in 2000 and 20% in 2003. There has also been a marked fall in applications – by 67% against their peak in 2002. This is interpreted as a reduction in abuse (Cm 6472:12,17), although it has elsewhere been acknowledged that many deserving cases may not have access to the services of traffickers increasingly necessary to gain entry to Britain (Blunkett 2003; CM 5387:52).

The conditions associated with different categories of protection provide one example of how a system of stratified rights can be linked to the process of governance. *Secure Borders, Safe Haven* (2002) granted immediate settlement for recognised refugees, but a later change[11] confined this to resettlement cases. Other recognised refugees and those granted humanitarian protection (HP) now have their status reviewed after five years, while Discretionary Leave (DL) denies settlement for a minimum of six years. These statuses carry full work and welfare rights, but family unification (newly granted for HP) is withheld from DL. The use of Temporary Protection as a device for dealing with specific crisis situations has also increased. Refugee agencies consider this shift towards more temporary and insecure forms of protection to exacerbate feelings of insecurity and trauma, and frustrate the integration process (www. refugeecouncil.org.uk accessed 11 July 2005). However, the expansion of categories, their graduated approach to settlement, and frequent redefinition, suggest growing difficulty in drawing a clear line between what might be termed the deserving and undeserving applicants,[12] one possible reason for the focus on deterrence as an aspect of control (Webber, 2004).

Support and deterrence

Welfare support for asylum seekers has been the focus of much policy attention and legal challenge throughout the NL government (see Morris, 2002; Sales, 2002; Webber, 2004). The system established under NASS (see Greater London Authority, 2005) was a subsidiary system of support which removed asylum seekers from the national welfare system, and established instead a tailored mode of provision set at 70% of standard benefit. Some refused asylum seekers could retain legitimate presence by seeking a judicial review of their case, and others may be unable to leave through illness or lack of documentation. They can apply for 'hard cases' support in the form of full board and accommodation outside London, conditional on monthly reviews of their case and proof of active efforts towards departure. Those with special care needs and minor children may still qualify for local authority support, and finally, there are various (expanding) forms of reception and detention, which raise additional human rights questions with respect to the right to liberty and a fair trial.

Despite the fact that asylum seekers wish to engage the absolute right to protection embodied in the Geneva Convention and the ECHR (now HRA), there was an attempt to maintain consistency with the language of contractual rights by reference to a 'covenant' with asylum seekers in the *Fairer Faster and Firmer* (1998) document. One conceded obligation on the government side was: 'to ensure that no asylum seeker is left destitute while waiting for their application or appeal to be determined' (CM 4018:36), though there was also a clear conviction that asylum seekers were being attracted to Britain by the benefits available. Bloch and Schuster (2002) provide data to contest this view, while Duvell and Jordon (2002) argue that an unregulated labour market and lax removal policies may be a factor, but increasingly welfare support comes with conditions and controls attached (Dwyer, 2005)

We have already noted the limitations imposed on government action by judicial intervention in response to the Conservative government's denial of support for late claimers. This culminated in the ruling[13] which upheld the recourse of dis-benefited asylum seekers to support under the NAA. Subsequent legislation under NL removed this possibility[14] and introduced instead a system of provision based on vouchers and dispersal; a system which was itself somewhat punitive and brought many problems in its wake (Sales, 2002). Among them was the threat of a Human Rights challenge to the voucher system on grounds of inhuman and degrading treatment, and vouchers have since been abandoned. The favoured provision in the 2002 White Paper was accommodation centres (or 'managed accommodation', Cm 6472:30), to provide 'end to end credibility' via induction, accommodation, maintenance and reporting systems, leading to either integration or removal, though these have not proved viable (Migration News Sheet, July 2005).

The idea of accommodation centres – undermined by local opposition – signalled a wish to segregate asylum seekers from the rest of society; a form of civic exclusion which has in part been achieved through both detention and dispersal. An official enquiry (Guardian, 2005b) has confirmed racism, casual violence and abuse at Oakington detention centre, while dispersal has created marginal groups, often housed in hard to let accommodation, the victims of local resentment and sometimes racist attack (see for example *Gezer*, EWCA). Though cut off from specialist support, asylum seekers become institutionalised to a degree which creates both practical and psychological problems for those who finally receive recognition (Sales, 2002; Dwyer, 2005). Furthermore, they were denied the opportunity to 'earn' their way to security, whatever their skills, when the possibility of employment after six months was abolished in the summer of 2002. Under EU law asylum seekers may now request permission to work after 12 months, but an earlier option to seek employment would offer an opportunity for meaningful activity, ease integration, demon-strate that asylum seekers are not a drain on public resources, and possibly defuse resentments and tension. The related tendency to physical and social separation for certain groups has been described by Rodger (2003:413) as an erosion of functional democracy and part of a 'decivilising tendency' in contemporary welfare.

Indeed, the 'covenant' with asylum seekers proved to be of limited life when a late amendment to the 2002 Nationality Immigration and Asylum Act (section 55) re-introduced the denial of benefit for in-country applicants who do not claim 'as soon as is reasonably practicable'. Stratified protection was also extended by a reservation to the UN Convention on the Rights of the Child, excluding the children of asylum seekers from its coverage (see Joint Committee on Human Rights, 2004, paras 92–94) and linked to the with-drawal of support from families of failed asylum seekers on receipt of a negative decision (Bloch and Schuster, 2005). This vulnerability to the erosion of rights underlines the fragility of the espoused 'covenant' with asylum seekers, and Hale (2004) has noted that the language of contract applies only in a situation of free consent. In so far as asylum seekers can opt out of the system, it is by reliance on similarly placed friends and relatives or by taking their chances in the informal sector of the economy, which some commentators are now predicting (Webber, 2004).

Civic stratification and asylum

Although asylum seekers are claiming an absolute right, the assumption of high levels of abuse has meant practices of control which make arrival in the UK prohibitively difficult. This policy was reinforced by the possible deterrent effect of the withdrawal of welfare support from late claimers, which was likely to be damaging to public perceptions of asylum seekers and hence their informal standing in society, Lockwood's 'civic deficit'. One claim made in the 1998 White Paper is that the work of Airline Liaison Officers in 1997 led to 1,800 refusals of boarding: 'saving the welfare system £14 million' (p. 25), which assumes that if allowed to travel all would have claimed asylum and attendant welfare support. A popular belief that asylum seekers are a major reason for over-burdened health and education systems (Lister, 2003) is there-fore unsurprising, and practitioners in the field have also voiced concerns about associations of criminality, the emergence of a vigilante culture, and a negative effect on race relations more generally (JCWI, 1998; Webber, 2004).

Though deterrent policies are presented as part of an attempt to draw a clear line between genuine cases and the rest, the expansion of categories of protection suggests that this distinction is increasingly difficult to make, hence the variety of statuses with different prospects of settlement. In fact, in Boswell's (2000) view, universal rights are at risk simply by virtue of the absolute numbers involved, rather than doubts about the genuine nature of their claims. Webber (2004) goes further and argues that to claim asylum is now almost counter-productive, with a large swathe of countries designated generally safe, reduced rights of appeal, deterrent systems of support, and limited availability of legal aid. Her prediction is that instead of alleged abuse of the asylum system by economic migrants, we will see asylum seekers present in a clandestine capacity but not bothering to register an application, preferring rather to occupy the lowest rung on the civic stratification ladder – that of clandestine presence.

This is a strange prospect for an administration whose term of office began with a trumpeting of rights and a commitment to build a human rights culture, underpinned by the passing of the HRA. In the case of asylum, the outcome has been a growing complexity manifest in expanding statuses of protection, severe deficits in accessing the status determination process, constrained social rights, and active exclusions from economic rights. These developments have not been part of a creeping erosion, but rather reflect a particular philosophy at work, which has meant that increasingly 'rights' represent a privilege which has to be earned. The granting of rights is therefore carefully balanced against contributions to society and as such offers the government a valuable tool in the management of population and society. The chapters to follow trace the history of legal challenges to the deterrent withdrawal of support from late claimers for asylum, which confront the pragmatics of control and its communitarian justification with the principles of cosmopolitanism. The role of judgement is critical to this history, and much of this volume is concerned with the nature and impact of judicial decision-making, explored via a series of cases in which two contrasting interpretive orientations come into conflict. The case history is presented as a microcosm of the tensions identified in the present chapter, and as both reflecting and shaping the direction of change in society. We therefore begin with a chronological review of the cases at issue, followed by an account of civil society involvement, and an analysis of the history in terms of competing legal paradigms. We then step back from the legal detail, to consider the social and political import of the rulings and to offer some thoughts on a sociology of judgement and a sociology of rights.

Notes

1 http://news.bbc.co.uk (accessed 24 March 2009).
2 www.ukvisas.gov.uk (accessed 21 April 2009).
3 Later extended to European Economic Area (EEA).
4 This eventually emerged as a Council recommendation under the French Presidency in 1995.
5 Explanatory note submitted by the Home Office to Parliament, 28 February 1995.
6 The study was referred to in the Home Office note on the Joint Action (see above) and included immigration officers, police, the Department of Social Security, Employment Services, the National Health Service, and housing authorities.

7 Neither did asylum seekers appealing against an initial refusal, though benefits were backdated if the appeal was successful.

8 Families with children deemed 'in need' could be given help in cash or kind for the children alone, and asylum seekers with physical or mental health vulnerability also qualified for support.

9 Cm 6363, Tables 4.1 and 5.4 combine to suggest about one-third.

10 Either Humanitarian Leave or Discretionary Leave, for which the key instruments are the ECHR, the Convention against Torture, and the International Covenant on Civil and Political rights.

11 Written Ministerial Statement, 19 July 2005.

12 In 2000, 11% were granted full recognition, 12% Exceptional Leave to Remain and 17% of appeals were allowed, totalling a positive outcome for around 35%.

13 M[1997] 1 CCLR 85.

14 Immigration and Asylum Act, 1999, para 116.

Chapter 3

Welfare asylum and the politics of judgement

In November 2005 the House of Lords (HoL) delivered a landmark judgement (*Adam*, UKHL), ending a 10-year period of legislation and contestation regarding the removal of welfare support from asylum seekers who do not claim on entry into national territory (late claimers). This history began with the Conservative government's attempt to remove benefits from late claimers by changes in Income Support Regulations (DSS, 1996), and ended with a HoL judgement on the application of Labour's 2002 Asylum and Immigration Act, yielding a sequence in which 'each step taken by Parliament has led to litigation' (*T*, EWCA, para 6). Of the 14 judgements in this case history, 11 went against the government.

One interesting question is what was at stake in these judgements, and why so many cases were necessary to bring the sequence to a final conclusion; this will be the focus of the present chapter. As we have seen, the policy at issue stems from government concern over asylum and immigration, and attempts at deterrence which collide with the assertion of fundamental rights. Thus challenges to its implementation implicitly raise questions about the boundary of our social and moral community, and highlight the role of the judiciary in determining the legitimacy of contentious policy measures. The case history spans a period of transition in Britain from the general principles of the Common Law to implementation of the Human Rights Act (HRA), the latter requiring public authorities to act compatibly with the European Convention on Human Rights (ECHR). Yet indeterminacy is to the fore in such a developing area of law (Dworkin, 2005), allowing considerable scope for judicial interpretation.

The following account of these cases documents an incremental process in which the application and interpretation of basic values and principles plays a vital role. The starting point for analysis is therefore the moment of judgement in each case; what issues the decision turns upon, what general principles the judges draw on, and the impact of such principles on the outcome. These questions can then be considered alongside more overt policy issues such as the force of collective interest as against individual rights, the way judges differ in their interpretation of these matters, and how these differences are resolved across a series of cases. Beyond these questions we find a more elusive terrain of further interest to policy analysts – judgement as political dialogue, which can be explored by close attention to both the rationale and delivery of each judgement. Legomsky's (1987) account of the judicial treatment of immigration law notes the significance of 'extra-legal' factors in shaping a judgement, and he includes here the force of political concerns. Accordingly, we can ask what legal and political strategies judges deploy in the formulation and delivery of their judgement, what political messages the judgements contain, and what impact they have on the application of policy.

Such questions open up the idea of judgement as part of a dynamic process that shapes our conception of social and political life, and establishes the parameters of acceptability. Analysis of these cases is therefore of great relevance to social policy, especially given the high success rate of the challenges. The judgements allow us to examine how far constraints may be placed on government action by virtue of recourse to general principles and fundamental rights, and they have powerful implications for the deterrent approach to asylum which has been a key aspect of policy over the last decade (Stevens, 2004; Webber, 2004). They also permit an assessment of the role of the HRA, as compared with common law principles, in challenging the implementation of such policy. Conversely, we can consider how far the judgements are constrained by government objectives, through an examination of the political concerns at issue and their handling by the judiciary. What is revealed is an insight into the role of judgement as part of a political exchange both between judges and with the government (cf Fredman, 2000) over permissible means of deterrence.

The context for the cases under consideration is an attempt by respective governments to harness the benefits system as a means to deter arrival, each instance of the withdrawal of support coinciding with a significant rise in asylum numbers (to 43,925 in 1996, and to 84,135 in 2002). In the case of both Conservative and New Labour policy in this area, justification for withdrawal was a claim to combat abuse, despite critical comment on the policy's failure to discriminate between genuine and non-genuine claimants.[1] It has been shown that late claims were more likely to succeed than applications on arrival,[2] and that the measure was based on misguided assumptions about how asylum seekers choose their country of destination, benefits playing a lesser role than that of traffickers and the availability of informal supports (Bloch and Schuster, 2002).

Such mis-matches of policy and practice have been highlighted by Juss (1997), who writes of 'cultural jurisprudence', and the need to judge policy in the light of the lived experience of those affected. The policy of removing support from late claimers offers a good illustration, and has been one aspect of a broader attempt to deter and control certain types of migration (Stevens, 2004), linked under New Labour to an emphasis on targets for the reduction and removal of asylum seekers (Düvell and Jordan, 2003). The erosion of welfare support as part of this process has been documented by Cohen et al. (2002) and Sales (2002), while my own work (Morris, 2002) has addressed migration and asylum policy in terms of a system of civic stratification, designed to attract or repel certain categories of migrant.

Judicial decision-making in the field of immigration and asylum has traditionally been driven by deference to policy priorities (Stevens, 2004), and shaped to a degree by conservatism and constraint (Legomsky, 1987). However, many writers (Woodhouse, 1998; Woolf, 1998; Stevens, 2005) see a recent growth of Judicial Review as marking increased judicial involvement in placing government policy under challenge. For Sedley (1995) this development has filled a 'lacuna of legitimacy' in the functioning of British politics, and has signalled a waning of the tradition of judicial deference in relation to welfare issues. Woodhouse (1998), for example, cites a number of cases reading positive rights to social support from protections such as the right to life, or to seek asylum, and she predicts an increase in judicial intervention to defend rights historically associated with the welfare state. The present history is therefore of particular interest, in dealing with welfare issues which are indirectly linked to the immigration aspect of asylum policy.

Early cases in this history were confined to interpretations of domestic law, albeit read against the Convention on the Status of Refugees (CSR) and the Common Law. Later cases post-dated the HRA and invoked an absolute human right, requiring the highest degree of scrutiny and offering little scope for qualification in terms of the national interest. Both before and after the passing of the HRA key judgements ruled against the application and effect of government policy, and below we examine their unfolding logic and policy implications. The account is interspersed with interview material from the solicitors and barristers involved in bringing the challenge, and their comments are deployed here to underline the critical legal and strategic moments in the case history.

Before the HRA

The early cases were noted in the previous chapter, and have been documented elsewhere (Feria, 1996; Gillespie, 1996; Scoular, 1997). However, they provide an interesting backdrop to the later HRA cases and are briefly summarised below, with particular attention to the political thrust of the judgements and the role played by general principles in the interpretation of domestic law.

The law of humanity

It all starts in 1996 when the Tory Government decides it is going to discourage asylum seekers by starving them and denying them access to benefits.

(Barrister 6)

The first case therefore arose from a challenge to the 1996 Income Support Regulations under the Conservative government, which abolished benefits for asylum seekers who did not claim asylum immediately on arrival, or were appealing a first decision. The challenge was initiated by the Joint Council for the Welfare of Immigrants (*JCWI*, QBD), alleging inconsistency with the 1951 CSR and the 1993 Asylum and Immigration Appeals Act. The High Court (HC) found no direct interference with rights conferred by the 1993 Act (Scoular, 1997), and that the removal of benefits did not amount to deportation, expulsion or *refoulement*.[3]

> In 1996 the judges were so very concerned not to overstep the limits of domestic law. ... so it was "is this *ultra vires* of this statute", and that was it.
>
> (Barrister 7)

Nevertheless, the Court of Appeal (CA) reversed the decision (*JCWI*, 4 All ER 385). Simon Brown LJ noted the questionable logic of the policy and accepted an argument of conflict with asylum seekers' right to status determination, contained in the CSR and confirmed in the 1993 Act. In his view enforced destitution of asylum seekers *did* amount to constructive *refoulement*, and could place the UK in violation of the CSR.

The ostensible core of the judgement was that statutory rights were not to be cut down by subordinate legislation, but the decision was much more broadly conceived, arguing that Parliament had made a full commitment to the CSR in the 1993 Act, granting fuller rights than asylum seekers had previously enjoyed, some of which would be rendered nugatory by the Regulations. Simon Brown LJ therefore identified an expansionary logic at work which would be undermined by the Regulations, and ruled that 'Primary legislation alone could achieve that sorry state of affairs' (p. 13). Criticism of the government went further, in describing the 'uncompromisingly draconian' (p. 13) effect of the Regulations which 'necessarily contemplate a life so destitute that ... no civilised nation can tolerate it' (p. 12). Simon Brown LJ also made reference to an earlier case (*R v Eastbourne*, 1803), which upheld an obligation to maintain poor foreigners by reference to the 'Law of Humanity', and moved beyond the core of the legal decision to state:

> So basic are the human rights at issue that it cannot be necessary to resort to the ECHR to take note of their violation.
>
> (p. 12)

In effect, the Law of Humanity gave moral weight to the decision, underlining the unacceptable nature of the policy, while Simon Brown LJ's comment on the ECHR issued an implied threat or warning of a bigger debate in waiting, to be played out in later cases.

[The case] put down a marker in relation to the ECHR. We can have a bigger debate but let's not have it now ... The real argument is black letter law but squeeze as much out of the Law of Humanity as you possibly can.

(Barrister 2)

Was the Law of Humanity a necessary part of the decision? I'm not sure it could have been really. I suppose it was underlining the point that that the predicament of asylum seekers deprived of support conflicted with a long standing common law tradition about how you treat people. ... it underlines the unacceptable nature of the treatment. Judgements will often have a greater effect than their narrow ratio.

(Barrister 5)

Though Brown LJ's opinion, supported by Waite LJ, was decisive, the dissenting opinion from Neill LJ struck a sharp contrast. It stressed the established treatment of persons from abroad as special cases, the primary purpose of the Regulations given rising public costs, and the need to strike a balance between collective interests and the rights of asylum seekers. These issues drive much of the ensuing history and Neill LJ's position is implicit in later attempts to re-establish the policy. Since this case turned on the legality of secondary legislation, it remained open to the government to confirm the policy in primary legislation, which in turn sparked further challenge.

The National Assistance Act

The 1996 Asylum and Immigration Act enshrined key aspects of the discredited Regulations in primary legislation (see Gillespie, 1996) and so overcame the negative ruling. The next case (M, 1 CCLR 69) turned upon S21 (1)(a) of the 1948 National Assistance Act (NAA), granting residential care to those 'in need of care and attention', now put to a use in apparent conflict with the purpose of the 1996 Act. Collins J, in his HC judgement, recognised the intention of Parliament to reverse the earlier JCWI decision (p. 13), but in failing to designate exclusion from the NAA they had left open the question of Local Authority liability. Since Parliament 'could have made (this) clear beyond doubt' (p. 15) the interpretive task was to uncover their intentions in the NAA, which was deemed a source of provision for those *unable to fend for themselves*. Resource constraints were ruled out of the picture and Collins J cited the JCWI case on the dilemma confronting asylum seekers without benefit and on asylum rights rendered valueless.

There was almost no conception in 1996 that there might be some kind of law that could trump a statute. We really ducked and dived before the Convention [ECHR] came into force, finding that 1948 act. The government thought they had completely repealed everything. They just made a mistake. No-one had ever dreamt that a completely healthy person could need care and attention under the 1948 act. It took them completely by surprise.

(Barrister 5)

As in the CA judgement on *JCWI*, once the legal core of argument was established there were a number of wider ranging references, notably to the Right to Life, and the Law of Humanity (*M*, 1 CCLR 69, p. 27). Emphasising that the judgement did not frustrate but implemented the will of Parliament as expressed by the NAA, it was declared impossible to believe that Parliament intended lawfully present asylum seekers to be left destitute and at risk of illness and death. If the intent was to deny all assistance then:

> [Parliament] must say so in terms. If it did, it would almost certainly put itself in breach of the ECHR and of the Geneva Convention.
>
> (p. 28)

The same judicial technique was in play as in the *JCWI* judgement on appeal, by reference to a broader argument awaiting a public airing. However, the subsequent CA judgement on *M* (*M*, 1 CCLR 85 CA), while arriving at the same conclusion, was cast in narrower terms.

In this CA judgement, delivered by Woolf LJ, the NAA was construed as 'an act which is always speaking', requiring a reading which addressed contemporary circumstances. Late claimers thus qualified for support under the NAA as a result of their particular predicament – lacking food and accommodation, without knowledge of the language or country, and under stress in pursuing an asylum claim. However, the judgement rested purely on a statutory interpretation of the NAA, making explicit the fact that provision could not be claimed by those simply short of money (thereby excluding undocumented migrants). It made no reference to fundamental Human Rights, the Law of Humanity, or the CSR, though its impact was explicitly linked to the practical circumstances confronting asylum seekers. The policy message was more limited as a result, but nevertheless made an explicit connection between the circumstances of asylum seekers and their need for basic maintenance. It may therefore seem surprising that the denial of benefit for late claimers should resurface some five years later, under a New Labour government. However, nothing in the judgements above prohibited the removal of asylum seekers from eligibility under the NAA, or the introduction of further deterrent measures.

Rights brought home

By the time the next case came to the courts the 1998 HRA had been passed and come into effect, securing the application of the ECHR in British law and making it unlawful for public authorities to act incompatibly with a Convention right (HRA, S6). The Act also had the potential to increase existing tension between the judiciary and the executive (cf Woolf, 1998):

> The judges said if you incorporate the HRA you are going to bring us into the centre of socially controversial policy, which is not where we are used to being. If that is what parliament wants we will do it, but the *quid pro quo* is you the politicians must accept that you have asked us to do the job and you cannot throw sticks and stones at us when we do.
>
> (Barrister 1)

At this point, late claimers for asylum had been explicitly excluded from the NAA but granted maintenance and accommodation under the 1999 Immigration and Asylum Act, via a system of dispersal administered by the National Asylum Support System (NASS) (Thomas, 2003). However, the 2002 Nationality Immigration and Asylum Act carried strong echoes of the 1996 exclusions. It *denied* the Secretary of State power to support asylum seekers who did not claim 'as soon as reasonably practicable' (S55(1)) but incorporated human rights principles by *permitting* support where necessary to 'avoid a breach of Convention rights' (S55(5)). However:

> If you introduce a system which has the potential to threaten people's article 3 rights at the same time as you introduce a piece of legislation through the HRA which gives people a claim if their rights have been breached then one thing will lead to the other.
>
> (Solicitor 2)

A number of rights were potentially at play in relation to S55(5) (Billings and Edwards, 2004) but article 3 was the most debated, with respect to whether enforced destitution amounted to inhuman and degrading treatment (IDT) and was therefore impermissible. The Joint Committee on Human Rights (JCHR, 2002) had already noted:

> It is difficult to envisage a case where a person could be destitute without there being a threat of a violation of Articles 3 and/or 8 of the ECHR.
>
> (para 15)

Eligibility for support under NASS was anyway confined to those destitute or likely to become so within 14 days; defined in the 1999 Act (S95(3)) as the absence of adequate accommodation or the inability to meet essential living needs. S55(5) of the 2002 Act implicitly assumed a gap between NASS destitution and any definition which might qualify for article 3 protection, without which the section would be meaningless. The effectiveness of the policy therefore hung upon the court's interpretation of IDT, and its application in the cases at issue, attaching powerful policy implications to the ensuing judgements.

Interpreting article 3

An assault on democracy?

In the first case to challenge disqualification from support under S55 (Q, EWHC) Collins J drew attention to a lack of Parliamentary scrutiny (para 5), registered Joint Committee on Human Rights (JCHR) concern (para 8), and queried the overall logic of the measure (para 14). However, the first element of the judgement was procedural. It found the interpretation of 'as soon as reasonably practicable' (ASRP) to be inadequate in neglecting the subjective element deriving from the power of agents over their charges and the possible trauma of flight. The policy impact of this finding is underlined by the Home Office (HO) argument that this interpretation would rob S55 of force and therefore undermine government policy. This argument was dismissed.

The decision on S55(5) carried greater import. Collins J recognised that 'Parliament (had) now in terms removed the Law of Humanity' (Q, EWHC, para 62),[4] thereby demonstrating the weakness of the Common Law in challenging government policy. Although the law of humanity had been described as 'anterior to all positive laws' (JCWI, EWCA, p. 12), it could not over-ride a statute:

> Because here we have the principle of ultimate parliamentary sovereignty so a statute always takes precedence. You would expect that a statute would be designed to be consistent with the law of humanity, but if it is not, it is the statute that prevails. ... That is why you need a constitution and that is the significance of the HRA
>
> (Barrister 6)

At this point there was indeed a possibility that the HRA could have a constraining force, and the idea that some Convention right was at issue was implicit in S55(5) itself; the judgement thus turned to article 3. The HO argument against entitlement to support under article 3 made reference to a European Court of Human Rights ruling (O'Rourke, ECtHR), which found that a British citizen living on the street in a state of poor health did not attain the 'requisite level of severity' (Q, EWHC, para 62) for a finding of IDT. This case was subject to scrutiny in later judgements, but Collins J looked instead to the 'real risk' test of article 3 applied by the ECtHR in cases of threatened deportation. Satisfied that real risk of a breach existed for the present claimants, he ruled that provision could be anticipatory, and that no attention had been given to human rights issues by NASS officials.

The Home Office position was always: we don't accept that these consequences will happen ... Which is where the absence of the guidelines comes in. If the Home Office had any idea of how they would resolve things, this was the time when a wise government could put its own position. But it was all done for rhetorical effect; all done to sound tough.

(Barrister 1)

The *implementation* of S55 was therefore found to be fundamentally flawed.

Collins J closed by recognising that his decision would weaken the anticipated effect of S55(1) but with a reminder of the intentions of Parliament in including S55(5), and a glancing reference to possible breach of the CSR (Q, EWHC, para 74). In fact, once more the strategic delivery of the judgement ranged more widely than the detail of the argument, in its implied criticism of the rationale of the policy, and in citing general principles which supplement the specifics of the decision. These include not only the rights enshrined in the ECHR, but also the Universal Declaration of Human Rights (UDHR), and 'the constitutions of many civilised countries' (para 87). Collins J also recalled the Law of Humanity, despite its acknowledged removal:

It would be surprising if the standards of the ECHR were below those believed 200 years ago to be applicable to the law of humanity.

(para 72)

So again, we find an implicit assumption of an expansionary logic to rights, as in the *JCWI* CA case.

Heated responses from press and Parliament (Bradley, 2003) supply the context for the subsequent CA decision, and David Blunkett's outrage was widely cited:

This measure is an important part of our asylum reform programme which is dealing with widespread abuse of the system ... Frankly, I'm personally fed up with having to deal with a situation where Parliament debates issues and the judges then overturn them.[5]

He claimed that as a result democracy itself was under threat[6] and thus seemingly challenged the role of the courts in interpreting the HRA in a manner which potentially undermined government policy.

Resolving a conundrum

The CA judgement on the HO appeal in Q (Q, EWCA) described the case as presenting a conundrum: 'Can the Secretary of State refuse support to the destitute without thereby subjecting them to inhuman treatment?' (para 3). Despite the praise for Collins' approach, his 'real risk' solution was over-ruled, the parliamentary evidence was held to be inadmissible, his reasoning was termed opaque, and there were important differences of detail in the treatment of S55(5). On S55(1) there was broad agreement; Philips LJ found the decision-making procedure to be neither fair nor fairly operated, and rejected the HO argument that S55 would become 'a dead letter' (para 39) as a result. However, assurances were offered:

> When appropriate procedures are in place ... it will be very difficult ... to discharge the burden of proving that it was not reasonably practicable ... to claim asylum any earlier.
>
> (para 42)

Thus far, the judgement reads as an endorsement of the policy, but Philips LJ then turned to the applicability of article 3 – the 'cutting edge of human rights jurisprudence' (Q, EWCA, para 52). The issue was whether failure to provide support could breach the negative obligation to refrain from IDT, or whether article 3 could only in extreme circumstances impose a positive obligation. The decision turned on the meaning of 'treatment', which implies something more than passivity, and Phillips LJ found that the denial of support under S55(1), in combination with a prohibition on employment, did indeed qualify (para 57). This gave the CA judgement a huge additional significance, linking withdrawal of support to the breach of a negative obligation and confirming the absolute nature of article 3 as a right which cannot be qualified according to circumstance. It placed the responsibility for creating destitution firmly with the government and made arguments of balance between policy concerns and individual rights groundless.

> Once they decide that it is treatment then the HO picks up the tab for the consequences. There may be a bit of debate about whether those really are the consequences. ... (but) that is the winning position ... In military terms, if I can plant my cannon on that hill, there may be some factual debate down the margins, but I'm going to dominate the discourse.
>
> (Barrister 1)

For a definition of inhuman and degrading the judgement turned to *Pretty*, an ECtHR case:

> Ill-treatment that attains a minimum level of suffering and involves actual bodily injury or intense physical or mental suffering. Where treatment humiliates or debases an individual showing lack of respect for, or diminishing, his or her human dignity or arouses feeling of fear, anguish or inferiority capable of breaking an individual's moral and physical resistance.
>
> (quoted in Q, EWCA, para 60)

As in the HC, weight was placed on the faulty procedure for applying S55(5), but having supplied the meaning of IDT, it remained to furnish a test and 'real risk' was deemed inappropriate. To meet the requirements of article 3 the asylum seeker must be:

> so patently vulnerable that to refuse support carries a high risk of an almost immediate breach of article 3 or 8.
>
> (Q, EWCA, para 68)

Hence:

> It is not unlawful for the Secretary of State to decline to provide support unless and until it is clear that charitable support has not been provided and the individual is incapable of fending for himself such that his condition is verging on the degree of severity described in Pretty.
>
> (Q, EWCA, para 119, viii)

This is the closest we come to a test in the CA judgement. According to Billings and Edwards (2004:98) the CA 'finessed' the application of article 3 restrictively, and the gap between NASS destitution and destitution for the purposes of article 3 was thus confirmed (dismissing a JCHR concern). In contrast to the *JCWI* case, where the legal tool available was to strike down the Regulations, attention was turned instead to *degrees* of suffering. We should also note that the emphasis lay not simply on withdrawal of support but also on the prohibition of employment, which precludes any application of the ruling to the indigenous homeless.

The full impact of the decision on 'treatment' becomes clear in later cases, but in other respects the ruling delivered a politically nuanced judgement which allowed both sides to claim victory.[7]

> So the government can say (the Courts) have upheld our policy and our policy is fine. But we and the rest of the immigration/asylum community claimed it as a victory as well, because the judgement was critical of the way the policy was being dealt with at the time.
>
> (Solicitor 2)

> Oh politically – this judgement is beautiful for that. All of these very hard lines about what we do as judges, so just back off. But having established that, they are saying within this sphere we really know about your concerns and we really think they are very important. This is the balance between Parliament and judiciary.
>
> (Barrister 2)

The judgement criticised procedure and determined the meaning of treatment, but allowed the policy to function by maintaining a gap between the NASS definition of destitution and destitution for the purposes of article 3. The judgement relied on the ECtHR for a *definition* of IDT, but without delivering a clear concrete test, setting the stage for further debate about the availability of charitable support, and the acceptable degree of anticipation for provision under S55(5). Hence, in policy terms, a caution had been issued that enforced destitution where employment was prohibited *could* breach article 3, but a further eight judgements were required to resolve the matter of where the line should be drawn.

A fixed or bright line?

> Q didn't really solve things. My feeling after Q was pretty much that the window dressing had been sorted out but the actual problem, the heart and soul of what this was all about, was really still there.
>
> (Solicitor 2)

A step towards specifying concrete conditions was taken in Kay J's HC hearing on the case of *S, D and T* (*S, D and T*, EWHC). Though one S55(1) decision was found to be flawed, the main burden of the judgement fell to addressing article 3, and applying the principles established in Q. Seeking a means to assess IDT, counsel representing the asylum seekers reformulated the Pretty definition into 10 ways whereby treatment could breach article 3. This reformulation included a distinction between physical and psychological suffering, and was supported by a submission that dignity is the core value of our society. Lord Hoffman was cited on the ECHR:

> Although there is not much trace of economic rights in the 50 year old Convention, I think it is well arguable that human rights include a right to a minimum standard of living, without which many of the other rights would be a mockery.
>
> (*Matthews*, para 26)

It was also argued that the purpose of S55(5) was to *prevent* a breach of Convention rights, and thus required anticipation.

The HO again relied on the ECtHR decision on *O'Rourke*, but Kay J dismissed the case as inapplicable since the claimant's suffering had been self-induced. Though the determining *level* of suffering was not explicitly addressed, Kay J did state that:

> The Q test of "verging on" connotes a degree of anticipation or, at least, a very fine temporal line.
>
> (*S, D and T*, EWHC, para 27)

On this basis, all three cases were found to qualify for support under S55(5) and in his closing paragraph Kay J set out parameters for an IDT test:

> Denied access to employment and other benefits, he will soon be reduced to a state of destitution. Without accommodation, food, or the means to obtain them, he will have little alternative but to beg or resort to crime. ... In those circumstances and with uncertainty as to the duration of their predicament, the humiliation and diminution of their human dignity with the consequences referred to in Pretty will often follow within a short period of time.
>
> (para 33)

This statement was the key aspect of the judgement:

> Para 33 became a very well known passage in which Mr Justice Kay set out words to the effect that it would only be a short passage of time before the consequences of street homelessness and destitution reduced someone to the level where article 3 was engaged ... (he) made it very clear what the position was.
>
> (Barrister 4)

The judgement thus moved closer to a concrete definition of IDT for S55(5) purposes. Humiliation and loss of dignity were critical, and they were placed in the context of contemporary values by reference to Simon Brown LJ's condemnation of 'a life so destitute that ... no civilised nation can tolerate it' (quoted in S, D and T, EWHC, para 33).

This still left scope for interpretation in the application of the ruling, though of the three individual cases in S, D and T only T was appealed, to yield a judgement later criticised by the HoL. Although Q (Q, EWCA) had established the absolute nature of article 3, Kennedy LJ accepted an argument for restraint:

> Because the allocation of resources is normally a matter exclusively for the executive, courts must be careful not to set too low the threshold at which the duty to act does arise.
>
> (T, EWCA, para 11)

This came close to turning an absolute right into a qualified right, to be determined by resource availability. Furthermore, HO counsel argued that a claimant must be able to present a stronger claim than the general mass of asylum seekers, or the situation would become unworkable, again a position more appropriate to a qualified right. The judgement was also significant in preserving the gap between destitution for NASS purposes and destitution which might trigger article 3 protection.

Eschewing any 'simple test' (*T*, EWCA, para 16), comparison was made between *S* and *T*. The case of *S* was recognised as inexorable – sleeping rough, forced to beg, and suffering psychological disturbance and weight loss, he was verging on the required degree of severity. *T* had mental health problems he did not recognise, and was living (with some limited funds) at Heathrow in breach of local by-laws. The conclusion was that: 'the boundary – which is not a fixed or bright line – lies somewhere between the two' (para 18), and *T* fell outside the scope of article 3.

> He had shelter, sanitary facilities and some money for food. He was not entirely well physically, but not so unwell as to need immediate treatment
>
> (*T*, EWCA, para 19)

Critical to this case is the question:

> What treatment can properly be said to have arisen when there is no more than the imminent threat or fear of maltreatment
>
> (*T*, EWCA, para 51)

The ultimate decision was based on a narrow interpretation of the Pretty criteria, and seems to privilege the physical condition of the claimant. Hence Billings (2004) argues that this judgement plays down the legal significance of T's loss of dignity (cf Carnwath in *Adam*, UKHL, para 107), whereas:

> You can still be humiliated living in an airport ... he was completely illegal and could have been arrested at any time for breach of the by-laws or the vagrancy act.
>
> (Barrister 5)

The first policy change followed some three months later, when the acceptable period for 'as soon as reasonably practicable' was extended from 24 hours to 72 (Refugee Council, 2004:11).

Wait and see or common sense?

Despite the rulings thus far, the application of article 3 was still unresolved for want of a clear test for the necessary level of severity (cf Cassese, 1991). The next four judgements demonstrate two contrasting approaches to how much suffering the application of section 55(1) could inflict before triggering article 3 protection. As we will see, the choice between them was critical in determining the feasibility of the policy in practice.

i) Zardasht

Newman J noted that a majority of asylum seekers share the facts of having no home, income, possessions, or money, of being strangers to the UK with no command of English, and being lonely, disorientated, anxious and vulnerable (*Zardasht*, para 5). In *M* it was precisely these features which qualified asylum seekers for 'care and attention' under the NAA. However, for article 3 Newman J applied a harsher test based on the *extent* of their effect; only in their 'heightened presence' would common features give rise to the 'necessary degree of severity' (para 7). He added: 'It may offend the social and moral values of others, but it is the law' (para 9).

There is no scope here for an expansionary view of rights, and in contrast to other decisions Newman J seemed to seal off the law from interpretation in terms of contemporary moral values. He reasoned that the purpose of S55 was to deny NASS support, which anyway required a test of destitution, and since individuals varied in their ability to cope, being destitute for weeks would not necessarily constitute a breach of article 3. A case must show 'discernible imminence that the state of severity is impending' (*Zardasht*, para 19), with precise detail pertaining to food, shelter, health and hygiene. Furthermore, if there had been significant food deprivation:

> there would be a measure of starvation and debilitation which any lawyer would have been alert to notice.
>
> (*Zardasht*, para 31)

Newman J's ruling came to be termed the 'wait and see' approach: the intention of Parliament was to deny support, law took precedence over moral reservations, the features common to destitute asylum seekers were insufficient to make a case, and the interpretation of fending for oneself was more restrictive than in the NAA. There must be discernible imminence of the *Pretty* criteria and the ruling thus endorsed a policy which led to destitution, requiring state action only in extreme cases.

ii) Limbuela

Collins J posed an alternative view in his HC judgement on *Limbuela*. He reviewed evidence of the claimant's cough, pain, dizziness, and feelings of trauma and humiliation, noting common sense suggests that sleeping rough was likely to exacerbate ill health and could have further psychological effects.

> In many of the statements where it wasn't possible to obtain psychiatric evidence, claimants would say I can't live like this. I would rather die than live like this. I'm going to die if I live like this for much longer.

People were very clearly traumatised by the situation they found themselves in.

(Barrister 4)

The claimant's attempts to access support were detailed, together with the denial of hostel accommodation for those with no recourse to public funds. This went against alleged availability of charitable provision, and lead to the conclusion that:

> If it is established that the claimant will be out on the street in winter, that no charity can assist him in that regard, and that although there is a possibility of some irregular food and washing, nonetheless, there is no real prospect of regular obtaining of such facilities, then the threshold is crossed.
>
> (*Limbuela*, EWHC, para 30)

The judgement closed with a reprimand: a great deal of public money was being spent on court proceedings and lawyers fees which a more flexible approach to S55 would reduce. In contrast with the *Zardasht* ruling, which applied only in extreme cases, the *Limbuela* case simply required evidence of no real prospect of support. The policy implications of the difference are profound as the 'common sense approach' all but closes the gap between NASS destitution and article 3 protection, stripping the policy of effect. Acknowledging his differences with Newman J, Collins J granted permission to appeal, but first came two further cases which each took a different position on the 'wait and see' and 'common sense' approaches.

iii) Tesema

Tesema's case was critical in testing out the permitted degree of suffering, as it concerned a claimant who had not yet experienced time on the street. The issue was presented as a 'test of the response of a civilised society to a pressing social problem' (*Tesema*, para 19) and echoing Kay LJ, Gibbs J implicitly placed the case in the terrain of social morals as well as law. The case was that the claimant was not fully fit, had experienced assaults and beating at home, was depressed and vulnerable, and though not yet homeless was distressed at the prospect. In contrast to the *O'Rourke* case, Gibbs J stressed the involuntary nature of homelessness in S55 cases. He also noted the different ways in which the *Pretty* criteria could be met, implicitly drawing attention to mental suffering and to fear and anguish. He then weighed the 'wait and see' approach against the 'common sense' effects of sleeping rough in winter.

Drawing on general principles beyond the letter of the law, he found it 'contrary to any reasonable concept of justice' (*Tesema*, para 59) to require someone to reapply for support when their condition had worsened, in the face of evidence that their basic needs could not be met. In contrast to Newman J he also found social and moral values to be central:

> The question of whether or not article 3 is infringed has to be determined on the basis of what a reasonable person, objectively applying the standards of a civilised society would find to be acceptable or otherwise.
>
> (*Tesema*, para 68)

The fact that *Tesema* had not yet slept rough was viewed as irrelevant to the fate he would face without support. The judgement also challenged the resource considerations implicit in Newman J's judgement:

> Whatever the extent of the problem, it does not follow that a decision compelling an asylum seeker to live and sleep in the streets in winter is other than a breach of article 3.
>
> (*Tesema*, para 67)

The case was significant in finding the *prospect* of destitution rather than the actual experience to meet the required threshold.

iv) Adam

Charles J's HC judgement (*Adam*, EWHC) began by noting that welfare issues are normally reviewed in the context of the statutory scheme, democratic accountability, efficient administration and the sovereignty of Parliament (citing *Runa Begum*, para 35). However, he also recognised (citing *Q*, EWCA, para 115) that the more substantial the interference with human rights the more the court would require by way of justification, and that the rights at issue were not confined to those of the ECHR but also included the CSR and UDHR. A challenge to the S55(1) decision was quickly dismissed and the judgement accordingly turned to article 3. The claimant had been unsupported and sleeping rough for four weeks, though displaying only those features common to many asylum seekers. Nevertheless, it was judged that the duration of his predicament, the medical evidence and the absence of support were sufficient to meet the threshold.

Despite his emphasis on rights beyond the statute, Charles J nevertheless followed Newman J, finding Collins J's rejection of the 'wait and see' approach to display only fine distinctions from 'real risk', and therefore to be out of accord with earlier authority. Thus, two of these four cases endorsed the 'wait and see' approach and two the 'common sense' approach. It remained for the CA and later the HoL to consider their relative merits, the point at issue being the degree of suffering which would require intervention from the Secretary of State; a matter which would determine the effectiveness of the policy itself.

Positive negative and absolute rights

The CA judgement on *Adam, Limbuela and Tesema* (*Limbuela*, EWCA) began with Laws LJ's dissenting judgement. This reopened the question of treatment in a manner which placed policy considerations to the fore. Laws LJ distinguished between article 3 breaches through violence by state servants, and violations stemming from acts or omissions by the state which expose the claimant to suffering, the key issue being the degree of direct state responsibility. There was a negative obligation on states to refrain from inflicting harm, but flexibility in article 3 to address other circumstances which might imply the need for protection and therefore a positive obligation. For Laws LJ only negative obligations were absolute, while positive obligations required a balance between 'the general interests of the community and the interests of the individual' (*Limbuela*, EWCA, para 61). The effect was to undermine the absolute nature of article 3 in the light of policy objectives.

The legal reality was presented as a spectrum whereby in certain cases government action which caused suffering was justifiable. In deciding where the balance lay account should be taken of the severity of the suffering, its origin, and government purpose. Laws LJ recognised the ECHR as a living instrument, with an elastic quality, but:

> It should (not) stretch so far as to impose on the signatory states forms of obligation wholly different in kind from anything contemplated in the scope of their agreement.
>
> (*Limbuela*, EWCA, para 73)

Declining to act in the face of destitution, when there were no additional considerations, was not a breach of article 3 (para 75). Having introduced government purpose into the equation, Laws LJ argued anything other than a 'wait and see' approach 'would plainly emasculate the effect of S55(1)' (para 78). He thus gave policy factors considerable weight, and notwithstanding the 600 asylum seekers who would suddenly be without support (para 79), allowed the HO appeal, with the admonition:

> We cannot don the mantle of the statute's practical administrators ... in order to save S55 from excoriation in the moral and political arena.
>
> (para 80)

This closing statement leaves hanging the role of moral principles in the interpretation of a statute, or as other judges have put it, an interpretation guided by the standards of civilised society:

> So does the theory of parliamentary sovereignty mean if it so wished parliament could adopt a policy to kill first born babies? Well they can't – which

tells you the concept of sovereignty is not an absolute concept ... Given the disgraceful attempts to promote more and more draconian law by this so called Labour government, you have had a growing recognition by the judiciary that sovereignty is not absolute.

(Barrister 3)

In the event, Laws LJ's was a minority position.

Carnwath LJ also adopted a policy focus, but to very different effect. He made reference to 650 cases awaiting a decision, the difficulty of applying the *Pretty* criteria, and the absence of any single test which could resolve the issue. *Q* was taken to establish that lacking charitable assistance and with no other means of fending for himself, a claimant would qualify for support without evidence of further suffering. However, Carnwath LJ queried other aspects of the decision in *Q* to argue that suffering by the destitute flowed from the absence of charitable support rather than treatment by the state. He therefore accepted the 'spectrum' analysis but nevertheless found a breach of article 3. In his view, the Convention required the state:

> To take measures designed to ensure that individuals within their jurisdiction are not subjected to torture or inhuman and degrading treatment.
>
> (*Limbuela*, EWCA, para 120)

For Carnwath LJ this implied more than acting as a long stop in individual case:

> If the scale of the problem is such that individual breaches can only be avoided by more general action, such action can and must be taken "for the purpose" of avoiding the individual breaches.
>
> (*Limbuela*, EWCA, para 122)

At odds with his endorsement of the spectrum analysis, Carnwath LJ then asserted the absolute and fundamental nature of article 3, noting the very limited scope for deference to the Secretary of State (*Limbuela*, EWCA, para 128). He found the approach of other judgements far too narrow for a problem that was systemic and related to the scale of numbers involved, such that individual solutions would not suffice. The third opinion, from Jacobs LJ, was on similar ground and also in agreement with the 'spectrum analysis', though finding this did not resolve the question of where on the spectrum a case fell. Jacobs, LJ went further than Carnwath LJ in advocating a systemic approach:

> One may not be able to say of any given individual that there is more than a very real risk that denial of food and shelter will take that individual across the threshold, one can say that collectively the current policy ...

will have that effect in the case of a substantial number of people … it must follow that the current policy is unlawful in violating article 3

(*Limbuela*, EWCA, para 149)

Hence he offered an approach which, instead of focusing on degrees of suffering, a spectrum of accountability, and individual rights, considered the collective impact of the regime.

The judgement overall found against the HO appeal and thereafter S55 was in effect suspended (JCHR, 2007, para 90), except in maintenance-only cases. However, there was still no clear specification of a concrete test, though this eventually came as a result of a further HO appeal, to the HoL.

Resolution

In the HoL appeal (*Adam*, UKHL) the statements of case[8] for each side show clearly contrasting orientations:

1. For the HO, an interpretation of the ECHR in terms of its original focus, an assertion of the limits of positive obligations, and an interpretation in the context of legitimate policy objectives and proportionality.
2. For the claimants, an emphasis on the ECHR as a living instrument, on the absolute nature of article 3, and on a defence of fundamental rights over and above policy objectives.

Lord Bingham opened by recognising that the policy and purpose of S55 were a legislative choice and therefore not at issue. The question was rather what was required by the ECHR, and he accepted the ruling in Q which confirmed the regime as treatment for the purposes of article 3. On the IDT threshold he recognised that while many factors could affect a judgement, being compelled to sleep on the street, OR being seriously hungry, OR being unable to satisfy the needs of hygiene would qualify. A concrete test was thus finally provided, while Laws LJ's spectrum approach was dismissed by Lord Hope as having no foundation in the jurisprudence of the ECtHR. For Lord Hope the application of S55(1) amounted to an intentionally inflicted act which removed from asylum seekers the ability to fend for themselves, and required positive intervention as a remedy. Where the state was directly responsible for the action this qualified as treatment, the prohibition was absolute, and there was no question of balance with regard to legitimate government policy.

The word *avoid* was identified as the key to when preventive action was required; 'it was not just a question of wait and see' (*Adam*, UKHL, para 62). Real risk was again deemed too generous, so 'verging on' and the 'imminent prospect' of a breach stood as the critical test. Lord Hope did not translate this directly into concrete indicators but identified a safety net of wide reach, embracing all sorts of 'inhumanity and degradation', thus making implicit reference to dignity (para 59). While Lord Scott agreed with the HO that treatment required more than failure, he found the whole regime imposed on asylum seekers to meet this test, and emphasis was again placed on the need to *avoid* a breach. In this each case must be judged on its facts, but:

> having to sleep out of doors would be a very strong indication that the threshold had been reached.
>
> (*Adam*, UKHL, para 72)

Lord Scott also stressed not only physical suffering but 'growing despair and loss of self-respect', and like Lord Hope made implicit reference to dignity. Similarly, Lady Hale read article 3 as a reflection of:

> The fundamental values of a decent society, which respects the dignity of each individual.
>
> (*Adam*, UKHL, para 76)

She also expressed unease with the spectrum approach, though recognising two types of state responsibility for suffering – the direct infliction of the suffering or the failure to provide protection. S55 was construed as a clear case of the first:

> The state has taken the Poor Law policy of less eligibility to an extreme which the Poor Law itself did not contemplate, in denying not only all forms of state relief but all forms of self-sufficiency.
>
> (*Adam*, UKHL, para 77)

Judged by the 'standards of our own society' (para 78) the result was deemed inhuman and degrading, and she endorsed the Bingham criteria.

Finally, for Lord Brown state responsibility was the key, with no room for policy justification. While recognising that S55 necessarily contemplates homelessness for some, and that there is only limited scope for any positive obligation to house the homeless, Lord Brown saw it as:

> Quite another [thing] for a comparatively rich (not to say northerly) country like the UK to single out a particular group to be left utterly destitute on the streets as a matter of policy.
>
> (*Adam*, UKHL, para 99)

He emphasised the deliberate nature of the state's involvement, and quoted the Prime Minister on rough sleeping as a scandal in a 'modern and civilised society' (para 99), thus invoking contemporary moral standards. Doubting the practical impact of the policy he found that the consequences must be regarded as intended and therefore inhuman and degrading, or unintended and involving hardship disproportionate to the policy's aims – though Billings (2006) sees the latter view as opening the door to proportionality. Either way, for Lord Brown street homelessness in this context crossed the article 3 threshold, such that T would also qualify.

The decision was unanimous, and the issue on which the judgement turned was the significance of state responsibility in engaging article 3. A rejection of the spectrum approach and the involuntary nature of the situation confronting late claimers confirmed S55 as treatment, and human dignity was endorsed as a central principle. The use of article 3 in these rulings thus strikes a contrast to the tradition of judicial deference in immigration law, and serves as a positive illustration of the impact of the HRA (cf Stevens, 2004). While there were references to the non-political nature of the judicial role (*Adam*, UKHL, paras 2, 14, 85), these were partially belied by indirect statements of moral censure (*Adam*, UKHL, paras 66, 77, 99), and an awareness of the broader significance of the polarised positions represented by the case (*Adam*, UKHL, paras 13, 53, 73, 101).

The politics of judgement

Taken together, the cases examined here provide a forceful illustration of the power of rights in challenging policy interests, and demonstrate the significance of general principles or background values in their interpretation (Dworkin, 2005). However, not all judges drew equally on such principles, and the present history reveals a distinctive pattern; the more expansive interpretations occur where judges take recourse to general principles, while restrictive interpretations are more closely confined by the words of a statute and policy imperatives. One role of the cases documented has therefore been in determining an appropriate framework, with judges variously making reference not only to justice, fairness, and dignity, but to the standards of civilised society, decency, and common sense. In so doing, they place their judgements on a policy of deterrence by destitution in the context of broader social values, which have a powerful bearing on the boundaries of social and moral obligation.

Dialogue has played a significant role in establishing this framework (cf Habermas, 1996), both in terms of judicial exchanges within and between cases, and in political dialogue beyond the courtroom, manifest in the strategic delivery of many judgements. This delivery may be ameliorative, with judgements protecting the coherence of legislation, or offering assurance that policy is viable if procedures are amended. It may emphasise government resource constraints or reprimand government profligacy, etc. But delivery can also underline issues of principle, as in critical comment on the lack of parliamentary scrutiny, the rationale of policy, its moral legitimacy, and even grounds for future challenge. In recognising these possibilities we begin to see the functioning of the judiciary not just in terms of their structural position in a system, but also as actors in a social and political exchange. The whole sequence of cases can be viewed not simply as the pursuit of legal reason, but also as an inherently political conflict (Unger, 1986) about the application and interpretation of the general principles which must govern policy choices. These issues are pursued in later chapters, but we begin the chapter to follow by looking at the complex process which lay behind the mounting of a challenge to section 55, and the role of civil society groups in identifying cases, furnishing evidence, and shaping the judgements.

Notes

1 See Memorandum to Social Security Advisory Committee, 1995; Lords Hansard, 17 October 2002, cols 976–1006.
2 Lords Hansard, 24 October 2002, col 1468.
3 Removal of asylum seekers to a situation in which their life or freedom is threatened.
4 By withdrawing eligibility under the NAA.
5 HL Hansard, 26 February 2003, col 239–40.
6 Guardian Unlimited (2003).
7 Beverley Hughes MP, HC Hansard, 24 March 2003, col 6; Independent (2003).
8 Arguments submitted to the HoL by counsel in advance of the hearing.

Chapter 4

Civil society and civil repair

This chapter considers civil society input to the series of legal judgements outlined in Chapter 3. Drawing on the ideas of Habermas (1996) and Alexander (2006), the chapter examines a history which pits fundamental rights against political intent, and explores the role of civil society actors in waging a legal campaign against a form of legislated social exclusion. The chapter thus illuminates a set of issues which arise from attempts to incorporate sociology into legal studies, and elaborates the scope for civil repair in the case of a group outside of citizenship and rendered marginal by the law. It shows how the actions of a small network of national non-governmental organisations (NGOs) and activist lawyers working through domestic legal institutions were able to forge a link between what Isin and Turner (2007:16) term everyday politics and cosmopolitan virtues. Such civil action may also begin to exemplify the broadened conception of citizenship embraced by these authors, and to demonstrate its association with the pursuit of universal rights.

Deliberative judgement and civil repair

> Legal theory moves within the compass of particular legal orders ... (but) cannot afford to ignore those aspects that result from the internal connection of law and politics.
>
> (Habermas, 1996:196)

Yet traditional approaches to adjudication have sought to sanitise the law from its underlying political structure (Harlow and Rawlings, 1984:256), and in doing so to deny the political nature of judgement. Habermas addresses this gap by seeking legitimacy in the law not through the nature of rules (Hart, 1961), or normative coherence (Dworkin, 2005), or any privileging of the judicial perspective, but rather through procedural certainty. In his account, the point of legal procedure is to provide a space for free exchange such that the process of judgement rests on a regulated contest for the best argument. This promotes contextual interpretation through the world views of actual participants, in a 'normatively rich' description which must nevertheless preserve the universal perspective underpinning valid norms (p. 229). Attention is thus drawn away from legal theory per se to the deliberative process, and hence the relationship between politics, the courts and civil society:

> The *interplay* of a public sphere based in civil society with the opinion and will formation based in parliamentary bodies and courts offers a good starting point for translating the concept of deliberative politics into sociological terms.
>
> (Habermas, 1996:371)

For Habermas (1996), the associational network of civil society provides a 'lifeworld' anchor for the public sphere, and he offers a model in which a sufficiently vital civil society can bring conflicts from the periphery to the centre of political concern. Hence:

> Civil society is composed of those more or less spontaneously emergent associations, organisations and movements that, attuned to how societal problems resonate in the private life spheres, distil and transmit such reactions in amplified form in the public sphere.
>
> (Habermas, 1996:367)

In this model, civil society plays a key role for deliberative politics, with voluntary associations influencing public opinion and acting as advocates for neglected issues and under-represented groups (p. 368), while the public sphere as a whole offers a space for the extension and radicalisation of existing rights (p. 370).

Habermas concedes that the very existence of social movements requires the formation of solidarities and publics which cannot be taken for granted, while their 'signals' are recognised to be generally too weak to redirect political decision-making. An exception occurs in perceived crisis situations, when civil society actors are deemed to assume enhanced influence in the public sphere, through both an appeal to officeholders and parliament, and to the critical judgement of a public of citizens (p. 383). This scenario places considerable weight on a view of the public audience as constitutive of the public sphere and therefore its 'final authority' (p. 364), and seems to leave no opening for movements with a hostile or unsympathetic public, especially if this hostility drives government policy. Yet Habermas also recognises the *courts'* potential for influence on elected assemblies, and notes that the political system may fail if its decisions can no longer be traced back to legitimate law. Though this point is not developed, it opens up a different route of action which further advances an interest in the inter-relation of law, political power, and civil society, as well-documented 'test case' action can testify (eg Prosser, 1983). Where public opinion cannot be invoked, and where fundamental rights are at stake, there is a critical role for the court as an interpreter of rights and a mediator between civil society and the state.

These issues come close to Alexander's (2006) recent interest in sources of social solidarity. He advocates a 'new' concept of civil society as a civil sphere of values and institutions which generates the capacity for social criticism and democratic integration; a conception close to that of Habermas. But while in the latter we find an implicit portrayal of civil society as an inherently positive force, Alexander gives more attention to the contradictory and fragmented nature of 'real' civil societies (cf Fine, 1997). For Alexander the discourse of civil society can be as repressive as it is liberating and can legitimate exclusion as well as promoting inclusion. Hence he notes (via Eisenstadt) that when universalism and abstraction are institutionalised they produce not only emancipation and inclusion but 'tension, alienation and a restless duality' (2006:22).

Elaborating this point, Alexander argues that in establishing the civil rights of all, democratic law evokes related but unsatisfied expectations of substantive equal treatment (cf Lockwood, 1996; Turner, 1988). For some this opens up the possibility of 'civil repair' by challenging injustice through the law, while for others the legal code represents the external coercive power of class, caste or state (cf Morris, 2002). Solidarity can be extended and judicial impartiality maintained only insofar as parties subject to the law are considered full members of the civil community (Alexander, 2006:186). So can the procedural certainty of Habermas's model be accessed as a means of 'civil repair' by peripheral groups that lack both a sympathetic public and full membership? What is the role of civil society in this process, and can it harness the power of 'universal' human rights in support of such groups? To answer these questions Habermas's insights on legal procedure must be integrated into a fuller understanding of civil society action, highlighting a possible disjuncture between 'public opinion' and a rights-based conception of 'public interest'.

Judicial Review and deliberative democracy

Judicial Review (JR) is a procedure for challenging in court the way that Ministers, Departments or public bodies make decisions, thus providing extensive powers of intervention for the judiciary. Its use has seen a dramatic rise since the early 1970s, viewed by some as filling a legitimacy gap in the functioning of British politics (Sedley, 1995; see also Woodhouse, 1998; Stevens, 2005). Applications rose from 160 in England and Wales in 1974, to 4,539 in 1998, with immigration matters consistently accounting for 50% or more of the total, while Treasury spending for JR between 1997 and 2003 rose from around £1.7 million to £6.2 million (HC Research Paper, 2006).

JR can be an intensely political process, and the names of individual applicants may disguise a wide range of interest group activity (Harlow and Rawlings, 1984; 1992). Prosser's (1983) account of CPAG test case strategy, for example, demonstrates the role of JR in contesting policy and harnessing the law as an instrument of social change. Such litigation allows for pressure group activity in the absence of a larger scale social movement and a concerned or sympathetic public, representing otherwise marginalised groups, and often combined with campaigning activities. While there has been hostility to the use of unelected judges to make political choices over where the public interest lies (HC Research Paper, 2006), there are counter-arguments. Judges are accountable by means other than electoral politics, through the publically available reasoning and logic by which they reach their conclusions, by the process of deliberation within the courts, and through the right of appeal to a higher court (cf Habermas, 1996:225–26). The courts have also traditionally deferred to democratic institutions in considering challenges (Fordham, 2007), though the Human Rights Act (1998) (HRA) has shifted the ground, requiring a greater intensity of scrutiny where fundamental rights are concerned. Hence, it has been argued that, under the Act:

> The courts are charged by Parliament with delineating the boundaries of a rights based democracy.
> (Clayton, 2004, cited in HC Research Paper, 2006:45)

The impact of the HRA on democracy has been much debated (Woolf, 1998; Fredman, 2000; Clayton, 2004) and it certainly places constraints on the elected legislature. Fredman, however, argues that parliament is an increasingly imperfect vehicle for participatory rights, and that the process of litigation can itself provide an opportunity for participation by means of argument before the court on the nature and scope of rights. Through litigation parties have the chance to present their own perspectives, while deliberation can be broadened by interest group participation, class action and specialist intervention (see Irvine, 2003). Given the absence of extended debate on the content or interpretation of rights contained in the HRA this is likely to play a central role in any application of the act. Hence:

> The challenge remains with litigators and the judiciary to use the opportunities presented to strengthen the exercise of participatory rights and enrich the ongoing debate about the meaning of fundamental rights.
> (Fredman, 2000:129)

Indeed, the precise meaning and application of article 3, which prohibits torture and inhuman and degrading treatment (IDT), lies at the heart of the cases under consideration in this study, determining the point at which the secretary of state must resume support for destitute asylum seekers.

The withdrawal of support from asylum seekers who did not claim 'as soon as reasonably practicable' (ASRP) (S55(1) of the 2002 Nationality Asylum and Immigration Act) was introduced by means of a late amendment in the HoL. It was allowed only 15 minutes' debate in the House of Commons (Willman, 2003), was not included in the White Paper preceding the bill (Q, EWHC, para 5), and was the subject of severe reservations by the Joint Committee on Human Rights (2002), which noted:

It is difficult to envisage a case where a person could be destitute without there being a threat of a violation of article 3 and/or 8 of the ECHR.

(JCHR, 2002, para 15)

The Committee also found the 'as soon as reasonably practicable' requirement to be 'unacceptably imprecise and lacking in objectivity' (para 17). The proviso contained in S55(5), which required intervention where necessary to avoid a breach of Convention rights, in effect acknowledged the potential for incompatibility with the HRA, invited judicial interpretation and handed deliberation to the courts.

The vehicle for civil society involvement was JR of government decisions under S55, and the following account of this challenge is based not only on the relevant judgements, but also draws on third party interventions and key items of evidence, supplemented by interviews with the NGO officers, solicitors and barristers involved. The dimensions of action examined here thus cover the emergence of a legal strategy, the accumulation of evidence and legal argument, and strategic interventions. These actions are then considered in the light of Habermas's model of deliberative judgement and Alexander's concept of civil repair, and as an instance of Isin and Turner's (2007) citizenship engagement in everyday politics in pursuit of cosmopolitan virtues.

The early cases

The first case in our history illustrates the role a special interest group can play in giving a voice to groups disadvantaged in the national political system (Harlow and Rawlings, 1992:319). It was brought by the Joint Council for the Welfare of Immigrants (JCWI) and later conjoined with an individual claimant, B. As we have seen, the case succeeded on appeal through the argument that Income Support Regulations deterring disentitled asylum seekers from pursuing their claim undermined rights inherent in the 1993 Asylum and Immigration Appeals Act. The judgement was also supported by reference to the 'law of humanity'.

The JCWI was granted leave to bring the case (prior to the appearance of the individual claimant) on the grounds of their legitimate interest as an advisory organisation, though in so doing they exposed themselves to the risk of costs; as an organisation they were ineligible for legal aid. Though their standing was contested the judge accepted that the JCWI's involvement advanced the public interest, accelerated a decision in bringing an early case, and thus performed a public service. Since changes to regulations do not require debate in parliament, the case served as the sole forum for debate in considering the following evidence:

- On the rationality of the provision, which neglecting legitimate reasons for late claiming and penalised genuine claimants.[1]

- On the experiential effect of the regulations in exposing asylum seekers to exploitation, in undermining their health, and in causing personal distress.[2]
- On the impact on voluntary organisations, given their limited capacity to help.[3]
- On the inconsistency with the Convention on the Status of Refugees (CSR) and the 1993 Act, through the claim of constructive *refoulement*.[4]

The case stands as an example of both a challenge on a point of law, and an instance of a forced policy change, albeit temporary. It was followed by a very different case, which arose when the discredited regulations were confirmed in primary law via the 1996 Act. This was lawyer led and an example of a 'revival case' (Prosser, 1983), bringing into play existing but largely inactive legislation by testing out possible recourse to the National Assistance Act for dis-benefited asylum seekers argued to be 'in need of care and attention' under the Act.

> It was just someone's bright idea and it emerged from talk within the legal community about this policy.
>
> (Barrister 7)

The judgement covered background information on the public cost of provision for asylum seekers (cited at $200 million) and the policy rationale for disentitlement, which were deemed insufficient to over-ride the purpose of the NAA. Voluntary sector organisations again played a vital role in furnishing evidence as, for example, on the paucity of charitable provision, especially free beds, and on the individual experience of dis-benefited asylum seekers.

We saw in the previous chapter that the passing and implementation of the HRA has considerably changed the terrain since these cases were heard. Coming some way to redressing the absence of a written constitution in the UK, the rights enshrined are less easily reversible than entitlements conferred in other legislation, such as the NAA or other instruments governing welfare provision. However, the rules of standing for JR under the HRA are narrower, such that 'sufficient interest' does not qualify and the applicant must be a victim (or potential victim) of the unlawful act (HC Research Paper, 2006). This excludes actions such as the *JCWI* case, and would seem to limit the possible input of civil society organisations. However, as we shall see, they continue to play a major role by promoting test case litigation, by providing evidence which shapes the interpretation of the law, and through their role as third party intervenors.

The campaign against Section 55

i) The emergence of a strategy

Though the response to S55 happened on three levels – public and parliamentary campaigning,[5] a legal challenge via JR, and practical help for those affected, legal action quickly assumed primacy. Despite a clear sense of outrage among NGOs, many soon concluded that public campaigning would have limited effect, given a perceived low level of sympathy for asylum seekers:

> Raising awareness and media campaigning is very, very hard, because to put it bluntly, not a lot of people care about asylum seekers and many don't necessarily see less tax-payers money going to support them as a bad thing.
>
> (Solicitor 2)

> This had to be done through the courts because asylum seekers are not a group which evokes much public sympathy. That is the significance of the HRA – if you look at who it has helped they are typically vulnerable groups with no alternative means of asserting their rights.
>
> (Barrister 6)

If the measure could not be removed then the intention was to make it inoperable, and a legal challenge was therefore co-ordinated by the Housing and Immigration Group (HIG), loosely associated with the Immigration Law Practitioners Association (ILPA) and a London Law Centre. The group was formed in 2001 as an informal forum for legal practitioners in immigration and/or housing, and was ideally placed to support action on S55. There were repeated references to a sense of revolt among practitioners:

> You just get a climate of outrage and everybody starts talking and thinking.
>
> (Barrister 7)

> There was certainly a feeling of outrage in the NGO community and amongst lawyers. The legal impetus obviously came from the lawyers, but the challenge was closely co-ordinated by a group of NGOs who tried to make sure that a proper case which tested all the issues could be brought forward.
>
> (Barrister 3)

HIG provided a kind of clearing house for information and support to people likely to be handling cases, and for thinking at a more strategic level.

> HIG was already up and running when S55 came along, and it was fantastic that it was there … There were two levels – trying to set up and develop a test case strategy and also dealing with individuals problems in the mean time, through the courts.
>
> (Barrister 2)

HIG was not, however, an immediate source of cases:

> What you really need is a funnel of grass roots advisors – like CAB, Refugee Council, Refugee Action etc., that people directly affected will go

to. They have to know about the issue, know about the class, and have access to people in the class affected.

(Barrister 2)

This is what emerged, as alongside the campaigning and legal strategising, asylum support organisations were simultaneously confronted by the practical effects of S55. The National Asylum Support System (NASS) (see Thomas, 2003) is implemented via an Inter-agency Partnership (IAP) in which six voluntary sector organisations[6] are funded by the Home Office (HO) to provide orientation and advice, and to process asylum seekers access to support and accommodation.

The most immediate impact of S55 was to place these organisations in the difficult position of turning away late claimers who did not qualify for support:

We ended up providing emergency support from the day centre. People were coming in and sleeping on the benches. Every night there would be six or seven people sleeping at the back in the car park and other people sleeping rough elsewhere. It was very difficult ... At the time we had to be gate-keeping emergency accommodation to stop people refused under section 55 from getting in, but still saying look this is how you can contest.

(NGO worker 7)

We were an organisation that never said no ... but with S55 we would sometimes be saying we can't help, we can refer you on, but quite probably they won't be able to help either ... people slept around this building and sometimes you would come to work and pass through cardboard boxes and realise there were people in there.

(NGO officer 8)

Since the disentitled asylum seekers were nevertheless turning up for advice one response was to feed back to the HO through NASS the feeling that the policy was not workable and was hitting the most vulnerable people hardest.

We were going back to them on a day to day basis and it increased their workload – the message to the HO was we are going to show you how many difficulties there are in implementing this legislation, and in our view, how many inaccuracies are involved. We felt that if we could annoy our local contacts enough with these issues they would probably start complaining to their managers. We used every possible forum that we could – thinking of it now, we are not campaigners but that was probably a bit of a campaign.

(NGO officer 8)

The other response was to refer people to solicitors to seek JR and an injunction for emergency accommodation, pending a hearing. This became a key source for the supply of test cases. So within the period of a few months which covered the passing of the bill into law and the hearing of the first test case there was a process of lobbying and campaigning against the measure. There was both trauma and a practical response at grassroots level, and the beginnings of a legal strategy through the networks connecting grassroots care, voluntary sector workers and the legal community.

Both Habermas (1996:368) and Alexander (2006:152) see civil society to be constituted through basic rights, as a sphere in which social subjects relate to each other and to social institutions as rights-bearing individuals. An alliance between voluntary sector organisations and activist lawyers can be seen as a latent feature of this sphere, which will come to the fore when rights are threatened, even in the face of public apathy or hostility. The emergent network of support workers and legal practitioners in the present case history provided the substance for much deliberative debate and the key to civil repair, working through JR to contest legislation regarded as inhuman and degrading. The picture is less that of a conscious plan, but rather a reactive process which unfolded with events as the system itself went into motion.

ii) Test cases and the 'blitz' campaign

The key to 'civil repair' in this history, and the locus of deliberative debate, has been a network of lawyers and voluntary associations working to contest legislation they regarded as inhuman. There was an early recognition of the need to challenge the policy by legal means and a search for a test case by some of the campaigning organisations, but it very soon became unnecessary to seek out cases:

> Within weeks of the legislation going into effect we had so many cases coming in that we had a rota of people working on requesting out of hours injunctions. Sometimes as many as ten a night.
>
> (Barrister 6)

Some effort was made by the NGO and legal community to develop a test case strategy, in which a key case or cases would test out the points of law at issue and determine the outcome of other pending cases:

> What you're doing as a barrister is saying time is our enemy. We want to get a case on as quickly as we can, because in the meantime all these other people who don't have access to lawyers and so on are all suffering. What you are looking for is a set of clients whose facts usefully illustrate the problem and only the problem.
>
> (Barrister 2)

However, the selection of a case for a full hearing from the large number granted permission is a process over which the contesting side have little control:

The big advantage the Home Office have is that it's much easier for them to concede cases, whereas we tend to have to litigate on bad facts because of our duty to the client.

(Solicitor 3)

The HO thus has the capacity to settle a strong case and so keep it from a public hearing. Nevertheless, after some correspondence with the court, the selection of cases for the first hearing, *Q and others*, was agreed upon and the application of S55 successfully contested (see Bradley, 2003).

By the time of this judgement, far from a search for cases, the mounting number of applications for review had become part of the strategy (cf Harlow and Rawlings, 1984):

It was one of the things that we had discussed before, that this might be quite an effective way of challenging, to show that all these decisions were leading to JR. The way it worked it was almost automatic that they got injunctions, and it was driving the court mad.

(NGO officer 7)

One factor enabling this escalation was the availability of legal aid, without which the whole history could never have happened.[7] The work was quite lucrative for the lawyers involved and so the litigation driving the challenge was ironically rather costly for the government:

I don't really think it was until the grassroots immigration firms picked up that these section 55 cases are really easy, that the big numbers started to go in. To bring a JR is much more lucrative for a solicitor than to bring an immigration appeal, or give benefits advice. But the government had legislated against appeal to an asylum support adjudicant for these cases.

(Barrister 5)

Several support organisations worked to establish a network of solicitors willing and able to take on cases, and effort was also devoted to providing support by the exchange of information and generic evidence:

We had check lists of what to ask someone when they come in, what kind of evidence and information to get and so on; everything to make it easier and quicker for people to deal with these cases. We decided we just had to swamp the HO with them.

(Solicitor 1)

There was inevitable judicial concern about the scale of the response. Collins LJ, in the High Court judgement on Q (*Q, EWHC*) noted that by the commencement of the first case some six weeks after S55 came into force,

150 applications had been lodged and one judge had personally dealt with more than 20 applications over a weekend. Eight months later, Kay J stated (*Q, D, H and others*, EWHC, para 2) that prior to S55, asylum support cases accounted for a minute proportion of the court's work. This had risen in 2003 to one quarter, accounting for approximately 800 cases in the then current workload and requiring the Court to act as a 'first-call dispute resolution'. Seven months later, in the Court of Appeal (CA) hearing on *Limbuela* (*Limbuela*, EWCA), there was concern from two judges that the 650 cases then occupying emergency accommodation would be on the streets without support if the application of S55 was upheld:

> The huge backlog of cases for JR was something which I think changed the mood in the higher levels of the judiciary ... A crisis was really developing on the back streets of London.
>
> (NGO officer 6)

A number of writers have begun to think about court proceedings as a deliberative process and as part of democratic debate (Campbell, 1998; Fredman, 2000; Clayton, 2004). As Alexander puts it:

> Collective demands can be addressed in other words not only in the court of public opinion but in the court of law.
>
> (Alexander, 2006:154)

However, it should also be recognised that this process begins outside the courtroom – through the mobilisation and selection of cases, influence over how cases are presented, the nature of evidence made available, and the way it is turned to address legal questions. We must therefore look to the interaction between the production of evidence and the process of deliberation, and in Habermas's terms (1996:229), the translation of a participant 'world view' into a legal argument.

Evidence and argumentation

Voluntary sector groups played a key role in furnishing evidence to contest S55 on three fronts. The IAP organisations had direct experience of the policy in practice and were well placed to question both its implementation and basic rationale. Secondly, a wider array of support groups were in a good position to comment on the (non)-availability of alternative charitable provision, and thirdly, their direct contact with dis-entitled asylum seekers meant they were able to address the article 3 impact of the measure. All three aspects of evidence drew on participatory knowledge which enabled the translation of policy and principles into lived experience and were crucial in shaping key judgements.

i) Rationality and procedure

The rationale of the policy and its ability to achieve its aims were closely criticised in the first HRA case (Q, EWHC), with evidence showing that late claimers were more likely to succeed than port applicants, and that the measure therefore failed to discriminate between the genuine and non-genuine. However, the reasons behind the measure were ruled out of the purview of the court, whose task was rather to determine the intention of parliament 'from the words it has chosen to use' (Q, EWHC, para 15).

Further evidence focused on the practicability and interpretation of the ASRP requirement, as experienced by those directly affected. An extensive witness statement from Refugee Action (of the IAP) details difficulties in accessing the initial screening process whereby a claim is registered, and the time, distance and costs involved in arriving at a screening unit. Evidence was provided on the desire to secure safe entry before claiming, ignorance of procedures, the power of agents over their charges, and the effect of trauma. Furthermore, Ministerial assurances[8] were cited, stating that credible reasons for claiming late would be accepted, that the trauma of the claimant would be taken into account, and that a reasonable period of delay would be permitted. The witness statement also noted HO reliance on initial screening which was conducted by an Immigration Officer, not by a NASS official.

As we saw in Chapter 3, the Q judgement in both the HC and the CA ruled that the decision-making procedure on ASRP was unfair, and in particular that the subjective state of the applicant and the power of the agent should be taken into account. However, once the procedure was amended the judges in Q, EWCA saw no reason the policy could not operate effectively – it was this element of the judgement which allowed both sides to claim victory. The issue was reopened by a subsequent hearing, (S, D and T, EWHC) (see Billings and Edwards, 2004), with a vast amount of evidence generated by the voluntary sector:

> We were asking how reasonable was it that some terrified asylum seeker following the instructions of an agent who has maybe threatened or intimidated them should see instructions posted on walls ... we had statements from refugee community organisations about what information people had or didn't have back home when they left ... and simple things like they are not going to look at a poster on a wall, because in their own country that is not how information is conveyed.
>
> (Solicitor 1)

The judge in S, D and T accepted these points, and in one of the three cases the ASRP decision was quashed, but this was the last decision which went against the government on the issue. Thereafter, attention and evidence gathering focused on the question of whether rendering asylum seekers destitute could breach their human rights, amounting to inhuman and degrading treatment (article 3).

ii) Inhuman and degrading treatment

We have seen how, in the appeal on Q, the article 3 decision rested on the question of whether given a prohibition on employment, removing rights to support constituted 'treatment'. This implicitly raised the issue of whether some other form of support might be available, notably through charitable sources. Here the voluntary sector organisations were ideally placed to co-ordinate evidence and Shelter played a key role throughout, due to the link between destitution and homelessness, and their recognised authority on this issue.

Among the evidence submitted was Shelter's witness statement, asserting that very few charitable services are on offer to those who cannot pay, and that most rely on the client's eligibility for Housing Benefit (HB) to fund the service:

> All the way through, the HO position was that there was no problem because the voluntary sector could fill the gap, so Shelter needed to show that this accommodation was not free and that it relied on funding through HB for which asylum seekers were not eligible.
>
> (NGO officer 4)

This was crucial in establishing a fundamental difference between asylum seekers and the indigenous homeless with full citizenship rights (see O'Rourke v UK). The witness statement from Refugee Action confirms this argument, and also notes that the asylum claim itself is undermined by the absence of provision, not least in disrupting official correspondence. There was further support from individual evidence submitted by solicitors, with the help of the voluntary sector:

> We gathered medical evidence, or evidence showing that the support organisations – day centres, church organisations, shelters and the like were not able to offer support. You almost had to go shopping – asking can you support me this evening, no, well can you just write this in a letter and so on.
>
> (NGO officer 1)

In the decisive CA judgement on Q, in which withdrawal of support was deemed to be treatment, evidence of the absence of charitable provision was clearly an important factor. The ultimate position on article 3 was that S55(5) would only be activated once it was clear that charitable provision was not forthcoming, and that the claimant's condition was approaching that described in the Pretty case (see previous chapter).

This set the stage for more detailed consideration of individual circumstances and the question of whether or not support was available. Fittingly, the case which followed on from Q (S, D and T, EWHC) was furnished with 650 pages of evidence, much of it supplied by a London Law Centre, and it yielded a more substantive judgement.

As in *Q*, the evidence covered the absence of significant support in the charitable and voluntary sector, but the emphasis placed on individual circumstances required a more experiential dimension – in effect an interpretation of universal norms through the world view of participants (Habermas, 1996:229). It was necessary to demonstrate with evidence that help had not been forthcoming, so a detailed account of attempts to seek support and of how the claimants had survived to date was required. Beyond this, the purpose was to demonstrate substantively that the threshold of suffering required for a breach of article 3 had been reached in each individual case:

> I spent 14 hours doing a witness statement for my client, to get every last detail of just how awful it was to sleep in the park for nine days. ... and just the degradation and humiliation – they had to pee in the bushes, went for days without washing. Some were Muslims so this interfered with their religious beliefs, and many of them were abused by people in the street. It was extremely humiliating; anguish was the thing coming across.
>
> (Solicitor 1)

This material was then translated into legal argumentation for the court, such that counsel for the claimants detailed the following ways (*S, D and T*, EWHC, para 22) in which the criteria specified in *Q* could be met: bodily injury, physical suffering, mental suffering, humiliation, lack of respect for dignity, a diminution of dignity, debasing treatment, fear which breaks moral and physical resistance, and feelings of anguish and inferiority. The much-quoted conclusion to the judgement was that although a refusal of support would not *inevitably* breach article 3, in the absence of employment or benefits, forced to beg and sleep rough, the necessary humiliation and diminution of their human dignity would *soon follow* (*S, D and T*, EWHC, para 33).

iii) How much evidence is enough?

The next significant cases came in a cluster of four which tested in more detail the nature and level of proof required to demonstrate that the article 3 threshold had been met. These were described in the previous chapter in terms of the 'wait and see' approach, which required evidence of the discernible imminence of the *Pretty* criteria, and the 'common sense' approach, closer to the *S, D and T* judgement, that in the absence of support or employment the threshold of suffering would soon be reached.

In the first of these cases, *Zardasht*, the issue was less about the nature of evidence than its absence, and the judge took the opportunity:

> To remind claimants and their lawyers what the application of the law in this area requires by way of evidence.
>
> (*Zardasht*, para 1)

The judge asserted that the intention of the act made clear that the features common to all dis-benefited asylum seekers were insufficient to make the case for a breach of article 3. In the judge's view, a fit young man could survive on the streets without crossing the article 3 threshold if he had food from charities, and some access to washing facilities, while help might also be available from friends or family. Hence: 'These factors must be eliminated by evidence' (*Zardasht*, para 13). Furthermore, one would expect a lack of food over a period of weeks to mean 'a measure of starvation and debilitation' (*Zardasht*, para 31), and this had to be demonstrated.

One contentious aspect of evidence in the case was a list of day centres for homeless people, and details of 'hostels online' submitted by a NASS case worker. The material originated with the Refugee Council (RC) but had since been withdrawn:

> The Refugee Council had compiled a list of night shelters, mostly from hostels online and were giving it out to people coming in for advice. So they were trailing across London to find that [without Housing Benefit] they were not eligible. The HO had got hold of the list and it was used to argue that there were places available ... They had no idea how homelessness worked.
>
> (NGO officer 4)

However, in a manner reminiscent of the 'actively seeking work' test for unemployed benefit claimants, the judge asserted that it must be made plain whether attempts had been made to access these facilities. A statement of no help forthcoming would not suffice, and so the *Zardasht* case failed.

The next case in the sequence (*Limbuela*, EWHC) cited evidence from Threshold Housing Advice confirming the HB requirement for hostel accommodation, while the list of day centres was held to be inadequate as evidence of the availability of food and washing facilities. The claimant also submitted evidence to show that:

> You can't always get fed but if you can it is quite a distance between meals. We worked out that you had to walk 30 miles a day to get two meals.
>
> (Solicitor 5)

Experiential detail of the claimant's begging and feelings of degradation was provided, with a supporting statement from Migrant Helpline (of the IAP). Given the irregularity of any other form of support, the judge held that it defied 'common sense' to insist on the further accumulation of evidence when:

> It is common ground that there is no possibility that [the claimant] will obtain overnight accommodation.
>
> (*Limbuela*, EWHC, para 29)

The difference between the judges in the *Zardasht* and *Limbuela* cases demonstrates a limit to how far evidence can take the argument. The issue by this point was less the nature and extent of the evidence than the reasoned interpretation of the right at issue (cf Habermas, 1996:226). Indeed, the other two cases in this sequence of four add little new in the way of evidence, but are revealing with respect to interpretive choice: in *Tesema*, who had not yet been on the street, an impending breach of article 3 was found on 'common sense' grounds, simply at the *prospect* of homelessness in these circumstances. In the other case (*Adam*, EWHC) the judge favoured a 'wait and see' approach, but found 'with some hesitation' (*Adam*, EWHC, para 88) that while there were no factors outside those common to many, the severity of the case after 24 nights on the street meant the article 3 threshold had been met.

In all three of the successful cases, *Limbuela*, *Tesema* and *Adam*, the HO argued that the evidence was insufficient to demonstrate a breach and lodged an appeal. As we have seen, the issue was finally resolved by a conjoined hearing, first in the CA and then in the HoL (see Billings and Edwards, 2006) – in effect a deliberation between judges via the appeal system. The voluntary sector input to these final cases is best considered under the broader heading of third party interventions, which in turn raise a further set of questions regarding civil society influence, public interest and civil repair.

Third party interventions

Third party interventions play a particular role in judicial procedure by allowing external parties with special expertise to intervene, often on the grounds of public interest.

> Intervention is quite a recent phenomenon. Basically the court started saying that it wanted certain interventions, that it found them very helpful, because a responsible intervenor could present the court with a bigger picture of the issues raised by a particular case, a wider perspective, bring its own expertise to bear, and bring its counsels expertise to bear. Courts are receptive to the idea that NGOs are worth listening to; they aren't partisan, they are in possession of particular facts, and they are able to address issues of principle.
>
> (Barrister 3)

An intervener can legitimise a case, lending legal and social significance by attaching its name, it can offer help to the court on a new or difficult area of law, and it can add a further perspective to those of the parties directly represented. The work of third party interveners is lent additional force by the *pro bono* contribution of the legal team.

For the CA hearing on *Adam, Tesema* and *Limbuela* (*Limbuela*, EWCA), Shelter's intervention was influential not only by virtue of its legal argument, but also its additional accompanying evidence:

> They provided that more general background which you need to get in but which is much more difficult to cover if you are a sole individual. You need those NGOs to put in all that evidence, and it is a mutually beneficial arrangement because it gives them a higher profile.
>
> (Barrister 7)

The evidence included a summary from the Director of Shelter on the absence of charitable provision, and a powerful witness statement on the suffering entailed from the RC, which was quoted extensively in the judgement. Supporting evidence was also provided on the danger to health, on attacks and abuse of asylum seekers, and on police concern over community relations, together with a collection of statements from community organisations about their inability to help. Much of this material was recycled from an earlier case (*S, D, and T*, EWHC).

The emphasis in the intervention itself was on the experiential dimension of the treatment meted out to the claimants, presenting all the various components of the criteria for IDT cited in *Q*, EWCA. It also addressed the absurdity of further evidence gathering, referring to the 'charade' of applying for charitable support in order to record its absence. The intention was rather to translate facts into experience, and the underlying argument was that individual suffering and exposure to IDT must be *inferred* from the evidence, thus requiring an interpretive act. This would reveal humiliation and debasement, exclusion from normal social existence, the enforced breaching of social norms, and loss of personal dignity, all exacerbated when simultaneously attempting to pursue an asylum claim. The decision went against the government, with Laws LJ dissenting, and the same bundle of evidence was then submitted for the HoL appeal. Shelter's intervention again emphasised the degree and nature of suffering under S55, but with additional argumentation on the absolute nature of article 3, notably that:

> Article 3 does not expressly provide for rights to be overridden to the extent necessary to achieve specified governmental objectives.
>
> (Shelter's intervention in *Adam*, UKHL, p. 3)

The HoL case (*Adam*, UKHL) also featured a joint intervention from Liberty and Justice which concentrated on abstract points of law. This intervention highlighted the argument that rights to protection under the Convention on the Status of Refugees (CSR) and the ECHR are undermined by an absence of support, and addressed the argument of Laws LJ, which translated article 3 into a spectrum of harm. According to Laws LJ, only intentional acts by the state were absolutely prohibited, while acts of omission in pursuit of lawful policy permitted some qualification. However, since article 3 confers *absolute* rights, the interveners argued that once a causal connection between the state's behaviour and ensuing suffering was established, then a breach could not be justified. Here the two interventions came together: the withdrawal of welfare support, given a prohibition on working and an absence of charitable provision, constituted 'treatment' and established a causal connection between S55 and the inhuman and degrading experience of those affected. The 'wait and see' approach was also criticised, as S55(5) permits intervention to *avoid* a breach of fundamental rights, and thus implies preventive action. Five Law Lords were unanimous in finding against the government.

Two prior interventions should be also mentioned. Liberty was involved in an earlier joint intervention with the JCWI in the case of *Q*, EWCA, supported by eight other organisations. The intervention questioned the rationality of the legislation, noted its effect in undermining rights conferred by the CSR and ECHR, and offered an interpretation of IDT. However, its significance lay as much in its collaborative nature, and the declaration to the court that it carried support from 10 different voluntary sector groups.

One further intervention (in *Q, D, H and others*), again from Shelter, addressed procedural issues pertaining to applications for JR. The submission recorded delays in NASS decision-making, failure to respond to written representations, a lack of prompt decision-making on emergency accommodation, and inappropriate use of the courts as gatekeepers to asylum support. It included expressions of concern at the large numbers unable to access legal advice, the procedural difficulties and delays in processing S55, and the waste of public funds in contesting decisions.

In sum, the varied interventions provided a channel for the expression of NGO concern about the implementation of S55, and made available evidence on the paucity of charitable provisions and the impact of the measure on the voluntary sector. They furnished experiential evidence pertaining to the application of article 3, abstract legal argument on a range of possible breaches of fundamental rights, and an informed critique of NASS procedure. In so doing, the interventions served as both an expression of interest on behalf of voluntary sector groups, a presentation of expert evidence and opinion, a source of assistance to the courts, and a broader representation of the public interest in upholding fundamental rights. But such claims have met with some criticism.

The courts as a deliberative space

An expanding use of intervention has been associated with the HRA, which draws the court into policy areas and creates a need for wider information and assistance. Yet it has been argued that the court cannot mimic parliamentary consultation (Hannett, 2003) or perform as a surrogate legislature (Harlow, 2002). Thus, a number of commentators express reservations about the status of third party interventions, the related politicisation of the courts, and the use of the courts to revisit political battles lost elsewhere (Hannett, 2003; see also Harlow, 2002; Fordham, 2007). These arguments, if they have force, apply not only to interventions per se, but to other forms of civil society involvement in the judicial process.

Cane (1995) agrees with many of the reservations, but recognises the role of the courts in protecting fundamental rights and therefore entertaining public interest challenges to official decisions. A public interest motivation is commonly inferred from a concern with legal principle rather than concrete outcomes (Hannett, 2003), though this opposition breaks down in the interpretation of human rights. Here advocacy can merge with a public interest in upholding human rights as a basic principle of our social system. In the *Adam*, UKHL judgement in the present history it is significant that the three cases were no longer 'live', in that two had been granted refugee status and one had received a final negative decision. The purpose of the hearing was not, therefore, to resolve these specific cases but rather to give legal guidance on the wider issue of how to interpret and apply article 3 of the ECHR.

In this process the court is not seeking to reflect a representative view of public opinion, but to establish the content of fundamental rights. The public interest lies both in determining human rights standards, and in how that determination is arrived at through deliberation in the courts. In the present study expert evidence has contributed to this process by supporting an expansive interpretation derived from participatory knowledge. However, if campaigners' perceptions are correct, this expression of 'public interest' is not at one with 'public opinion', leaving it open to argument that the proper place for the determination of rights lies with Parliament. Hence, Campbell (1998) asserts that the prime locus for democratic deliberation is the total community of persons affected by political power, though note that asylum seekers have no direct voice in the parliamentary process. Furthermore, where parliament has failed in this role – see, for example, the abbreviated debate on the bill and the contrast between its expressed intent and actual implementation – and where *absolute* rights are at stake, the court has a duty to intervene, and by default fills a deliberative gap. In the case history at issue here, the form of the legislation itself invites judicial determination, leaving it for the courts to decide when a breach of article 3 would occur.

The present chapter has explored the role played by civil society groups in prompting litigation on this matter, and in furnishing evidence and argument, though the mobilisation recounted in this narrative was called into action as much by events as by intent. If the foundations of civil society are the fundamental rights which structure relations between individuals, and between the individual and social institutions, as Habermas suggests, then the legal process is inherent to the functioning of civil society. Where the political process (including public opinion) is insensitive to breaches of these rights it is almost inevitable that the matter should find its way to the courts in pursuit of civil repair.

The process by which this has happened, by means of the dynamic response of concerned organisations and activist lawyers, may be taken as an example of the linkage between democratic virtues expressed in 'everyday politics' and cosmopolitan virtues of concern for the vulnerable and excluded. Such a linkage is endorsed by Isin and Turner (2007:5,16), who wish to stress the role of citizenship in cultivating civic virtues and democratic values, and the essential compatibility of citizenship and human rights. This may be seen as a key component in transforming 'cosmopolitanisation' into cosmopolitanism (Beck, 2006). The argument is illustrated in the present case study by the daily interaction of NGOs and community organisations with disentitled asylum seekers, and the use of this contact to powerful effect in a legal (and political) campaign against the dispossession of a vulnerable group. Such action is indicative of a broadened conception of citizenship which emphasises public engagement in the civil sphere as a dimension of societal membership, an example of Isin and Turner's (2007:13) argument that:

> Citizenship remains important as an active domain of democracy and as the principle expression of being political ... it should be regarded as a foundation for human rights and not as a competitor.

In the present study this engagement has been part of a process of civil repair, asserting the rights of a group excluded from citizenship and corresponding precisely to the subject of Kant's 'cosmopolitan right'; a right to hospitality for those who cannot be turned away without risk of their destruction. Thus civil society action undertaken on their behalf exemplifies an aspect of cosmopolitan virtue, and its capacity for incorporation into participant citizenship. It implicitly serves to challenge the consolidation of an 'enclave society' (Isin and Turner, 2007:11), in which securely placed citizens live alongside but untouched by a threatening 'other'. In fact, the history has conversely shown how citizens may take up the international responsibilities and obligations incurred by the state to disrupt Arendt's paradox (1979:297) whereby the 'right to have rights' will often depend upon membership of a (national) political community (Isin and Turner, 2007:13). We thus begin to see how Isin and Turner's notion of a cosmopolitan citizenship might serve to 'undergird a broader and pragmatic conception of human rights' (p. 7) through struggles over redistribution and recognition which extend beyond borders (p. 14).

There is one element of this process, however, which remains unresolved. In the cases at issue here the courts have offered a means of recourse to a marginal group for whom there appears to be little public sympathy. For civil repair to be fully achieved this absence would need to be addressed, which raises one further question – that of the relationship between the granting or withholding of rights and public standing. While the narrative recounted here suggests that low public esteem may both encourage and be fed by the erosion of rights, it remains to be seen if the restitution of rights through the courts can contribute to enhanced public status. To put this in Habermasian terms, the role of the courts in will formation could be a vital final stage in the process of civil repair, bringing public opinion more closely into line with a rights-based conception of public interest. To return to Isin and Turner (2007), such a linkage could open up the route to a more cosmopolitan citizenry, by endorsing a more expansive conception of human rights.

Notes

1 Furnished by the Social Security Advisory Committee (SSAC) and the Citizens Advice Bureau.
2 Furnished by the United Nations High Commission for Refugees (UNHCR), CAB, and claimant B's witness statement.
3 Furnished by the CAB and JCWI.
4 Furnished by the UNHCR.
5 Including reports documenting the problems: Mayor of London, 2004; Inter-agency Partnership, 2004; Refugee Council, 2004.
6 Refugee Councils for England, Wales and Scotland, Migrant Helpline, Refugee Action and Refugee Arrivals Project.
7 Legal aid has since been severely curtailed (Guardian, 10 March 2008).
8 HL Deb, cols 978–81, 17 October 2002.

Chapter 5

An emergent cosmopolitan paradigm?

This chapter continues the analysis of cases challenging the withdrawal of welfare support from late claimers by further considering their implications for recent sociological debate on cosmopolitanism. We have seen how Isin and Turner's (2007) call for a citizen engagement with cosmopolitan ideals may be exemplified by the civil society action documented in the previous chapter. We now turn to the process of judicial interpretation, and here key cases are revisited in the context of socio-legal theory and examined for signs of a 'national' or 'cosmopolitan' paradigm in judicial interpretation. The focus of the chapter is therefore on how the national resistance to growing asylum numbers was confronted by claims to a universal right, and on how far the normative ideals of cosmopolitanism can be identified in the ensuing judgements.

Beck and Sznaider (2006) have called for a reconceptualisation of the social sciences by means of a 'cosmopolitan turn' which would challenge the 'container theory' of society associated with methodological nationalism. Border crossing and other trans-national phenomena are argued to have undermined an assumed correspondence between national and social boundaries, 'denationalising' national spaces and requiring a new conceptualisation of society. Fine (2007), in this context, indentifies a denaturing and decentring of the nation-state, as part of a desire to emancipate social science from bounded national presuppositions. To this end, Beck and Sznaider advocate a reflexive cosmopolitanism which would reconfigure existing cosmopolitan ideals into concrete social realities. However, in so doing they recognise nationalism as a co-existing (and conflicting) force, and acknowledge a distinction between the normative ideal of cosmopolitanism and the full achievement of a cosmopolitan condition.

One stage in the emergence of a cosmopolitan outlook has been a rejection of the false dichotomy of 'internal' and 'external' forces – itself symptomatic of methodological nationalism (Grande, 2006), in favour of a cosmopolitan constellation which combines both dynamics (cf Habermas, 2001). For Beck and Sznaider this amounts to 'globalisation from within', illuminating trans-nationality inside the nation-state itself (cf Levy and Sznaider, 2006), and for Fine (2007), the engagement of existing forms of political community in a transformative cosmopolitan project. The cosmopolitan moment therefore arises when principles inform practice (Beck and Sznaider, 2006:10), but this possibility invites more detailed questions on the relation between normative ideals and their empirical realisation.

The development and implementation of human rights have provided one reference point for such questions, along with an allied interest in the transformation of national sovereignty (Levy and Sznaider, 2006). Human rights are cited as one example of multiple trans-national forces associated with a cosmopolitan legal frame, such that their consolidation denationalises concepts of legitimacy and contributes to a reconfiguration of sovereignty (cf Meyer et al., 1997; Held, 2004). With the incorporation of international legal norms into domestic regimes, we have a concrete case of the blurring of internal and external factors, seen by some as the basis for a global citizenry – which Fine (2007) terms the 'credo' of cosmopolitanism (see Habermas, 2001). Hence the argument (eg Douzinas, 2000) that human rights have the ability to create new worlds by pushing and expanding the boundaries of society, identity and law.

Another related empirical referent for cosmopolitanism has been the growth of cross-national migration and asylum seeking, though this border crossing plays an ambivalent role. Grande (2006:104) sees migration as a polarising issue, revealing a structural cleavage between nationalism and cosmopolitanism, such that it is precisely 'the lowering and unbundling of national boundaries which renders them more salient'. While Beck and Sznaider suggest that in defending the human rights of foreigners and strangers people may feel they are defending their own identities, Douzinas has argued that the plight of the refugee puts claims of the universalisation of rights to the test. Where Beck and Sznaider see 'cycles of cosmopolitan sympathy', Fine (2007:43) sees rather a dilemma for citizens in choosing between their own national interpretations of constitutional principles and a more distant cosmopolitan view. As Habermas (2001) notes, a peculiar tension arises between the universal meaning of human rights and the local conditions of their realisation.

Beck and Sznaider hint at this ambivalence in their recognition that a single phenomenon may be analysed at a variety of levels:

> In the cosmopolitan constellation sociology is then concerned with the formation of post-national and cross national bonds, or who belongs and who does not, and how inclusion and exclusion arise.
>
> (Beck and Sznaider, 2006:21)

The distinction between cosmopolitan norms and cosmopolitanism as an extant condition lies at the heart of these questions and opens the path for sociological investigation of empirical issues which may highlight tension, lag or contestation when explored at different levels. Human rights and cross-border movements provide a good illustration; while a trans-national focus will centre on the presence of asylum seekers, pursuing their claim to human rights protections, a national focus highlights political concern over welfare policy and immigration control. One forum in which these levels come into confrontation, and where the relationship between normative ideals and empirical reality has been played out, is the courts, via struggles over the lived experience of asylum seekers.

Rights and controls

This chapter therefore reflects upon the case history documented thus far from the perspective of cosmopolitanism; a history which weighs the impact of a policy driven by government concern to reduce public spending and limit 'abuse', against fundamental rights of access to asylum and freedom from inhuman and degrading treatment (IDT), thus reflecting the national/cosmopolitan tension noted above.

Habermas (1996:507) finds 'frighteningly accurate' Arendt's diagnosis that stateless persons, refugees and those deprived of rights would come to symbolise the twentieth century. The plight of asylum seekers brings into potential conflict a set of concerns about national resource issues, identity and security, with a more cosmopolitan set of ideals and obligations stemming from human rights guarantees. Indeed, Douzinas (2000:365) has argued:

> The refugee is so radically different from us that no similarity can be found or equivalence constructed ... (he/she is) a frightening symbol of the totalisation of difference and of the denial of affinity and points to those realms which civilisation cannot change.

The cases in the present study test this assertion by challenging the enforced destitution of asylum seekers, and seeking a response which is acceptable to a 'civilised society'.[1]

The context for varied government attempts to withdraw support from asylum seekers who do not claim on entry was a rapid growth in the numbers,[2] though they have since fallen markedly. With rising applications, asylum was increasingly linked to issues of control rather than protection, and 'successful' policy was measured in terms of reduced applications,[3] on the assumption that many claims are abusive and encouraged by the availability of benefits.[4] The withdrawal of support from late claimers (a majority of claimants) was part of a more general strategy to harness rights as a tool of governance, as documented in Chapter 2. This was to be achieved through the elaboration of a system of 'civic stratification' (Lockwood, 1996; Morris, 2002) whereby different legal statuses have differing associated rights, reflecting the 'desirability' or otherwise of varied categories of migrant. Rights thus become implicated in the process of managed migration and the removal of welfare support from 'late claimers' therefore constituted an erosion of rights with a view to deterrence (Webber, 2004).

The enforced destitution which followed represented a new embellishment in an already complex system of classification, and undermined the rights of a group precariously positioned in the hierarchy of civic stratification. In the course of this development, two commonly cited features of cosmopolitanism are potentially brought into conflict – the expansion of trans-border movement, and the consolidation of universal rights. As we argued in Chapter 3, by testing the limits of our national obligation to support and maintain asylum seekers the cases in this history in effect serve to draw the boundaries of our moral community. While Nash (2007) highlights the imagining of communities beyond the nation, there is also a case for the reimagining of community within the nation.

Analysing judgement

Socio-legal thinkers have for some time been wrestling with issues deeply implicated in cosmopolitan debate, notably the respective roles of legal principles (Dworkin, 1986), political interest (eg Altman, 1986), and deliberation (Habermas, 1996) in shaping judgement. The link is clearly illustrated by the current case history, which has involved the application of basic principles to a government policy that brought immigration control and human rights into conflict. This conflict was resolved by extended deliberation over two opposing paradigms of interpretation; the 'cosmopolitan' and the 'national', and the organic emergence of a judicial cosmopolitan outlook. The history neatly reflects Habermas's insight (1996) into the processual rather than the substantive basis of legal legitimacy, and a brief background to his argument will be helpful for the analysis to follow.

Much socio-legal debate on judgement has revolved around the scope and nature of judicial freedom, and Dworkin's work (1986; 2005) is of particular interest, given his focus on the role of general principles in interpretation of the law. In Dworkin's approach, rules and statutes provide the content of law, but their interpretation and application is informed by background principles, which are called into play in areas of uncertainty. In reaching a conclusion, a judge will seek to make the larger system of law coherent *in principle*, or to read the law as if created by a single author – the 'community personified' (Dworkin, 1986:225). The identification of core principles – human dignity and equal worth in the field of human rights, and their application to particulars, must therefore play a vital role in case analysis, but so too must judicial disagreement.

Dworkin accepts that judges differ in their interpretation and application of principles, that their own moral and political convictions are engaged, and that there is no way to prove the best decision. He also concedes that in reality judges belong to rival political traditions, that their interpretations are honed by different ideologies, and that legal paradigms shift over time, but finds in this no threat to his 'integrity' approach to judgement. Yet according to Michelman (1986:24) Dworkin neglects 'the most universal and striking characteristic of the appellate bench, its plurality'. He therefore leaves open to empirical analysis the role of dispute and dialogue in the rendering of a judgement, and as our case history shows, this is particularly salient in a developing area of law such as human rights.

A contrasting approach is found in the critical legal studies tradition, which actively embraces conflict and contradiction such that the judge is confronted by a choice whose outcome is not dictated by the law (Altman, 1986:217). The argument of this approach is that ideological controversy lies at the heart of politics and is inevitably reproduced in the law, which will reflect those conflicts present in the wider society. While tending to uphold established relations of power and privilege, the law itself is fraught with contradiction and compromise, and the principles of law exist as a site of ideological struggle (Unger, 1986; Norrie, 1993). We find an example in Beiner's (1983:143) discussion of judgement as intrinsic to political life, which cites the example, central to our case history, of whether national or universal solidarity takes precedence. A potential conflict here suggests a tension in Dworkin's idea of the 'community personified'.

While it may be recognised that judges look for the most convincing legal principles in seeking resolution to a case (Dworkin, 1986), the 'critical' position is that principles may conflict, and their interpretation will anyway be shaped by a judge's ideological predisposition. For Altman (1986:235) an important advance of this approach has been the effort to take seriously the conflicting ethical visions and principles argued to infuse legal doctrine, while Unger (1986:18) notes that among such conflicts lies a broader contest about differing visions of society:

> Modern legal doctrine ... works in a social context in which society has increasingly been forced open to transformative conflict. It exists in a cultural context in which ... society is understood to be made and imagined rather than merely given.

In addressing such debate, Habermas (1996) takes a position which finds legal legitimacy less in the content than in the process of law. He thus steers a path between Dworkin's quest for coherence in the law through the application of principles, and a 'critical' view of law as inherently contradictory and conflictual. Pursuing Dworkin's argument that principles are often called into play in the application of the law, especially in hard cases, he emphasises the plurality of judicial opinion and the role of deliberation in forming a judgement. For him this suggests a theory of legal argumentation grounded in procedural principles that 'bear the brunt of the ideal demands' which in Dworkin's account fall on an individual judge (Habermas, 1996:225). Judicial decisions are thus seen as part of a co-operative search for truth which establishes legitimacy through deliberation rather than legal certainty.

Habermas suggests that this deliberation can be informed by prevailing paradigms of law:

> The legal paradigm determines how basic rights and constitutional principles are to be understood and how they can be realised in the context of contemporary society.
>
> (1996:195)

He identifies the two most successful paradigms of modern law as bourgeois formal law (classic liberalism) and welfare state 'materialised' law (social welfare) (cf Kennedy, 1997), but proposes what he calls a third paradigm, in the form of a proceduralist understanding of law, whereby:

> legal paradigms can open up for one another and prove themselves against a variety of competing interpretations
>
> (Habermas, 1996:222)

He is therefore making the case for a new paradigm in the analysis, understanding and *conduct* of judgement, rather than for a *substantive* paradigm as exemplified by the liberal and social welfare models. However, it may be that through this proceduralist approach we can begin to identify in deliberative debate an emergent and substantive *cosmopolitan* paradigm. Indeed, Habermas himself does not dispense with substantive paradigms, for:

> A proceduralist understanding of the law ... reckons from the start with discursively regulated competition between paradigms.
>
> (Habermas, 1996:223–24)

He also emphasises the need to place the law in its social context, such that legal interpretation is conducted not just with reference to the legal corpus, but 'within the horizon of a currently dominant understanding of contemporary society' (1996:388). He therefore opens up an approach which allows us to identify differing substantive paradigms, while recognising the importance not just of a judge's implicit image of society but also of judicial deliberation and paradigm shifts over time.

Addressing tension within the law

The approaches sketched above need not be mutually exclusive, and though each suggests a different means of addressing tension within the law, all can inform the history considered below. Dworkin emphasises the search for coherence as a subjective act by the judge; the critical legal school seeks out political interest and contradiction; while Habermas emphasises procedure and deliberation. Taken together they can inform a distinctively sociological contribution to an understanding of the present history by guiding the analysis of concrete cases, set in the context of the wider political environment, and measured against emergent cosmopolitan ideals. We can begin analysis of this history by seeking the roots of a paradigm struggle in the unfolding content of the law itself.

The CA judgement on the first case in our history (*JCWI*, 4 All ER 385) warrants brief comment as two emergent paradigms are already prefigured. The cosmopolitan moment in this judgement is driven by parliamentary commitment to the Convention on the Status of Refugees (CSR) in the passing of the 1993 Act, and more precariously through a Common Law principle, the 'law of humanity' (*Eastbourne*, 1803), whereby foreigners should not be left to starve. A dissenting opinion did not hold sway but was significant in its strong assertion of a national interest perspective, stressing the need for balance between collective interests and the rights of asylum seekers, and the objective of the contested Regulations to limit rising public costs. The tensions implicit in these issues recur in later cases and are addressed in the pages to follow in terms of a paradigm struggle between a 'national' and a 'cosmopolitan' perspective.

Though the Regulations were subsequently established in primary law, through the 1996 Asylum and Immigration Act, late claimers were then deemed eligible for local authority support under the National Assistance Act (*M*, 1 CCLR 85, CA). However, we have seen that such domestic provision is vulnerable to change[5] when not also underpinned by more fundamental human rights obligations; hence Beck and Sznaider's (2006) stress on the internalisation of trans-national forces *within* the nation-state itself as one element of cosmopolitanism. Commitment to the CSR through the 1993 Act offers one example, as does the incorporation of the European Convention on Human Rights (ECHR) into domestic law via the Human Rights Act (HRA) (Home Office, 1998).

Indeed, the ECHR may be seen as one attempt to embody the ideals of cosmopolitanism in a legal instrument. The UK was already formally committed to the Convention, being the first country to ratify this Council of Europe Instrument in March 1951 (Simpson, 2004). However, the passing of the HRA was critical in giving British judges the opportunity to rule on the Convention in British courts, and this chapter explores the ensuing struggle over the interpretation of article 3 in terms of an emergent paradigm split. The broader significance of this history as a European issue of some reach is heightened by inclusion of the denial of welfare to late claimers as an acceptable policy in the European Directive on minimum standards of treatment for asylum seekers (Council Directive 2003/9/EC).

We have seen how Section 55 of the 2002 Nationality Immigration and Asylum Act (Home Office, 2002) raised a potential human rights problem soon after the implementation of the HRA, by withdrawing support from late claimers for asylum, but incorporating human rights principles to *permit* support where necessary to 'avoid a breach of Convention rights' (Section 55(5)). In so doing, it opened up the question of application and interpretation of the ECHR. The legislation cannot quite be construed as a contradiction in critical legal terms, since Section 55(5) gives clear priority to the HRA. Nevertheless, the clause is symptomatic of an underlying tension, and contains implicit recognition that human rights could be breached by withdrawal of support.[6] However, the meaning and application of Section 55(5) was left to the courts, and while human rights principles have been paramount in interpretation, deliberation over their precise purchase again reveals the paradigm split apparent in nascent form in earlier cases.

The ensuing dilemma raises some interesting issues in relation to legal theory. Alexander (2006:185) has argued – citing Unger (1986) – that the critical legal emphasis on the role of law as a reinforcement of inequalities of power and wealth, and a tool for social control 'barely recognises the possibilities of civil repair'. However, Unger himself goes further, by indentifying a transformative potential in the law such that conflicts between ruling ideals and established arrangements can be pushed 'by gradual steps towards ever more drastic ways of reimagining society' (Unger, 1986:19). Both writers see scope for using the law as a means to attack the patterns of power and privilege that it elsewhere protects, and this is a possibility which runs through the present case history. By looking at the forces for and against cosmopolitan expansion, moments of tension, and means of resolution in concrete cases, we can begin to show what it means to argue that 'we do not live in a cosmopolitan age but in an age of cosmopolitanism' (Fine, 2007:19). Publicly available legal judgements on the challenge to government policy on asylum seekers provide us with a perfect tool.

Contours of two paradigms

The challenge to withdrawal of welfare support from late claimers raised critical questions for human rights jurisprudence, and we noted earlier Lord Hoffman's view (*Matthews*, para 26) that economic rights may be necessary to give meaning to other rights. Yet the precise boundary of rights is contestable, and while Lord Justice Laws (*Limbuela*, EWCA, para 73) recognised the necessary 'elastic quality' of the ECHR, he cautioned against an interpretation which introduced obligations not contemplated in its original conception. The point at issue was whether, and under what circumstances, a right to basic maintenance could be read into a convention designed with civil and political rights in mind. While both sides in the dispute are seeking a resolution which renders the law coherent (cf Dworkin, 1986), the nature of the human rights obligation is contested, such that differing interpretations reflect a tension implicit in section 55 which is then played out in the judgements (cf Altman, 1986).

The two aspects of section 55 pull in different directions with immigration control and resource concerns, on the one hand, and consistency with human rights, on the other, re-running the conflict noted in earlier cases. Since there is scope for both a restrictive and expansive approach with reference to rights, we can look to the content of the judgements to ask how far differing positions reflect contrasting paradigms of interpretation.[7] While a majority of judgements lean towards the more expansive position, there is sufficient disagreement to warrant the question. To explore this issue, an open reading of the full range of judicial opinion[8] first identified the critical features of each opinion, or the arguments on which the opinion turned. It was only then that the paradigms were constructed, by grouping together related positions which were interpreted in terms of the national/cosmopolitan divide to yield the polarisation presented below. The internal coherence of these groupings is reflected in their tendency to support either an expansive orientation to the welfare rights of late claimers (the cosmopolitan position) or a more restrictive orientation (the national position). While individual judges in this case history weigh the arguments on both sides, their expressed opinions lean towards one or other paradigm. No single opinion contains all features of either paradigm, but their cumulative effect suggests the emergence of a cosmopolitan position which may be viewed as an outcome of the whole history, and therefore of an organic process of deliberation.

Cosmopolitan paradigm

1. Emphasis on the absolute nature of article 3.
2. Prioritising of fundamental rights over policy concerns.
3. Recognition of the role of social rights in realising civil and political rights.
4. Greater intensity of review of welfare issues where human rights are at stake.
5. Reference to a range of trans-national instruments and other national Constitutions.
6. Judgement exercised with reference to the standards of 'civilised society'.
7. Emphasis on the protection of human dignity.
8. Singling out for special treatment deemed a special affront to human dignity.
9. Emphasis on the uniquely vulnerable position of asylum seekers.
10. Identification of an expansionary logic in the development of human rights.

National paradigm

1. The absolute nature of article 3 to be confined to cases of direct state violence.
2. Emphasis on the purpose of legislation in combating abuse of the asylum system.

3. Recognition of resource allocation as a matter for the executive not the judiciary.
4. A defence of legitimate public concern over resources.
5. An emphasis on striking a balance between the community and the individual.
6. An emphasis on the high threshold of suffering required to breach article 3.
7. A view that an expansive approach to article 3 undermines government policy.
8. Recognition of government powers and duties relating to immigration control.
9. A view that if features common to all asylum seekers trigger article 3 rights the situation would be 'unworkable'.
10. The need for caution in extending the ECHR beyond its original scope.

What is at stake in these two paradigms is thus, in Fine's terms (2007:127), the relation between the social norms of an immediate national community and those of a more distant world community of world citizens. Both perspectives are arguable and informed by aspects of established jurisprudence, but might also be read in terms of ideological predispositions (Altman, 1986:230). However, this does not necessarily conflict with Dworkin's account of judges seeking consistency in the law, while at times drawing on their own moral viewpoints. The tension is perhaps best presented in Weiler's (1992:69) recognition of the judicial role as:

> shaping and developing the binding normative framework within which it operates ... an important voice in the overall rhetoric which is constitutive of the political culture of the polity.

In Habermas's 'procedural paradigm' the court provides a deliberative forum for determining which interpretation prevails, and this can – as in the present history – involve a dialogue between judges not only within but across cases. Fredman (2000) sees this as a positive aspect of the HRA, whereby challenges under the Act provide a focus for deliberation about the content of rights and thus enhance the democratic process. This is an interesting claim, given the assertion from Douzinas and Warrington with McVeigh (1991:17) that politics holds the power to impose one idiom whereby:

> Those people and groups that have no power to establish their interests will always remain unrepresented and unrepresentable.

So how far has the cosmopolitan paradigm served to support challenges to the disentitlement of a vulnerable and excluded group? Here we revisit some of the material from Chapter 3 to examine how the two models sketched out above are manifest in the delivery of key judicial decisions.

Decisive moments

A central question for the present history has been whether the enforced desti-tution of asylum seekers could amount to a breach of article 3,[9] that is, whether the right was engaged at all. The deciding aspects of judgement turned on: i) the conceptualisation of 'treatment', and ii) the level of suffering deemed to meet the 'inhuman and degrading' threshold. The cases considered below represent critical moments in the unfolding deliberation on these matters.

i) Treatment

At the heart of deliberation about treatment lay the question of whether withdrawal of support could be construed as a positive act by the state, and the determining ruling was in the Court of Appeal (*Q, EWCA*) which found:

> The imposition by the legislature of a regime which prohibits asylum seekers from working and further prohibits the grant to them, when they are destitute, of support amounts to positive action directed against asylum seekers and not to mere inaction.
>
> (para 57)

The reasoning behind this decision emphasised the vulnerable position of asylum seekers, who could not be removed, and were compelled to remain to press their claims, but were denied the means of survival (*Q*, EWCA, para 56). Against argu-ments from the Attorney General (*Q*, EWCA, para 52) that failure to act could never constitute treatment, and recognising that something more than passivity was required, the judgement ruled that the whole package of measures to which late claimers were subject amounted to treatment within the meaning of article 3.

The engagement of a fundamental human right was further confirmed elsewhere in the judgement (*Q*, EWCA, para 115), which endorsed a greater intensity of review where human rights were engaged (as compared with statutory welfare schemes), and noted that this applied not only to the ECHR but also to the CSR and the Universal Declaration of Human Rights. The judgement therefore displays a number of elements of the cosmopolitan paradigm: it took an expansive approach to interpreting the ECHR, reinforced by reference to other international norms, affirmed that positive obligations could be drawn out of article 3, and noted its absolute nature (*Q*, EWCA, para 53), thus ruling out qualification by reference to policy considerations.

This decision on treatment provided a baseline for the six cases that followed, but was revisited in a later case by Lord Justice Laws' dissenting CA judgement (*Limbuela*, EWCA). This opinion displayed many features of the 'national' paradigm, and urged caution in expanding the application of the ECHR to areas beyond those originally contemplated. Laws LJ's distinction between type a) breaches of article 3, consisting of violence by the state or its servants, and type b) breaches, resulting from acts or omissions by the state was deployed to undermine the absolute nature of article 3. In his view, the absolute prohibition only applied to type a) breaches, and in distancing the state from responsibility he implied a different conception of treatment than that adopted in Q, EWCA. Posing the question of whether withdrawal of support is a direct act or a failure to protect, Laws LJ argued that it was the latter, and as such could be 'capable of justification' if arising 'in the administration or execution of lawful government policy' (*Limbuela*, EWCA, para 68).

Thus, suffering due to circumstances arising from a lawful policy decision should only attract the protection of article 3 when it reaches a 'high degree of severity', and account should be taken of government responsibilities in relation to immigration control. Laws LJ made reference to the need to balance community interests and individual rights (*Limbuela*, EWCA, para 73), and noted that the finding of an article 3 breach at the prospect of life on the street would 'eviscerate' the policy (para 58). Broader moral considerations were written out of the picture (para 80). The opinion thus offers a closely argued instance of the national paradigm in operation via the interpretation of article 3, dismissed in a later judgement (*Adam*, UKHL).

ii) The requisite level of severity

We saw in Chapter 3 that in addition to ruling on 'treatment', the judgement in Q, EWCA provided criteria for 'inhuman and degrading', drawn from a European Court of Human Rights ruling in a rather different case (Pretty v UK). Having provided a definition, however, Q fell short of specifying concrete indicators, and the final criterion offered seems tautologous – the applicant must be 'so patently vulnerable that to refuse support carries a high risk of an almost immediate breach of article 3 or 8' (para 68).[10] A further eight judgements were required to resolve this matter but the 'national' and 'cosmopolitan' tendencies eventually polarised around the two High Court cases, *Zardasht* and *Limbuela*.

In *Zardasht*, since the features common to all dis-benefited asylum seekers were deemed insufficient to make a case[11] further evidence was required as to the *extent* of their effect (paras 5–6). Emphasis was placed on the intentions of Parliament with respect to late claimers in expressly denying the benefit available for other destitute asylum seekers (para 10). The judgement therefore leant towards the national paradigm, and to overcome the primary purpose of the policy, evidence was required to show that a sufficient 'state of severity' (para 19) had been reached, such as signs of debilitation or starvation (para 30) – hence the 'wait and see' approach. In later representation (*Adam*, UKHL) it was argued by the appellant that:

> Such an approach is necessary to give effect to the legitimate policy of the legislation, and cannot itself be held to be such an extreme approach as to be inhuman and degrading.[12]

The opposing judgement on *Limbuela* viewed this position as 'distasteful' and took instead a 'common sense' approach. If a claimant could show that reasonable steps to find support had failed, and they were left with only 'begging and hoping', and sleeping rough with no money, then this was sufficient to make the case. The same line was followed in the subsequent judgement (*Tesema*, EWHC), which was firmly expressed in terms of the cosmopolitan paradigm. While recognising the resource problems involved, the judge saw these as irrelevant to the key issue of 'basic and rudimentary' human rights standards, to be resolved by applying the 'standards of civilised society' (*Tesema*, EWHC, para 68). Hence:

> A decision which compels a person to sleep on the streets. ... without basic shelter and without any funds is normally inhuman and degrading. To subject an unwilling person to such treatment ... humiliates and debases the individual affected.
>
> (*Tesema*, EWHC, para 68)

We have noted a further case (*Adam*, EWHC), which supported the 'wait and see' approach but found that the IDT threshold had been met.

The conjoined appeal on *Adam*, *Tesema* and *Limbuela* (*Limbuela*, EWCA) confirmed these judgements (with Laws LJ dissenting), two of the three judges being swayed by the 600+ cases awaiting a decision, who would be on the streets if the government's appeal succeeded. On further appeal, a House of Lords (HoL) judgement (*Adam*, UKHL) finally delivered key criteria: being compelled to sleep on the streets, OR being seriously hungry, OR being unable to satisfy the needs of hygiene. The justificatory principles repeatedly cited are the standards of civilised/decent society (*S, D and T*, EWHC, para 33; *Tesema*, EWHC, para 19; *Adam*, UKHL, para 76), and respect for human dignity (*S, D and T*, EWHC, para 33; *Adam*, UKHL, para 76; para 94). Yet despite the apparent precision of language – variously referring to 'a sufficient level of degradation' (*Q*, EWCA, para 52), 'the necessary degree of severity' (*Zardasht*, EWHC, para 7), and 'the required minimum level of severity' (*Adam*, UKHL, para 56), there is nothing to explain how the principles cited translate into concrete criteria (cf Cassese, 1991), other than a position rooted in one of the two opposing paradigms. Thus, any justification of the outcome by reference to principles cited begs a further set of questions about how the principles were applied.

Reflexive judgement

Jackson (1991) argues that there is no straightforward deductive logic at work in relating legal rules to recorded facts, but rather a process of 'inter-discursivity'. Hence, the application of law to fact is not a one-way process; the more abstract the rule the greater the difficulty of application, and the greater the need for narrative illustration of conceptual legal codes. In fact, the opposition between 'wait and see' and 'common sense' makes manifest the limits of evidence, since two judges adopt conflicting positions as to evidential requirements. This impasse also demonstrates the limits of deliberation, for what further scope is there for deliberative debate when two opposing paradigms yield decisions based on incompatible justifications?

However, Jackson also argues that justification of a decision is not the same as an account of how the decision was made, the latter being a private act while justification is a public act. Furthermore, a judge is not only required to arrive at a conclusion, but to carry through a process of persuasion, and for Jackson this will depend on the 'fit' of their conclusion with a pre-existing stock of narratives. In the present case history this 'narrative' role is played by the two opposing paradigms, but such a 'fit' can only persuade if there is an already dominant position. The argument thus becomes more difficult to apply in a case of developing law, which provokes a paradigm struggle over interpretation. The 'private' element of the decision remains obscure, but some informed speculation as to its nature is possible.

While the national/cosmopolitan split is reflected in different evidential requirements on the part of judges, the presentation of evidence nevertheless served to confront judges with concrete instances of suffering against which to test their abstract criteria of IDT. It could therefore have a bearing on the 'private' moment of judgement, and Chapter 4 has shown how a powerful component in these cases was the submission of evidence from strategically placed elements of civil society – NGOs, law centres, and community groups. Writers have looked to civil society at international level to compensate for undeveloped representational systems (Habermas, 2001; Fine, 2007), but civil society organisations can play the same role domestically, where asylum seekers are not directly represented in the polity. Habermas (1996:429) has argued that normative standards can develop:

> only in those public forums where individuals have the chance to recount their lived experiences of repression and disrespect ...

In the absence of other fora, the courts perform this function, while civil society evidence can supplement a claimant's case and enhance the deliberative role of the courts.

The intervention on behalf of Shelter in the CA judgement on *Adam, Limbuela and Tesema* (*Limbuela*, EWCA), also cited by the HoL (*Adam*, UKHL, para 36) recognised the difficulty of moving beyond objective facts (such as the absence of charitable provision) to address the actual conditions into which asylum seekers had been driven. The intervenor argued that to achieve this shift required the drawing of inferences from evidence, and relating these back to determining criteria (see Pretty v UK). The submission included the following description of sleeping on the streets:[13]

Every part of your body in contact with the ground will hurt. If it is cold or raining and you do not have adequate protection you will experience the sensation of freezing and you will feel completely miserable – especially if you are hungry or feeling sad. Some kind of bodily injury is inevitable.

(para 9.1)

This leads to a further argument that:

To require special and detailed evidence of intense suffering in circumstances when any ordinary person would suffer intensely, entails regarding the person as less than ordinarily human.

(para 9.1)

The circumstances of the dis-benefited asylum seekers were described as an exclusion from ordinary social existence, and the imposition of such conditions was viewed as an act of social ostracism This was seen to be necessarily inhuman and degrading, and especially demeaning when the victims were attempting to pursue a fundamental right.

In the same CA case (*Limbuela*, EWCA) a witness statement from the Refugee Council was quoted at length (para 92) and also cited by the HoL (*Adam*, UKHL, para 36):

On one occasion I had to tell a group of three homeless asylum-seekers to leave the building on a Friday evening during a torrential downpour with nothing more than a blanket each, a food parcel (most of the contents of which had to be cooked) and a list of day centres. When I saw them the following Monday their condition had deteriorated considerably, their clothes were filthy, they had started to smell, and had been unable to find any of the centres listed.

(*Limbuela*, EWCA, para 92)

The purpose of such evidence and argumentation is partly epistemological; to invite identification and so enable judgement through an act of imagination which goes beyond deliberation. It serves to disrupt what Weiler (1992:69) calls the 'banalization of suffering' which comes from treating people as cases and categories within a bureaucratised administrative system. This imaginative identification has been claimed as a further element of the cosmopolitan perspective, stemming from a distinction between determinate and reflexive judgement; the former refers to the application of general principles to a set of particulars, and the latter to the capacity for deciding without fixed rules. Outlining this distinction in the context of cosmopolitan thought, Fine (2007:125) cites Arendt's connection between reflexive judgement and 'common sense' or 'enlarged mentality'. These concepts have a particular salience here, given the polarised judgements on IDT, and Arendt's (1978:257) conception of this 'critical thinking' is telling:

> (By) force of the imagination it makes the others present ... it adopts the position of Kant's world citizen. To think with the enlarged mentality.

Common sense is not simply the 'self evident', but rather thinking on behalf of others by entering their experience; a sense 'common to all', comparable with the 'collective reason of humanity' (Arendt, 1978:268). The idea is perhaps close to Habermas's depiction of an ideal speech situation:

> characterised by the intention of winning the assent of a universal audience to a problematic proposition.
>
> (1996:228)

This thinking beyond codified rules is thus a necessary feature of the emergent cosmopolitan paradigm, insofar as the latter requires thinking on behalf of all humanity. In the present cases such a process begins to address the 'private' dimension involved in the application of principles, without evoking the personal predisposition of the judge. It also seems to overcome a stalemate in deliberation over two opposing paradigms in relation to IDT, and to underpin the references to dignity and civilised standards finally given concrete expression in the HoL.

Cosmopolitanism: the normative meets the empirical

The last step in this analysis must be to consider the broader effects of what appears as a success story in terms of the realisation of cosmopolitan values, and the achievements of deliberative judgement. Douzinas (2000:365) has highlighted strategies of disavowal and denial of rights that construct the asylum seeker as a 'threatening other' in a graded and ranked conception of 'humanity'. We have seen an example of this in the deterrent treatment of asylum seekers according to the timing of their claims, and noted the conflictual forces apparent in a measure which introduces such controls alongside an assertion of human rights. We have also seen these tensions reproduced in the national and cosmopolitan paradigms manifest in competing interpretations of article 3. Dworkin (2005:205), however, has argued that a government which professes to take rights seriously must honour the majority promise to minorities that their dignity will be recognised and upheld, and would seek 'coherence' in the law on this basis.

In the present volume we have traced the conflictual nature of government policy on welfare for late claimers, and the assertion of basic principles in the face of government resistance. We have also shown how this confrontation yields a case history in which the guarantee of human dignity (through protection from IDT) triumphs over the status ranking of humanity. However, the concluding judgement, which gives substantive content to this guarantee, emerges only after collaborative, if conflictual, dialogue across a complex series of cases. This process of deliberation was brought to its close by a reflexive exercise to determine the concrete meaning of human dignity, and hence the boundaries of our moral responsibility and collective humanity.

Before ending this chapter some consideration should be given to the extent and effect of this outcome; to how far a seemingly 'cosmopolitan' judgement moves us towards the realisation of a cosmopolitan society. Such judgement carries a symbolic force, but equally symbolic is the fact that the last word lies with the legislature, as the HRA does not empower the courts to strike down legislation. In practice, the legislation remains intact, and Section 55(5) saves the policy from a declaration of incompatibility with the HRA, though its application has been greatly limited by the judgements detailed above. Nevertheless, a report from the Joint Committee on Human Rights (JCHR) (2007) some five months after the HoL judgement, drew attention to the continued refusal of support to late claimers who did not require accommodation and so requested maintenance-only support.[14] The HoL criteria for a breach of article 3 are not confined to homelessness, but include hunger and lack of facilities and could therefore apply to this group, though they did not feature in the cases documented here. Indeed, theirs would have been a harder case to fight, and their absence from the present history highlights a certain pragmatism in the process of challenge, whereby only 'winnable' cases will have their day in court. Furthermore, the rulings have no purchase for the indigenous homeless, and would read differently were asylum seekers granted the right to employment. Neither do the judgements affect the estimated 26,000 failed asylum seekers (Guardian, 2008) living in destitution but unwilling to return to their country of origin. Destitution remains a legitimate policy tool in the government's dealings with this group, and would be much harder to overturn.

The history discussed in the present paper therefore has only limited impact in forging the transition to a 'cosmopolitan' society. However, it has served to draw attention to the law as an exemplary focus of analysis for wider debates concerning cosmopolitanism, and as a site where the normative and the empirical come together. This chapter has shown how legal recourse by disentitled asylum seekers has generated a struggle between cosmopolitan ideals and national control over conditions of entry and access to resources. The struggle has drawn attention to a body of socio-legal theory commonly overlooked by cosmopolitan theorists, which addresses the sometimes contradictory nature of the law, and the role of judicial deliberation in reaching a solution. The argument of this chapter has been that in the present history such deliberation can usefully be construed as a contest between paradigms of interpretation, the national (restrictive) and the cosmopolitan (expansive). It has also suggested that while evidence cannot resolve a paradigm disagreement which generates differing evidential requirements, it can offer an aid to reflexive judgement through access to the human experience at issue. In the present history this has been critical in identifying the threshold of suffering for a finding of IDT. Thus, while border crossing and the elaboration of human rights instruments have both been features of Beck and Sznaider's (2006) 'cosmopolitanisation', a focus on the legal process can contribute to an understanding of how the two come together. Such a focus compels us to consider how the gap between the normative and empirical manifestations of cosmopolitanism has been negotiated in practice. The chapter to follow continues with this theme, and looks at the ways that the concept of 'civic stratification' can help to bridge the conceptual and empirical gap between the ideal and the practice of cosmopolitanism.

Notes

1 For example, *S, D and T*, EWHC, para 34; *Tesema*, EWHC, para 19.
2 From 2,353 in 1980 to a peak of 84,135 in 2002 (MPI data hub).
3 An Immigration and Nationality Directorate press release, 27 October 2003, is headed 'Asylum Measures to Build on Success in Halving Numbers', www.ind.homeoffice.gov.uk (accessed 3 November 2003).
4 See HC Hansard, 20 February 1996, col 160; Lords Hansard, 17 October 2002, col 979.
5 It was withdrawn by the 1999 Immigration and Asylum Act.
6 This possibility had already been highlighted by the Joint Committee on Human Rights (23rd Report of Session 2001–2, HL 176; HC 1255, para 15).
7 The term paradigm seems preferable here to 'ideal type' since the paper addresses modes of legal thought rather than concrete social phenomena, and is engaging with existing sociological debate on this issue (eg Habermas, 1996).
8 The total 14 hearings contain six judgements leaning towards the 'national' interpretation and 16 to the 'cosmopolitan' (five of these in the final HoL case). I include the four cases preceding the HRA in this analysis.
9 The cases also covered deliberation on the meaning of 'as soon as reasonably practicable' and on article 8 – respect for private and family life, but the core issue has been article 3.
10 Article 8 was taken to add little to the article 3 arguments.
11 Despite an earlier ruling that asylum seekers qualified for National Assistance for precisely these reasons.
12 Case for the appellant, in *Adam*, UKHL, p. 50.
13 Shelter's written intervention in *Limbuela*, EWCA.
14 People accommodated by friends or relatives. This option was removed in 2002.

Chapter 6

Civic stratification and the cosmopolitan ideal

This chapter further explores the features of cosmopolitanism, but shifts the emphasis from the power of cosmopolitan norms to the broader empirical question raised by Beck as to the extent of the 'cosmopolitanisation' of society. He has argued (Beck, 2006) that trans-national migration and the consolidation of human rights are features of an emergent cosmopolitan society in which we see a *blurring* of distinctions with respect to the rights of citizens and non-citizens. This chapter, however, suggests that the presence of non-citizens on national territory has in fact been accompanied by an *expansion* of distinctions, as evidenced in the system of civic stratification. The functioning of such a system of differentiated rights is considered alongside the social construction of particular groups as targets of policy and as objects of public concern. However, the chapter also explores the significance of judgements which have effectively placed a limit on the acceptable extent of erosion of rights in this process. In so doing it considers the interplay of formal entitlement and informal status in the process of change, and the implications of the whole account for cosmopolitan thinking.

The significant presence of migrants and asylum seekers in sometimes reluctant host countries has for many (Soysal, 1994; Smith, 1995; Beck, 2006) signalled the uncoupling of nation, state and society, especially when that presence is underpinned by claims to universal human rights. This combination of factors has led Beck (2006) to challenge the 'methodological nationalism' associated with territorial understandings of society, and to advocate instead a 'methodological cosmopolitanism'. Such an approach, he argues, would recognise what he sees as the increasingly 'mythic' status of the nation, and the trans-national realities and causalities which are coming to be seen as a universal norm (p. 28). We considered one example in the previous chapter, in relation to the position of asylum seekers and an emergent cosmopolitan paradigm of legal interpretation. In stating his position, however, Beck distinguishes between cosmopolitanism as an ideal and 'banal cosmopolitanism' – a condition of really existing 'cosmopolitanisation', which may be passive, latent or unconscious (p. 19).

Bred of the everyday disruption of bounded national spaces, this cosmopolitanisation is seen as a side effect of global forces, not actively chosen and sometimes consciously resisted. Thus, cosmopolitanisation may transform the 'experiential spaces' of the nation-state from within, though often against popular and political will (p. 101). For Beck, this tension inevitably raises the question of how the nation-state deals with difference, and while much of his discussion turns on culture and identity, he recognises that other issues are in play, as global inequalities and trans-national conflicts reappear within the national space. The figure of the trans-national migrant is central to the picture he paints; one in which 'explosive questions' arise over the distinction between foreigners and nationals, or citizens and non-citizens, and their status in relation to different kinds of rights (p. 27).

In making these observations Beck seeks to promote an imagining of the national and the trans-national as interlocking and mutually constituting; not an either/or but a both/and perspective, or a world of cosmopolitan nationalism (p. 49). Universal human rights are argued to play a key role in this configuration, superseding the national/international distinction and, according to Levy and Sznaider (2006), carrying the potential for a denationalised understanding of legitimacy. Human rights, they argue, provide a globally available basis for legitimate claims making, and can contribute to the reconfiguration of sovereignty whereby the treatment of citizens (and others) is no longer the exclusive domain of the state. Beck and Sznaider (2006) go further, by seeing in human rights a domain in which the interests of citizens and foreigners may coincide (cf Isin and Turner, 2007).

However, Fine (2007) has noted the danger of treating cosmopolitanism as a law of nature, without exposing its rational necessity to scrutiny or debate, and indeed Beck and Sznaider recognise that there is no necessary relation between internal cosmopolitanisation and the development of a cosmopolitan consciousness. They find that normative theories of cosmopolitanism tend to ignore society and its 'more banal forms of everyday life' (p. 22), and they therefore pose the advance of both internal and external cosmopolitanisation as an empirical question. In similar spirit Grande (2006) speaks of a new architecture of governance, though not yet a 'cosmopolitan state', in which the nation-state plays an important and indispensible part but no longer stands for 'society' in the traditional sense. He sees structural opportunities for the emergence of a cosmopolitan political authority, but argues that its realisation lags some way behind.

Grande, like Beck, therefore underlines the need for empirical research in which the task is not to weigh state autonomy against the force of external constraints, but to explore the ways in which internal and external features of cosmopolitanism can function in combination. Again human rights are cited as an example, whereby the legitimate powers of the national state may be necessary to carry through changes initiated elsewhere – though it may of course be the national state itself which is the object of scrutiny and challenge. While new oppositions will emerge that are not aligned with the traditional structures and cleavages contained within national boundaries, they are still most likely to be articulated and dealt with at national level (Grande, 2006:103). The 'container' view of society is, however, rejected (Fine, 2007:7), in favour of an empirical enquiry into how new dialectics of de-nationalisation and re-nationalisation unfold, and how national and trans-national forces mingle to create cosmopolitan spaces.

The present chapter pursues these and related questions in the context of our cases, showing how the history holds an interest beyond the detail of the judgements themselves. The underlying policy, embraced on different occasions by both Conservative and Labour governments, sought to grapple with what were then growing numbers of asylum seekers[1] and in response had asserted a restrictive definition of the national interest. In line with Grande's (2006) observations above, we therefore see how the national state is pre-eminent in the allocation and administration of rights, unless and until its power is challenged through judicial authority. A central device in this process of management is not so much what Beck (2006:39) terms a 'blurring' of distinctions with respect to rights but rather their expansion, through the elaboration of a complex system of legal statuses – what we have here termed civic stratification (Lockwood, 1996; Morris, 2002). The present chapter outlines the concept more fully, before considering the construction of asylum seekers as a 'target group' within this system, and the implications of the outcome of legal challenges for cosmopolitan thinking.

Civic stratification and target populations

According to Lockwood (1996) one reason social stratification has been so central to sociology is in illuminating the question of how much inequality may be tolerated or rejected in a given society. However, he goes beyond traditional conceptions of social class to recognise citizenship and its attendant rights as one potential and neglected source of inequality, such that:

> The ethos and practice of citizenship is at least as likely as class relations to structure groups interests and thereby fields of conflict and discontent.
>
> (p. 536)

This possibility inevitably raises questions about the granting and denial of rights to non-citizens, and therefore has direct bearing on any enquiry into degrees of cosmopolitanisation.

A crucial step in Lockwood's argument is the role of citizenship rights in securing social integration, in part through the legitimation of inequality, whereby equal citizenship status compensates for market inequalities (Marshall, 1950). However, Lockwood poses the question of when such integration might come under challenge, and explores the scope for inequality in entitlement and access to the basic rights which citizenship itself confers. Though the focus of his enquiry is the internal functioning of national citizenship, Lockwood's question becomes more pressing in the context of ongoing 'cosmopolitanisation', driven by the presence of non-citizens on national territory. While citizenship acts as both a status of inclusion for members of the national community, and a device of exclusion against others, cosmopolitanism threatens to disrupt the national orientation of this system and to usher in a rights revolution (cf Soysal, 1994). So how does this potential play out in practice?

Lockwood outlines two axes for plotting inequality with respect to rights; one refers to formal entitlement and is expressed in terms of the presence or absence of a right (inclusion/exclusion), the other refers to possession of moral or material resources – or more loosely social standing, which can enhance or reduce access to or enjoyment of a right (gain/deficit). This schema contains vast analytical potential and the following points have implications for both a general interest in cosmopolitanisation, and the more specific topic of the rights of asylum seekers:

1. Firstly, the whole complex of rights is open to manipulation by the state and its officials in the pursuit of policy goals, revealing the potential for a close alliance between rights and controls. Entitlement to rights can be granted as rewards or inducements, as in recent attempts to attract highly skilled workers through preferential immigration rules and residence entitlement (eg Home Office, 2005:16, 22). Conversely, exclusion from rights can be used as a deterrent, and we have seen an example with respect to the denial of work and welfare rights for certain categories of asylum seeker. Deficit may occur where prejudice means rights are administered in a punitive manner, as in the treatment of those deemed 'undeserving' within the benefits system (Morris, 1994), or the scepticism which seems pervasive in the asylum and asylum support system (Stevens, 2004). Such deficit can have the effect of both deterrence from making a claim and exclusion from the full enjoyment of entitlement.[2]

2. Secondly, Lockwood's schema reveals the scope for a potential link between formal entitlement and status, or public standing, in its informal guise. One possibility is that rights acknowledge or confer public standing, acting as a statement of respect and/or desert. The example of highly skilled migrants serves again in this context, since a more nuanced presentation of economic migration has meant enhanced social standing for those at the upper end of the skills spectrum, in contrast to the low skilled and/ or undocumented general worker (Home Office, 2005:16). Conversely, the denial of rights can serve to undermine public standing, and the general suspicion which now surrounds asylum seekers is one example. This suspicion grew as numbers rose through the 1980s and 1990s (Stevens, 2004), and contrasts sharply with a more positive image of the refugee in the politics of the Cold War era (Bloch and Schuster, 2002; Cohen, 1994).

3. Thirdly, the elements depicted in a) and b) above, together contain the beginnings of a theory of change with respect to a scheme of rights. This

is explicit in Lockwood's account, in so far as he argues that the possession of moral and/or material resources can lead to enhanced entitlement. Such a connection is often at work in the process of claims making, whereby public campaigning can heighten respect or moral acceptability, which may be followed by an improvement in formal recognition and rights. Early feminism, and more recently the gay movement, provide clear examples of this process (Lister, 2003; Plummer, 2006). However, unless this recognition is balanced by some understanding of the corresponding scope for a contraction of rights then it runs a risk common to much theorising in the field – the assumption of a necessarily expansive dynamic, a problem recognised by both Turner (1990) and Fine (2007).

4. The schema as presented by Lockwood has no explicit means of dealing with the contraction of rights, though this possibility is implied by the discussion above, which provides some clues as to how contraction might come about. We could look, for example, for a deterioration in the moral resources or public standing of a group, such as suspicions surrounding the long term unemployed as their numbers rose (Morris, 1994), or the public discrediting of asylum seekers through the allegation that a majority of claims are 'bogus' (see below). We could also look to the possibility that this process may be harnessed as a political ploy, an argument explicitly developed by work on the social construction of target populations (Schneider and Ingram, 1993). More generally speaking, some theory of change – both positive and negative, is a necessary foundation for any assessment of claims about cosmopolitanisation.

Target populations and policy design

The construction of particular social groups as targets for policy initiatives holds considerable potential for the understanding of social change, and provides a dynamic illustration of some aspects of the civic stratification argument. Schneider and Ingram (1993) have argued that the social construction of target populations is an overlooked political phenomenon whereby the images of particular groups can be harnessed by purposive aspects of policy. The intent of such policy is often to enable or coerce behavioural change, but these images may in turn be absorbed by the general population, serving to legitimise policy and win electoral support. It is argued that an important calculation for politicians is the way that social constructions may influence their prospects of re-election, and assist their claims to address widely acknowledged public problems.

In fact, the social construction of certain groups can also be an important element in the creation and depiction of such problems (cf Kaye, 1994). Public officials must explain and justify their actions to the public by articulating a vision of the public interest and showing how a proposed policy is logically connected to widely shared public values. Four types of target population are argued to emerge from this process (Schneider and Ingram, 1993) – the advantaged, on whom positive benefits are conferred; the contenders, who can mobilise for improvement; the dependants, who are rendered passive and powerless; and the deviants, who are subject to punishment and/or coercion. Hence, it is suggested that policy makers draw ever finer distinctions, dividing particular groups into the deserving and undeserving, to yield a picture which displays many features of Lockwood's account of civic stratification.

Like Lockwood, Schneider and Ingram are also interested in acceptable degrees of inequality, and they pose the question of how far inherent contradictions within the policy process will lead to cyclical patterns of correction. This may happen through public reactions against overly advantaged groups, or principled challenges to overly punitive constructions. In the latter case, groups may harness public sympathy to refute their negative image and mobilise for improved treatment, producing pendulum swings in policy content. However, Schneider and Ingram also note that there is no inherent self-correction in the policy process, as social constructions once firmly embedded can be difficult to dislodge. Indeed, policy itself is an important factor in shaping both public perceptions and internalised identities, such that groups portrayed as dependent or deviant may fail to mobilise. Stigmatised by the policy process, they will often lack public support and hence the will or capacity to take collective action (cf Lockwood, 1996:46).

Schneider and Ingram argue that while contenders have sufficient power and influence to blunt the imposition of negative policy, powerless and negatively constructed groups are more commonly driven to court action in pursuit of their rights. Furthermore, they suggest that the application of constitutional principles in defence of negatively viewed groups may be difficult to sustain in the context of widespread belief that such groups deserve to be punished and respond best to such policy. Finally, they also suggest that the process of targeting, especially in pursuit of electoral support, can sometimes account for apparently illogical policy, as the negative construction of a group in policy terms may serve political ends while having no obvious practical impact.

Immigration policy is cited as a good example of social construction in operation. It is also argued that some social constructions are stable over time, while others are subject to continual debate and manipulation. Asylum seekers are a case in point, and in Schneider and Ingram's terms have moved over time from being contenders to dependants and eventually, as we see below, to deviants. Asylum policy also provides an example of the construction of finer distinctions within the group, such that their differential treatment constitutes an instance of civic stratification. This has been evident not only in terms of the expanding possible outcomes of an asylum application – which now include rejection, toleration, temporary protection, discretionary leave, humanitarian protection and full recognition as a refugee (Morris, 2007), but also in various attempts to build support policy around a distinction between 'at port' and 'in-country' claimants.

Applying the concepts of civic stratification and target populations, there are therefore a number of inter-related questions we can ask about the evolution of the policy itself, the legal challenge that ensued and the possible public impact of the whole process. Lockwood's argument directs us to the formal inclusions and exclusions operating with respect to rights, and their possible connection with informal aspects of social standing, such that the diminution of rights both confirms an existing lack of status and further weakens that position. His argument also invites consideration of the acceptable limits of inequality and thereby the scope for challenge, and he has noted the importance of judicial review as a basis for 'civic expansion' through enhanced access to rights.

What Schnieder and Ingram's argument potentially brings to this configuration is the political motivation lying behind policy which targets particular groups for negative or positive treatment. This lends a dynamic political force to the schema outlined by Lockwood, and potentially illuminates the relationship between rights, controls, and public sentiment. Both pieces invite questions about the erosion of rights and the circumstances and scope for challenge, returning us in more nuanced form to questions posed by Beck about the relation between the cosmopolitan ideal and banal cosmopolitanism. Research to date has documented the rise of deterrence in immigration and asylum policy (Bloch and Schuster, 2002; Morris, 2002; Stevens, 2004) and the role played by erosions of support (Sales, 2002; Webber, 2004). However, the policy warrants closer examination with respect to civic stratification, target populations, and their possible contribution to an understanding of cosmopolitanisation. We can therefore explore the policy background to welfare and asylum by posing questions about the stated and hidden purpose of the legislation; the message it conveys with respect to the social status of the target group; any related irrationality in the framing of the policy; the moral and material resources enabling a challenge; and the outcome with respect to the contours of rights.

Asylum seekers as a target population

Asylum seekers who claim asylum from inside the country rather than at an arrival point must have entered in some other capacity, and this has made them a target for suspicion. Some insight into the process of targeting can be gleaned from parliamentary debate around the introduction of key items of legislation aimed at this group. We have already noted the critical policy moments in this history – the introduction, under a Conservative government, of secondary regulations removing late claimers from entitlement for income support in 1996; the enshrining of key elements of these regulations in primary legislation via the 1996 Asylum and Immigration Act; the restoration, under New Labour, of support for late claimers via the National Asylum Support System (NASS) in 1999; and finally a third attempt to remove support from late claimers through section 55 of the 2002 Nationality Immigration and Asylum Act.

The issue central to all measures was expressed in a parliamentary question on the 1996 regulations:

> Does my right honourable friend agree that the government should not encourage bogus asylum seekers who are not escaping persecution but are merely interested in benefit.[3]

The underpinning rationale for the regulations was set out in an explanatory memorandum to the Social Security Advisory Committee (1995) and based on a classification of asylum seekers into at-port and in-country claimants (late claimers), the latter normally gaining entry on condition of no recourse to public funds. It was then assumed that this group were drawn to Britain by the availability of benefits should they subsequently claim asylum and they were made a target for suspicions of abuse, supported by an association with 'deceitful' means of entry.[4] A further association was made between mode of entry and the validity of the asylum claim such that late claimers, who made around 70% of all claims, were deemed 'bogus'. The purpose of the regulations was then presented as an attempt to address the growing trend for non-genuine applications by reducing the attractiveness of the UK for economic migrants, thereby reducing costs to the tax payer. The method for pursuing this aim was the removal of benefits from late claimers and those pursuing an appeal, and the message to the public was:

> The proposals ... will have a significant effect in safeguarding the interests of the UK by reducing the attractiveness of this country to those who are essentially economic migrants not refugees fleeing political persecution.
>
> (Department of Social Security, 1995:10)

Drawing on Schneider and Ingram we can identify both stated and hidden purpose here, and trace a process of classification and targeting which recurs in all debate on the issue. In line with their observations we find an underlying irrationality in the chain of reasoning, which lies in the ineffectiveness of the measure for distinguishing between genuine and non-genuine cases. This points to the possibility of some hidden purpose behind the stated intentions, and certainly the unstated effect is to feed public concern about asylum, undermine the credibility and standing of late claimers, and create an impression of vigorous government action. Charges of this hidden purpose appeared when the Asylum and Immigration bill was debated in parliament, where it was argued that the real motive was its electoral 'potential to hurt', and that it pandered to xenophobic voters by using the 'race card'.[5] The bill was condemned by Jack Straw[6] as 'unbalanced and disproportionate', and misleading about the extent of abuse of the asylum system. There were also charges that the measure was punitive and would create a new underclass, stigmatising and criminalising all refugees.

We see here an illustration of civic stratification in action, by the targeting of a subgroup for punishment via reduced entitlement to welfare rights, and by tying this erosion to a lessening of their public status through accusations of deceit and abuse of the system. In Schneider and Ingram's terms, late claimers for asylum had been moved from dependants to deviants.

From deviants to dependants, and back again

Given New Labour opposition to the 1996 measure it was no surprise when in 1999 they reinstituted maintenance and accommodation rights for all asylum seekers via NASS. They also promoted a commitment to human rights and embraced the aim of building a culture of rights, through the passing of the HRA in 1998. However, as we have seen, the 2002 Nationality Immigration and Asylum Act carried strong echoes of the 1996 exclusions in denying support for asylum seekers who did not claim 'as soon as reasonably practicable' (S55(1)). Under New Labour this was one aspect of a spectrum of policies which promised a greater capacity to grade all forms of migration into good and bad varieties, with accompanying mechanisms of control (Morris, 2007).

The measure was made more complex by the incorporation of Section 55(5) which was necessary to secure consistency with the HRA. It was also more nuanced in design and presentation than the 1996 measure, in part through the use of the concept of 'reasonably practicable', which ostensibly offered the opportunity to explain and justify any delay in claiming. Nevertheless, while the National Assistance Act had provided a safety net for disentitled asylum seekers in 1996, the removal of their eligibility for such support left only recourse to the ECHR (via the HRA) for those falling foul of Section 55(1). When briefly debated in the House of Lords (HoL),[7] the policy was argued to address costs to the tax payer, which had risen to £1 billion per year, and to reduce illegal migration and manipulation of the asylum system.

Broadly speaking, the argument depended on the same classification and reasoning applied by the previous government, seeking to discriminate between the genuine and non-genuine by means of a rather blunt tool. The denial of support to late claimers was argued to assist genuine cases by increasing the likelihood that the non-genuine would return home, and to discourage claims from those simply seeking to extend their stay. The measure thus cast suspicion on late claimers, who were assumed to have been supported and living somewhere until the time of their claim. One expression of the purpose and rationale of the bill was:

> To win wider public support for our duty properly to consider claims for asylum. Part of that means that all reasonable steps must be taken to minimise fraud and abuse.[8]

Again the rationality of the policy was queried by its opponents,[9] who doubted the effect of a measure unlikely to be known in advance by most applicants and cited Home Office (HO) research showing that benefits are not the principle factor in asylum seekers choice of destination.[10] Subsequent debate presented data showing a slightly higher rate of success among in-country than port applicants,[11] and also questioned the feasibility of the policy objectives:

> The Prime Minister has said that he wants to see a 50% cut in the number of applications ... That target is ludicrous. It is something over which we have no control.[12]

The hidden purpose of the measure was identified – that by treating people badly others would be deterred,[13] while later debate also revealed a link with ease of removal and administrative convenience:

> People prefer, and are advised, to make their claim for asylum once they have entered the country rather that at the port as it then becomes more difficult to deport them.[14]
>
> (cf Feria, 1996)

We have seen how a further classificatory issue emerged with respect to the Section 55(5) safety net, and the question of what level of destitution would warrant support under article 3 of the ECHR (protection from inhuman and degrading treatment). Hence, parliamentary debate made reference to critical comments from the Joint Committee on Human Rights (JCHR) which queried the notion of 'degrees' of destitution,[15] and found it difficult to envisage destitution without some threat of a breach of article 3.[16] We therefore see civic stratification at play both in the distinction between at-port and in-country claimants, and in the matter of what degree of destitution would warrant support under article 3. Late claimers were targeted as suspicious in terms of both the validity of their asylum claim and their genuine need for support. The administrative treatment likely to be meted out was hinted at in observations on NASS personnel in Scotland, who were described as second-rate civil servants, low paid, angry and jealous of their clients.[17] Thus, the punitive treatment of late claimers with respect to their formal entitlement seemed set to be amplified by the informal treatment they would encounter in its implementation (cf Stevens, 2004).

The dynamics of contraction

The parliamentary debates documented above sketch out the dynamic of a contraction or erosion of rights, which moved through a series of stages. First came the elaboration of a social problem – in this case the high numbers of asylum applicants, followed by the discrediting of a sub-category of claimants, those applying in-country. This was achieved by allegations of 'deceitful entry', a false association with non-genuine claims, and a misleading assertion of the attractions of benefit, all of which were to be addressed by the policy. The fact that the policy's irrational design could not plausibly address the stated objectives of reducing false claims and aiding genuine asylum seekers suggests some other purpose at work. The public discrediting of asylum seekers, an appearance of vigorous government action and a gain in public support are all likely candidates, and in some sense interlocking.

In Lockwood's schema an expansion of entitlement can flow from a process whereby moral resources are brought to bear in the consolidation of rights. However, some informed speculation about the reverse dynamic is also possible. Kaye (1994), for example, has noted the role of political parties in agenda setting, and in the transition from the identification of a social problem to the construction of an institutional response. Such work points to the role which politicians can play in constructing the very problem they seek to address, prior to the introduction of some remedial measure, and we have discussed the treatment of late claimers as one example. What then can be said about the implications of this process for public attitudes towards asylum seekers, and their perceived moral worth or public standing? The status of late claimers is eroded by both the construction of the problem and the nature of the measure introduced in response – in Lockwood's terms, an association between a contraction of their rights and an erosion of their moral standing seems likely.

Recent work on the British Social Attitudes survey (McLaren and Johnson, 2004) documents an increase in anti-immigration sentiment throughout the 1990s which saw a dramatic rise in asylum applications. The explanation offered by McLaren and Johnson turns on the role of the media, not in any immediate and direct manner, but rather by virtue of the negative government statements which are central to press coverage of the issue. Revealingly, anti-immigration sentiment among labour voters rose from 58 to 71 % over the period 1995–2003,[18] and while higher education has traditionally been associated with a more positive sentiment, degree holders with anti-immigrant views also rose from 35 to 56%. The authors conclude that there has been a 'culture shift' throughout society, with the change being greatest among groups which previously expressed a relatively favourable view of immigration.

The argument above does not exclude the possibility of an independent media influence working alongside government statements and policy, and one indication of this is the guidance issued by the Press Complaints Commission in 2003 on the coverage of issues relating to refugees and asylum seekers.[19] In evidence to the JCHR, the United Nations High Commission for Refugees (UNHCR) called for a strengthening of such guidance and expressed particular anxiety about the tabloids' alarmist reporting on asylum issues. There was also a caution to politicians about the need for balanced presentation of asylum issues, and concern that:

In the United Kingdom asylum seekers – and the refugees among them – have increasingly become tools for politicians, or have been turned into mere statistics by the popular press. Asylum seekers are easy to demonise. They are foreign, so an attractive target for those who are suspicious of, or actively dislike, foreigners or minorities with foreign origins.

(JCHR, 2007:Ev 429)

What seems to be at work is a cyclical process whereby politicians seek to discredit the target group – late claimers for asylum, as a preliminary to measures of deterrence which erode their rights. This erosion in turn legitimates the public's negative perception and potentially feeds into a diminution of the public standing of the target group. Though ipsos-MORI data[20] suggest that asylum and immigration lacked any real salience for voting from 1995 to 2005, by 2006 it appeared in third place among the top 10 important issues. However, their data[21] also show wide divergence in attitudes, depending on age, education and region, suggesting that reservoirs of sympathy could well exist alongside more negative perceptions. So can we find any theoretical or empirical indication that an undermining of the public status of asylum seekers could be arrested?

From deviants to contenders?

In Lockwood's schema social integration is achieved by the integrity of democratic, market and welfare state relations, and secured on an individual basis through the guarantee of political, civil and social rights. It is the delivery of these rights which provides a legitimate foundation for the system as a whole. However, as we have observed, this framework was devised as part of an analysis of the functioning of citizenship, and its coherence is potentially threatened by the presence of those outside of citizenship and thus excluded from the polity. The access of such outsider groups to the rights associated with citizenship is therefore a matter for political determination via a process in which the outsiders themselves have no direct voice, unless such rights can be claimed as universal human rights.

Lockwood recognises the possibility of expansion for groups denied access to rights, fuelled by the moral and/or material resources which can be brought to bear on either the political process or public opinion. He identifies one such area of campaigning as human rights activism, which we have seen to be central to the struggles of late claimers for asylum. However, both Lockwood, and Schneider and Ingram see excluded groups as disadvantaged by a negative public image, often associated with the very policy which confirms and legitimates their formal exclusion. In Lockwood's scheme, they already suffer from 'stigmatised deficit', while:

lack of incentive, capacity and opportunity to engage in collective action is further diminished by the indignity of the status itself.

(Lockwood, 1996:546)

Such groups are the least able to accumulate moral force and to mobilise for change.

Nevertheless, both Lockwood, and Schneider and Ingram see court action as offering a possible recourse for those too marginal or stigmatised to command public sympathy or support. Thus Lockwood argues that for civic activists seeking to establish new rights, judicial review has become an ever more frequent feature of the process, while Schneider and Ingram note that the most beneficial outcomes for disadvantaged groups have been achieved through court action to secure their rights. So legal action can offer the possibility of challenge to formal aspects of exclusion and disentitlement among the lower reaches of the civic stratification hierarchy. Can it also correct the informal erosion of public standing by virtue of what Lockwood calls the 'indignity of the status itself'?

This topic has become a matter of interest for Alexander (2006) in his argument for a new conception of the civil, as a sphere built around solidarity and commitment to a common secular faith. In an argument which complements the civic stratification approach, he suggests that we must rethink the law as a form of symbolic representation. Alexander recognises that law often serves to legalise exclusion and domination, as in the formal aspects of civic stratification, and we have seen above that there can be a degree of manipulation in this process. However, he argues that divisions can be healed through a process of civil repair, in which individual injustices transcend their particularist nature to become interwoven with universal themes. This process suggests to Alexander an active civic role which extends beyond the selection of political representatives to that of their monitoring and control.

The ascendency of human rights and their consolidation in domestic law provides one possible vehicle for this control, such that judicial rulings on government action become part of the democratic process. They enable legal forms of civil repair and thus play a role in securing the legitimacy of the democratic system. However, for this process to function as Alexander hopes the subjects of regulation must be equal actors in the quest for justice, and research on immigration law shows this has not traditionally been the case (Legomsky, 1987; Stevens, 2004). Nevertheless, the growing accessibility of human rights law has expanded legal recourse, while also requiring a higher level of scrutiny than other aspects of the law (Stevens, 2004). Thus, argues Alexander:

Legal interpretations by judges are one way of crystallizing changes in civil regulation.

(p. 191)

Similarly, both Lockwood, and Schneider and Ingram argue that where power, stigma and disadvantage work towards exclusion, the courts may offer a means of correction. Thus:

> In the course of social conflicts, individuals, organisations and large social groups may be transferred from one side of the social classification to another.
>
> (Alexander, 2006:234)

This possibility raises the additional question of whether judicial decisions can reverse some of the negative effects of civic stratification and targeting, in both their formal and informal guises.

Judicial opinion and civic status

Judicial views on the legitimacy of policy have the potential to confirm or undermine associated status issues, and a number of the judgements on challenges to disentitlement for late claimers rehearse points covered in parliamentary debate. They variously note the aim to withdraw support from non-genuine claimants and those with alternative resources, to reduce costs to the taxpayer, to deter non-genuine applications, and to discourage economic migration.[22] However, a number of the judgements also recognise the policy's inability to effectively distinguish between the genuine and non-genuine, or to enhance efficiency.[23] Thus one HoL judge stated:

> It is in reality unlikely that many claims will be made earlier as a result ... Nor do statistics suggest that late claimants make a disproportionate number of unmeritorious claims.
>
> (*Adam*, UKHL, para 101)

Provided that the aims of the policy were legitimate, however, the method of pursuing those aims, or the reasoning behind them, was deemed beyond the purview of the court.[24] Nevertheless, the airing of these issues in court gave further public exposure to a measure little debated in parliament, while confirmation of the flawed nature of the policy itself could serve to offset its negative status impact.

The early cases brought against S55 placed great emphasis on procedural fairness. This underscores Lockwood's point that not only can the formal content of a measure shape the public standing of its recipients, but so too can the manner of its administration. Parliamentary debate had already raised questions about the quality of NASS decision-making (cf Stevens, 2004), but this received closer consideration in some judgements. Hence Collins J (*Q*, EWHC, para 3) noted that 40% of appeals on maintenance decisions by

NASS[25] were successful, highlighting their poor quality, while he later remarked that the approach to S55:

> Has been coloured by an assumption that a failure to claim at the port will itself be justification for refusal.

(para 56)

Similarly, Kay J in *Q, D, H and others* emphasised the need for proper instruction to officials:

> So that they do not resort to generic stereotyping regardless of accepted evidence to the contrary.

(*Q, D, H*, para 9; cf *S, D and T*, para 16)

The appeal judgement in *Q* stressed the importance of 'fairness' both for the applicant and for the public interest (*Q*, EWCA, para 71), especially given the 'potentially draconian effect' of the measure. Yet the judge found the decision-making system to fall short, sometimes rejecting the credibility of claimants 'out of hand' (para 100).

Such observations draw attention to the punitive nature of the decision-making procedure, which placed an onus on the claimant to prove that alternative support was not available. There were negative views on the requirement to present evidence of failed attempts to secure charitable support, described by Shelter's intervention in *Limbuela* (EWCA) as a 'charade' and 'waste of public funds'. The requirement of repeated submissions until the requisite level of suffering had been reached was described as 'distasteful' by Collins J (*Limbuela*, EWHC, para 32), and 'contrary to any reasonable conception of justice' by Gibbs J (*Tesema*, EWHC, para 59). Evoking a distinction between the deserving and undeserving, Lady Hale condemned the whole policy as having:

> Taken the Poor Law policy of 'less eligibility' to an extreme which the Poor Law itself did not contemplate.

(*Adam*, UKHL, para 77)

A minority of judges showed some deference to resource constraints, making reference to the need for restraint in resource allocation (*JCWI*, 4 All ER 385, p. 9; *T*, para 11), and for caution when applying the ECHR in the area of social rights (*Limbuela*, EWCA, para 73). However, other cases stressed the particular predicament of asylum seekers as strangers in a strange land (*M*, 1 CCLR 85 CA, p. 23), resourceless and vulnerable when denied the possibility of both employment and maintenance (*S, D and T*, para 33). The hearings also provided an opportunity to detail the abject circumstances of claimants denied support. So, for example, S (in *S, D and T*, paras 28–30) showed signs of psychological disturbance and malnutrition, after sleeping rough for nine days; *Tesema* (para 21), having suffered beatings and assault at home, and experienced stress and trauma at the prospect of homelessness, was described as unfit and depressed; *Adam* (EWHC, para 16) had been sleeping in a car park, fearful of assault and surviving on one meal a day; etc. Indeed, the heart of the case history rested on an interpretation of such details in determining the level of suffering which would meet the high threshold for article 3 protection under the ECHR.

While the judge in *Zardasht* required proof of a high degree of severity, beyond that common to all disentitled claimants, others viewed deterioration to the requisite level of suffering as a matter of 'common sense', once someone was deprived of employment and basic maintenance (*Limbuela*, EWHC). In the HoL the very nature of the policy was argued to contribute to this conclusion, by the singling out of a particular group for treatment which left them 'utterly destitute on the streets as a matter of policy' (*Adam*, UKHL, para 99). The very prospect of living cashless and without shelter was described in the HoL (*Adam*, UKHL, para 78) as both inhuman and degrading by the standards of our society.

A cosmopolitan outcome?

The paper began with a reference to Beck's distinction between the cosmopolitan ideal and really existing conditions of 'cosmopolitanisation', alongside Grande's argument that the nation-state continues to be pre-eminent in the allocation and administration of rights. It was suggested that one way to pursue these issues in the form of an empirical enquiry was through the concept of civic stratification, which has been applied in the present chapter to an analysis of legislation on the welfare rights of late claimers. This has been given dynamic form by attention to the relation between its formal and informal aspects, and through a linkage with the concept of target populations.

In tracing the construction of asylum seekers as a target population, we have seen how successive governments have justified the denial of welfare rights for late claimers by constructing an association between in-country claims and multi-faceted abuse of the system. By this means late claimers have been shuffled between the categories of 'dependant' and 'deviant' according to changes in government policy, and we have suggested the possibility of a consequent shift in their public standing. While the formal dimension of civic stratification is expressed in terms of legal entitlement, a further dimension refers to the informal status of a group in terms of public esteem. The granting of a formal entitlement in some sense confirms the general standing of a group, but the withdrawal of such a right, especially on grounds of fraudulent behaviour, will inevitably reduce their public esteem. However, this argument raises the corresponding possibility, that a series of successful challenges to the withdrawal of welfare from late claimers could go some way towards repairing their public standing.

The outcome of the legal history seems to offer some indication of an emergent cosmopolitan ethos at work. Expressed in terms of civic stratification, the conclusion is that there are limits to which the erosion of rights in a system of differentiated entitlement can descend. Although the policy itself could not be over-ruled as irrational, or struck down as inconsistent with the HRA, it could be held to standards of humanity which its implementation had failed to meet. This applied both to the level of degradation to which someone could be permitted to sink before engaging the protection of article 3, and also to the manner in which the system was administered. In Lockwood's terms, the disentitlement itself, the procedure formally applied, and the respect informally denied each fell below acceptable levels of humanity, fairness and dignity. The judgements therefore went some way towards restoring both the exclusions and the deficits entailed in the regime; to converting asylum seekers from deviants to contenders; and to moving 'cosmopolitanisation' in the direction of cosmopolitanism.

The present history has demonstrated the possibility of challenging government policy, even for those without appreciable moral and material resources, by virtue of access to basic civil rights and just procedure. The judgements documented here deal principally with formal rights, notably to fair procedure and to protection from inhuman and degrading treatment. However, each of these rights also asserts the basic worth of the individual in a way which offers some degree of reparation for the status denial contained within the policy and heightened by its mode of administration. The judgements counter the construction by the government of a specific target group, whose rights had been eroded and whose moral worth had been impugned. Whether the sentiments expressed will have a broader impact on popular opinion is another matter, which depends on some engagement of the public imagination. However, some fragile signs of spontaneous local opposition to such measures (Guardian, 2008) show they may find some fertile ground.

Notes

1 Key policy changes in 1996 and 2002 each coincided with a peak in asylum applications (43,925 in 1995 and 84,135 in 2002) MPI data hub.
2 Civic gain refers to the less common reverse dynamic.
3 HC Hansard, 20 February 1996, col 160.
4 Though the Geneva Convention prohibits penalties for illegal entry.
5 HC Hansard, 22 February 1996, col 547.
6 Then Shadow Home Secretary.
7 Lords Hansard, 17 October 2002, cols 976–1006.
8 Lords Hansard, 17 October 2002, col 991.
9 Not least on the difficulties of implementation, as, for example, those who travel clandestinely on the backs of lorries and have no opportunity to claim at port.
10 Lords Hansard, 17 October 2002, cols 976–1006.
11 Lords Hansard, 24 October 2002, col 1468.
12 HC Hansard, 26 February 2003, col 81WH.

13 Lords Hansard, 17 October 2002, col 986.
14 HC Hansard, 26 February 2003, col 73WH.
15 Lords Hansard, 17 October 2002, col 989.
16 Lords Hansard, 24 October 2002, col 1465.
17 Lords Hansard, 17 October 2002, col 985–86.
18 New Labour came to power in 1997 and continues at the time of writing in 2009.
19 www.pcc.org.uk/news/index.html?article=OTE = (accessed 7 July 2008).
20 www.ipsos-mori.com/content/importance-of-key-issues-to-voting.ashx (accessed 6 December 2008).
21 Ipsosmori.com/content/british-views-on-immigration.ashx (accessed 6 December 2008).
22 For example, *JCWI* QBD; *Q*, EWCA; *S,D and T; Limbuela*, UKHL.
23 For example, *JCWI* QBD, p. 8; *JCWI*, EWCA, p. 3; *Q*, EWHC, para 14; *Q*, EWCA, para 25.
24 *JCWI*, QBD, p. 8; *Q*, EWHC, para 15.
25 This does not include S55 decisions which are not appealable.

Chapter 7

Cosmopolitanism, human rights and judgement

Contemporary writing on cosmopolitanism has argued that the social changes associated with globalisation require a new outlook which would recognise the permeability of national borders and challenge our conception of society as a nationally bounded entity. This chapter steps back from the detail of our case history and considers the role of judgement in more general terms, as a critical moment in bridging the gap between cosmopolitan ideals and a social reality which is much more conflictual. We see how the uncertain content of rights plays a key role in this process, revealing the dual nature of rights as both a social product and a social force.

We earlier observed that Beck (2006) has identified three dimensions of a 'cosmopolitan outlook': the normative, the methodological, and the empirical. The normative content is captured by the notion of the 'world citizen' (Habermas, 2001) as indicative of membership in a world community fuelled by a cosmopolitan empathy and underpinned by the principles of universal human rights (cf Isin and Turner, 2007). The argument is not that the nation-state would be redundant in a new cosmopolitan order, but rather that it would occupy a critical position in the crafting of forms of belonging and entitlement through a set of binding co-operative procedures and global responsibilities, to foster a transformed consciousness of citizens (Habermas, 2001). For Fine (2007:39), however, this raises the question of:

> How to understand the relation between cosmopolitanism as a transformative project and actually existing forms of political community.

The present study has therefore considered how far the contemporary application and interpretation of universal human rights can successfully harness cosmopolitan ideals to challenge the exclusionary policies adopted by a national government seeking to enhance control over entry by means of deterrence.

Habermas sees the driving force of a cosmopolitan movement to rest heavily on demands for change from below, and he looks to a transformed consciousness of citizens which could impose itself on both domestic policy and on global actors through an engaged civil society which stretches beyond national borders. In embracing the principle of constitutional patriotism, he argues that adherence to constitutional ideals – such as popular sovereignty and human rights, could hold together an otherwise fragmented national population (1998:118). Thus, where human rights are institutionalised in constitutional norms, he suggests they can provide both a legal framework for the conduct of national politics, and a basis for the development of a more expansive, cosmopolitan citizenry. Constitutional patriotism therefore promises to transform the basis of national sentiment and identity in line with cosmopolitan ideals, to render what Fine (2007:44) terms:

> A self-reflective form of loyalty to the constitutional principles of the state that relativises our own way of life, grants strangers the same rights as ourselves and enlarges tolerance and respect for others.

For Beck (2006), one outcome of this process would be a cosmopolitan empathy, which would not replace national empathy but rather presuppose it, and transform it into a cosmopolitan nationalism.

The methodological dimension of the cosmopolitan outlook echoes some of these normative arguments, challenging a methodological nationalism which implicitly associates the idea of society with that of the bounded national state. The related research question is to what extent national spaces have truly become denationalised, and how far cosmopolitan ideals are being translated and reconfigured into concrete social realities. The endeavour is to illuminate the forms of trans-nationalism which are arising within the nation-state (Beck and Sznaider, 2006), and in so doing to clearly distinguish the normative from the empirical. A methodological cosmopolitanism must therefore be sensitive to the porous nature of national boundaries – to the social, political and economic forces which breach these boundaries, and to the ways in which dualities such as national/trans-national, universal/particular, and global/local are being deconstructed, conceptually and in practice. There must, however, be a corresponding awareness of possible local/national resistance to cosmopolitan trends, which might challenge the normative enterprise.

It is at this point that the empirical level of cosmopolitanism comes into play – through Beck's (2006) distinction between the cosmopolitan ideal and the lived reality of cosmopolitanism, which throws up ambiguities not fully addressed at the normative level. As we have seen, international migration provides a key example, and Beck suggests that the distinction between citizenship rights and universal human rights may be suspended as a result of the claims of trans-national migrants. If he proves correct then Arendt's paradox would finally be overcome. However, the extent to which human rights can fill the breach of national exclusions from entitlement is an empirical question requiring an exploration of mobilisation and contestation with respect to rights, and an understanding of the process of their interpretation. While the incorporation of human rights instruments into domestic law may be taken as one example of what Beck terms cosmopolitan nationalism, or cosmopolitanisation from within, the realisation of these rights might first require a disruption of more narrowly constructed policy, conceived in terms of the national interest. Thus Beck's hoped for 'trans-national nationalism' (p. 63), which would open up previously exclusive political and public spaces, may first have to confront conflict and resistance, rather than any assumed cosmopolitan empathy.

It is this realisation that drives Beck and Sznaider's (2006) distinction between cosmopolitan norms and cosmopolitanism as an existing reality, in which nationalism and cosmopolitanism might come into conflict. Reservations could accordingly be raised about Habermasian faith in a cosmopolitan citizenry, or constitutional patriotism, as the source of an expansive response to the presence of non-citizens on national territory. Hence, Fine (2007:40) issues a caution over the idealisation attendant on cosmopolitan conceptions of political community, and rather emphasises the role of political judgement on the part of ordinary citizens. However, this will not necessarily be exercised in support of cosmopolitan ideals, which may well provoke a struggle with more narrowly perceived self-interest. As Beck and Sznaider (2006) recognise, there is no guaranteed connection between the internal cosmopolitanisation of national societies and the emergence of a cosmopolitan consciousness, subject or agent. Similarly, when Habermas endorses a cosmopolitanism bred of constitutional patriotism, there is the accompanying spectre of a democratic outcome which goes against the extension of rights to non-citizens and results instead in a form of national protectionism. While Habermas (2001) recognises that poverty, income disparity and social disintegration threaten the integrative capacities of liberal societies, and that this lends some urgency to the cosmopolitan project, they could just as easily prove its undoing.

Human rights and cosmopolitanism

Cosmopolitan writers see a close connection between the drive for cosmopolitan ideals and the emergence of legal instruments intended to deliver universal human rights. The institutionalisation of human rights is thus a first step in translating cosmopolitan norms into empirical reality. If cosmopolitanism represents the ideal underlying recognition of a universal human condition, and its need for freedoms and protections, then guaranteed legal rights constitute a necessary part of its realisation. They are also seen by some as the basis for a move towards a de-nationalisation of legitimacy (Soysal, 1994; Levy and Sznaider, 2006) and a reconfiguration of sovereignty itself. This would mean that states retain their sovereign functions but are no longer the sole source of entitlement, which can rest instead on the global reach of human rights principles. The outcome is a shift towards a cosmopolitan sovereignty, whereby the institutionalisation of human rights becomes a source of state legitimacy and signals an uncoupling of the nation and the legitimate grounding of claims to rights. The contours of sovereignty are thus redrawn.

However, in practice, the most certain guarantee of rights still comes first from citizenship, and to a lesser but significant extent from permanent residence in a particular legal community. The extent to which others within but not of that community can lay claim to ostensibly universal rights introduces a tension identified by Habermas (2001). While many states have accepted the universal declaration of human rights and supporting international conventions, their application and meaning occupy a contested terrain. For Beck (2006) the campaign for worldwide recognition of human rights marks the beginning of an institutionalised cosmopolitanism, but Fine (2007:73) is alert to the limits of this process. These limits lie both in the uncertain content of human rights law, and in the problem of conceptualising human rights in purely juridical terms. Fine's argument is that we need to leave space for the political field of judgement, and though his hope is that this will be exercised in a cosmopolitan spirit, such an outcome cannot be guaranteed.

We have seen how Douzinas (2000) actively embraces the uncertain element of human rights, arguing that this indeterminacy has a positive aspect, granting to human rights the ability to re-imagine social boundaries. For him, human rights have the potential to create new meanings and values as novel subjects and situations lay claim to their protection, and as new rights are brought into being by a 'performative declaration'. This argument provokes an ironic reversal, in which he argues that we are always persecuted by the refugee, through our concrete encounter with their absolute need:

> The other arises in my field of perception with the trappings of absolute poverty, without attributes, the other has no place, no time, no essence, the other is nothing but his or her request and my obligation.
>
> (Douzinas, 2000:350)

There is again an echo of Arendt's writing here, and the implication is that there will always be a gap between the principles embraced by universal human rights, and their legal expression at any given time (cf Bobbio, 1996).

Ethical responsibility is argued to precede the codification of human rights, rather than to derive from them, hence giving force to the argument that their practical realisation will never be exhausted. It is here that indeterminacy comes into play, for the open language of rights makes their content amenable to political argumentation. We may institutionalise the ethic of responsibility for others, but the form and extent of that responsibility remains unspecified; while a claim to rights relies upon a corresponding ethical impulse, the role of the law is to concretise the ensuing obligation. However, Douzinas sees no clear and unambiguous principle of interpretation for determining a content which can never be fixed:

> The undecidability between the strict requirements of legal logos and the
> indeterminacy of human rights is both a structural characteristic of legal
> discourse and the moral element in the operation of the legal system
>
> (Douzinas, 2000:368)

For him, this is a key source of strength, allowing human rights to evade the
limitations and constraints of legal certainty and to offer a powerful 'popular
imaginary' which may be taken up in the name of as yet unimagined causes
and constituencies.

This argument means that the unspecified boundary of rights opens up a
space for the political judgement that Fine has called for, and we start to see
human rights as part of a social and political process involving contestation
and requiring interpretation whose cosmopolitan outcome is by no means
assured. National–trans-national forms of conflict are one common focus of
dispute, as Beck (2006) has argued, citing the suspicion which commonly
attaches to cross border migrants. This raises an empirical question about the
force of human rights as a source of entitlement for those whose legitimate
presence on the national territory is contested. As Donnelly (2003) has argued,
human rights norms have been internationalised but their implementation and
delivery lies largely at the national level. He has also suggested that rights will
only come to prominence when they are in some way at issue – questioned,
threatened or denied, and in such cases human rights principles provide a
moral foundation to strengthen or extend existing entitlement, or to resist its
erosion. However, the open nature of their conception requires not just political judgement in the broad sense, but legal judgement which has a narrower
remit while being broadly political in its implications.

Judgement and rights

If we accept the above argument about indeterminacy and human rights then
their concrete realisation entails both levels of judgement – the political and
the legal, though Fine has challenged this distinction. He argues, in relation to
humanitarian interventions, that:

> Law and politics are two sides of the contemporary cosmopolitan coin:
> they bring together institution and outlook, judgement and understanding.
>
> (Fine, 2006:64)

However, these two arenas of judgement, the political and the legal, may
well conflict, as the present case history has shown, such that cosmopolitan
principles are brought to bear in challenges to the implementation of an
exclusionary policy framed in terms of a narrowly defined national interest.
The exercise of judgement is therefore required in translating norms into
practice. Our discussion so far has suggested that rights, and especially

universal human rights, are not confined to narrow conceptions of legality in their origins, application or interpretation, and this position is supported by Dworkin's (2005:xii) distinction between background rights and institutional rights. The former refer to rights that hold 'in an abstract way' against decisions taken by the community or society as a whole, while the latter refer to rights that hold against the decisions of a specific institution. Thus, while human rights may take an institutional form when given effect in specific legislation (such as the Human Rights Act (HRA)), they are an expression of the broader background principles of human dignity and equal worth (Donnelly, 2003:27).

Concepts such as these, however, require interpretation and where there is indeterminacy concerning the content of human rights in their legal expression, then the process of judgement becomes critical. In Dworkin's (2005:5) terms, 'there are issues of moral principle that lie behind an apparently linguistic problem', and so controversial decisions about community morality may turn on an appeal to concepts which themselves are susceptible to different interpretations (Dworkin, 2005:127). The argument has implications not only for the concrete application of human rights guarantees, but also for more general questions about the status of cosmopolitan ideals and the scope for their realisation in practice. This is especially the case given the argument addressed in Chapter 5, that the law is fraught with contradictions which cannot be resolved by the application of principle (Unger, 1986) and which therefore entail judgement that is political in nature. While there may be debate about the motivational aspect of judgement in terms of the background and political orientation of judges (Legomsky, 1987; Griffith, 1997), the political *implications* of differing interpretations are beyond question.

We can find in legal judgements differing conceptions of the boundaries of our moral community, and this matter offers a fruitful avenue of enquiry for scholars of cosmopolitanism, turning attention to possible indicators of an emergent cosmopolitan outlook. A number of commentators of contrasting persuasions (Unger, 1986; Habermas, 1996; Dworkin, 2005) have noted the role of differing social visions or legal paradigms, such that within conflicting interpretations of rights we can find differing conceptions of human association. Hence:

> The focused disputes of legal doctrine repeatedly threaten to escalate into struggles over the basic imaginative structure of social existence.
>
> (Unger, 1986:17)

We would expect such struggles to reflect ideas and ideals already at play in more mundane social interactions, while the role of judgement over these competing visions will appear in legal decisions about the content of rights. We can see here how such judgement might be broader than the detail of the law, in the sense expressed by Douzinas (2000:368), who states:

Human rights cannot be reduced to categorisation and classification and their content is not given to categorical presentation.

In a more substantive context, Griffith (1997) has observed that the generality of provisions in the European Convention on Human Rights (ECHR) inevitably means that judges will be drawn into political decisions, and into defining the interests of society as a whole, and not simply those of the majority. Thus, Sedley (1995) has argued that human rights are by nature political, in seeking to condition how states treat individuals (and not only their citizens). Where the interpretive flexibility of human rights is put to use in challenging government measures against a vulnerable group then we see an example of what Dworkin (2005:205) terms the majority promise to minorities. The capacity of human rights to offer protection to otherwise powerless groups can therefore be seen as an extension of democracy, and this is especially the case if the group concerned is denied other forms of direct representation through the parliamentary system. The occasion of legal judgement in the present history has acted as a forum for participation and an arena for public deliberation about the content of human rights from the perspective of those excluded from parliamentary debate (Fredman, 2000).

Judgement conducted in this way can be a source of social change, opening up new areas of interpretation and application for human rights, as in the extension of the ECHR to address social as well as civil and political rights. In fact, Sedley (1995) has argued that the answers given by the court are functions of a larger social and political debate, in which case, judgement can provide a critical measure of the purchase of cosmopolitan values in a given society. The judicial interpretation of rights is therefore a vital dimension of any attempt to compare the empirical state of the cosmopolitan condition with the normative ideals of the cosmopolitan outlook.

Judgement as a social process

The institutionalisation of rights is itself part of a social process (eg Plummer, 2006) which proceeds through a number of stages. These can be described as the moral assertion of a claim, the accumulation of public credibility and support, the recognition of the claim by policy makers and legislators, and finally its institutionalisation. The removal or erosion of a right is also likely to spark a similar process of moral opposition and a drive for public support, though where the latter is not forthcoming then redress through the courts offers an alternative route. In such cases it may be a positive legal decision which helps to shift the tide of public opinion, rather than popular campaigning over contested government policy.

There is some support for such a conception of rights from a variety of socio-legal theories. Dworkin (2005), for example, argues that individual rights are political trumps which can be asserted when a collective goal is not sufficient to deny them, or to impose on individuals some loss or injury. Such a right can be claimed against a specific policy by drawing on civil rights which grant the right to a decision by the court, and on background principles which underpin the operation of the legal system (such as fairness and justice). While emphasising the quest for coherence in the law, Dworkin nevertheless recognises that background principles themselves require interpretation and that there is scope for differing views, reflecting different political moralities. However, a more critical approach to law (Unger, 1986) takes up this point, seeing scope for alternative visions of society embedded in the interpretive decisions which fall to judges. For Douzinas (2000) it is precisely this openness which is the strength of human rights, and hence the argument that the principles underlying human rights offer a resource to the vulnerable (Levy and Sznaider, 2006) as unanticipated interpretations emerge to assert the rights of those otherwise excluded.

Habermas (1996) argues that moral reasons enter the law via the democratic procedures of the law giver and through the political communications of the public sphere, with the political process acting as a theatre of debate about which principles a community should accept. However, judgement is called into play when the law is challenged, and such challenge will often have its origins outside of parliament, in public protest or social movements, and may seek to harness the power of the courts to secure social change. Where such protest has real purchase it will often rest upon uncertainty in the content or application of the law, and where such uncertainty exists, we have seen how Habermas looks to regulated competition between paradigms of understanding and interpretation via the courts. This paradigm struggle forms an aspect of his procedural approach, and offers an incipient theory of change, inviting the question of how new paradigms emerge and gain ascendency, for 'Rights are a social construction which one must not hypostatize into facts' (Habermas, 1996:226).

Neither judges nor legal theorists have difficulty accepting that interpretations of the law will change as society changes, and that such change can be manifest in a paradigm shift (eg Dworkin, 1986). Thus Habermas (1996) emphasises the connections linking the legal system with its social environment and dominant pre-understanding of society, whereby the law represents an answer to perceived challenges of an extant social situation, containing an implicit diagnosis of our times. For Habermas legitimate law flows from an unsubverted public sphere rooted in the lifeworld via networks of civil society, so while a paradigm may be discerned in important court decisions it arguably has its origin elsewhere. Paradigm change must surely therefore reflect experience of a kind which challenges established perceptions of the social world, and if Beck is correct, the forces of cosmopolitanism could represent one such instance. The law via the courts may then become a battleground over changing interpretations of fundamental rights.

Habermas (2001), as we saw, places great weight on the role of citizens in compelling their leaders to address the obligations of cosmopolitan solidarity, and his discussion of civil society and the public sphere envisions a public audience possessed of final authority (1996:364). However, he gives no explicit attention to the presence of those who lack a political voice and who fail to generate public sympathy, though the access of this excluded population to basic civil rights is itself significant. Their possession of rights before the law frees them from reliance on popular authority and opens up the possibility of legal challenge when other basic rights are denied. Alexander (2006:154) perceives such challenge as:

> Demands for more symmetry between the claimants' putative legal standing in civil society and their putatively uncivil status in another sphere.

Implicitly he is also suggesting that endorsement of claims in the court can have a further effect in changing the public climate through an assertion of the worth of the claim. We see an echo here of Lockwood's (1996) argument whereby the formal recognition of rights may reverse an informal status deficit for the claimant, thereby completing the circuit which connects politics, law, society and judgement. This nexus also recalls Honneth's argument about the importance of recognition for individual self-realisation. However, as Alexander has observed, the law as an expression of the coercive power of class, caste or state, can also create exclusions and this insight offers a starting point for the sociological analysis of judgement.

Judgement in political context

Writing on the geography of civil society, Alexander (2006:196) has argued:

> Nationalism can be conceived ... as the socialisation of space that is demarcated by the territorial limits of states.

He goes on to argue that this territorial fixing of society produces its own enemies, and generates suspicion over arrivals from outside its boundaries which fragments and distorts civil society at its roots. The divisions that it generates are then often given substance in politics and law which designate differing classes of person in terms of rights and belonging (cf Morris, 2002). The starting point for understanding judgement in the cases at issue here is this political context, which sets up two potentially opposing positions that approximate the national and the cosmopolitan paradigms outlined in Chapter 5, and which we have seen manifest in debates about asylum and welfare.

Griffith (1997) has argued that conflict between the judiciary and the executive, apparent in Britain since 1990, stems from government adoption of harsh policies and actions:

> which they must have known were on the margins of legality. In other words they have taken a view of where the public interest lies which does not accord with the judicial view.
>
> (Griffith, 1997:xvi)

Griffith depicts the judiciary as one of the principle organs of democracy – both upholders of the law and protectors of individuals against a powerful executive, whose voice is the voice of the community, not of government or the majority. He therefore sets up a distinction between the public interest, conceived as the interests of the community as a whole, and the national interest or the interests of the state, which might be more narrowly defined (p. 296) (see also McHarg, 1999). He also notes a recent readiness to deny validity to government actions less on the ground of illegality than 'from a sense of injustice and unfairness', in defence of those 'least able to help themselves' (p. 332). Destitute asylum seekers are cited as one example. Griffith was writing before the passing of the HRA, but the implementation of this Act has concentrated attention on the tension between perceptions of the national interest and the application and interpretation of fundamental rights; though where absolute rights are at issue this question of balance should not arise.

The logic underpinning various attempts to deny welfare support for late claimers was reviewed and questioned in the early hearings on challenges to the measure (*JCWI*, QBD, and 4 All ER 385; Q, EWHA and EWCA), and summarised in the Adam, UKHL (para 2). The picture of the political debate which emerges is of legislative measures adopted to stem a rise in the number of asylum claims, allegedly driven by economic migration. Such arguments were one attempt to defuse the tension between the desire to limit asylum numbers and conflicting obligations under both domestic statutes and international human rights law. In the case of S55, this tension was apparent in the legislation itself, and once its implementation was challenged it fell to the courts to resolve what was in practice a highly charged political dilemma. This was then worked out against the background of a traditionally restrictive approach to immigration and asylum by the UK government and judiciary. Questioning claims of an emergent post-national society (Soysal, 1994), Joppke (1998:110) has argued that there has been an increased willingness and determination by states to assert their sovereignty over immigration, even at the cost of equating genuine asylum seekers with economic migrants. He also states that advocates of a more open asylum and immigration regime stress human rights principles while remaining silent about the popular groundswell of support for tighter controls. Writing before the passing of the HRA, he was able to argue of Britain that:

> Due to the domestic weakness of human rights provisions and actors and a zealous and instant equation of asylum-seeking with immigration, state sovereignty prevailed easily, without a major challenge.
>
> (Joppke, 1998:113)

The cases at issue here illustrate the extent to which that situation has now changed.

Conservatism or activism?

Writing over 20 years ago, Legomsky (1987) described an 'all-embracing conservative tilt' in judicial decisions in the area of immigration, which exhibited 'great deference to the administrative bodies whose decisions have been challenged' (p. 255). This was ascribed in part to the general restraint with which judges have viewed their role, including a hesitation to defy public opinion in a climate of general hostility to immigration (p. 242). This restraint was seen as a form of conservatism with respect to preservation of the values and institutions at the core of our society (cf Griffith, 1997:8). However, such an account leaves open the possibility that some values might be assertively defended should government action be felt aggressively to undermine them, turning conservatism into activism. Furthermore, the passing of the HRA meant a change in the level of scrutiny of public bodies, which as Lord Irvine (2003:308) put it:

> Delivers a modern reconciliation of the inevitable tension between the democratic rights of the majority to exercise political power and the democratic need of individuals and minorities to have their human rights secured.

Griffith (1997) has argued that immigration cases exemplify the kinds of social and political choices at issue when weighing fundamental rights against arguments of state interest – and as Joppke (1998) notes, asylum has increasingly been seen in terms of immigration. The cases in the present history have generated a series of oppositions: policy as against principle, immigration control as against fundamental rights, and national resources as against universal humanity. They have raised questions about the degree of social support necessary to fully realise the civil guarantee of a right to seek asylum, and about the acceptability of enforced destitution in human rights terms. Allegations of abuse of the asylum system have been used to argue against entitlement to welfare, while fundamental rights have been called upon to set limits on the acceptable erosion of such support. Even before the passing of the HRA, Griffith (1997:317) cited the *JCWI* case as an example of 'new found robustness' when the judiciary was faced with a government action it did not approve. While one tradition of socio-legal thought has attempted to link judicial conservatism to the social and political background of judges (for discussion see Griffith, 1997:294; see also Logomsky, 1987) this does not account for their ability and readiness on some occasions to uphold a challenge to government action in support of the vulnerable.

Such conflict is held to occur where the government takes a view of the public interest which does not accord with the judicial view, though Griffith argues that the definition of public interest is itself a political matter which permits a variety of answers. He sees the public interest as wider than the interests of the state, not dictated by the majority view, and thus capable of embracing the protection of minorities. However, again prior to the passing of the HRA, he stated that in practice:

> Only occasionally has the power of the supreme judiciary been exercised in the positive assertion of fundamental values.
>
> (Griffith, 1997:342)

The cases at issue here, in invoking the HRA, have proved one such occasion, described by Palmer as an unusual instance in which judicial deference (to the government) has taken second place to human rights. The passing of the HRA has constrained the government to act in a manner compatible with the ECHR, and in the cases at issue here has brought an absolute right into play.

Absolute rights in particular require a higher level of scrutiny than other statutes and, as Palmer (2007) argues, bring values and principles to the fore, but in so doing open up the task of interpretation. Thus even absolute rights entail decisions which contain a political element, as elaborated by Habermas's discussion of the nature of legal paradigms. In his account, a paradigm reduces legal complexity and gives guidance as to the appropriate outcome of a particular case, but can also be equated with the judge's implicit image of society. In Chapter 5 we saw the example of an emergent cosmopolitan paradigm, set against a more traditional national orientation, suggesting that paradigms represent not just a view of an existing social relations, but a means of shaping them for the future. By guiding the interpretation of a right, they both recognise and foster change within the law and in society more broadly, offering 'an answer to the perceived challenges of the present social situation' (Habermas, 1996:388).

While Habermas sees contest between such paradigms as an essentially political dispute, he also sees it as part of a process of democratic deliberation:

> This dispute concerns all participants and it must not be conducted only as an esoteric discourse among experts. ... (who) cannot use their professional authority to impose one view of the constitution on the rest of us. The public of citizens must find such a view convincing.
>
> (Habermas, 1996:395)

So an interesting sociological question must concern the source of new legal paradigms, not just in legal argumentation but in the movements of social groups affected by the law; the means by which a 'public of citizens' might exert their influence on the outcome of judgement.

Civil society activism

For Habermas (1996) civil society provides the lifeworld roots of a public sphere, through an associational network which acts as both a sounding board and a warning system, grounded in a general public of citizens. The role of the public sphere for the political system is thus to identify and dramatise problems, and to offer solutions in such a way that they are taken up in the parliamentary complex. Constituted through basic rights of assembly, association and expression, the public sphere provides the space for a possible expansion of existing rights by communicative action. Civil society is therefore constructed by the law, through the guarantee of civil freedoms, while also offering a means of influencing the law, such that:

> the constitutional state is not a finished structure but a delicate and sensitive enterprise whose purpose is to realise the system of rights anew in changing circumstances.
>
> (Habermas, 1996:384)

A vibrant civil society is argued to address a public audience possessed of final authority, and the key question for Habermas (1996:330) is whether it has sufficient vitality to bring marginalised conflicts to the centre of political concerns.

In this model, therefore, the pressure of public opinion can compel the formal political consideration of an issue. However, Habermas has noted the importance of civil society groups as advocates for those under-represented in formal processes, and he attaches special significance to their willingness to take a universalist stand on behalf of those otherwise marginalised. The point is not pursued, but where vulnerable groups cannot carry public support then, as suggested by Lockwood (1996) and Schneider and Ingram (1993), being endowed with civil rights they will have access to the courts as an alternative avenue of influence. In Habermas's procedural understanding of the law as a deliberative space we see an opportunity for such groups to participate indirectly in the political process through the legal system. For those denied a political voice, legal procedure can offer a means of participation and representation through a challenge to measures which may carry majority support but which deny the rights of significant minorities. As Fredman (2000:101) argues:

> A properly constructed ... bill of rights can open up new avenues of participation and increase democratic control.

The courts thus provide the space for deliberation about the content of rights, and to explore the question of who has entitlement to which rights, thus providing a legal mechanism for the resolution of a social and political conflict.

Much cosmopolitan writing attributes a central significance to the development of public support for an expansive resolution to such ventures. Habermas (2001), for example, calls for a fostering of cosmopolitan solidarity among citizens which can impose itself on domestic policy; Beck (2006:5–6) speaks of a 'cosmopolitan pity' for the suffering of others which forces us to act; Levy and Sznaider (2006) write of the importance of embedding particular historical memories of abuse in global human rights imperatives; while Beck and Sznaider (2006) see people drawn into cycles of cosmopolitan sympathy, even against their will. There is an acknowledged ambivalence as well, however, and Beck (2006:44) concedes that 'an optimist of the cosmopolitan outlook can be a pessimist of the cosmopolitan mission', while Fine (2007) notes the dilemma confronting a citizenry faced with opposing national and cosmopolitan orientations. Cohen (2001) goes further, addressing the capacity for popular denial in the face of atrocities and suffering, and public feelings of moral inadequacy in place of political critique. It is this perspective, rather than cosmopolitan sympathy, which is perhaps more telling for the present history, given the absence of significant levels of protest against the enforced destitution of late claimers for asylum, compelled to live on the street and beg for survival whilst attempting to claim a fundamental human right.

In so far as the policy at issue was designed to court public opinion through the appearance of tough government action to control immigration, it signals some problems for Habermas's idea of public opinion as a final authority for civil society action. In fact, the case history documented here shows how, with the help of advocacy groups, the civil rights of late claimers rather than public support were instrumental in securing the protection of their human dignity through the courts. The account therefore highlights Alexander's (2006) view of the double-edged nature of the law, as both an instrument of social division and a source of 'civil repair', such that when fundamental rights are denied there is a call to account by recourse to higher level principles.

As we have seen, higher level principles themselves require interpretation, and in his discussion of legal paradigms Habermas cautions that they are vulnerable to ideological distortion and can harden when closed off from radically new situations. In his view, a closed paradigm occurs when there is an institutionalised monopoly of interpretation, such that the law loses its ability to adjust to changing situations. For Habermas, the openness of a paradigm is enabled by the role of participant perspectives in facilitating a contextualised interpretation of principles, rooted in the experience and worldview of those affected. In line with this perception, the present cases show how civil society advocacy played a central role in calling for interpretive flexibility to extend protection under the ECHR to incorporate social support. In this endeavour, they were active not only in co-ordinating the legal challenge and bringing cases to court, but also in envisaging, collecting and presenting the relevant evidence, providing a participant perspective, and offering expert intervention.

Writing over 15 years ago, Harlow and Rawlings (1992) saw the rule-bound nature of mass society as producing escalating challenge about the meaning of rules, and even of the 'public interest'. They also predicted a rise in group activity from minorities disadvantaged in the national political system. In this regard, advocacy organisations have an important role in the mobilisation and representation of vulnerable groups otherwise lacking the resources or knowledge to mount a legal challenge. Such litigation provides the opportunity for pressure groups to pursue social reform in the absence of a larger scale social movement and a concerned or sympathetic public (see Prosser, 1983). It has been of particular significance given the position of asylum seekers, who are 'in' but not 'of' the national community; they have a legitimate presence in the country while their claim is being considered but no direct political voice.

While a view of the courts as a participatory space has for some generated concerns about the politicisation of litigation (Harlow, 2002; Hannett 2003), others (Arshi and O'Cinneide, 2004) have supported the competence of courts to manage this process. Indeed, under the HRA the courts are charged with the more overtly political task of determining the content and boundary of fundamental rights. Fredman's (2000) reaction to concern over this political role lies in the characterisation of judicial decision-making as a process of deliberation, enriched by the contributions of litigants and interveners, which returns us to a Harbermasian argument about the deliberative nature of judgement. This is highlighted in the present history by the substantial evidential input from civil society organisations, and the unfolding of a final outcome across a series of cases which required a total of 24 separate judicial opinions, and was informed by interventions from four prominent non-governmental organisations (NGOs). This deliberative process moved the judiciary by incremental and sometimes conflictual steps towards a final judgement which was based less on the application of formal rules than on reflection over the lived experience of a vulnerable group.

Legal argumentation

We have seen how, prior to the HRA, early cases in this study were decided with reference to domestic statutes, though with background support from broader principles. However, the HRA, in enacting the ECHR domestically, set standards to which public bodies must be held, and the later judgements required an application of these general standards to the particular circumstances of disentitled asylum seekers. The ECHR has been described (Browne-Wilkinson, 1998) as a code of moral principles, posing a set of moral questions to which the courts must give moral answers. This view entails a conception of the Convention as a living document with respect to the social and political realities of the day. Among those realities in the present instance stood political concern about immigration control and the presence on national territory of asylum seekers whose claim to national resources has been placed in question. To pose the issue in this way invites a balancing between definitions of the national interest and the legitimacy of late claimers' right to support, unless this right is construed in absolute terms, which should eliminate any such qualification. Thus, a critical step in the present history was whether this absolute right was engaged.

Legomsky (1987:223) has stated:

> There can be little doubt today that a judge frequently has a practical choice between two or more alternative dispositions of a particular case.

He adds that although the proffered explanation for any specific choice lies in the legal doctrine expounded in the opinion, in many cases this does not seem especially persuasive. In fact, where justification lies in the application of a particular principle, then the explanatory task simply shifts to another level – that of how the principle is applied. Once the HRA had been invoked in the present history, the ostensible issue was a) whether the enforced destitution of late claimers amounted to 'treatment' for the purposes of article 3, and if so, b) whether the treatment was inhuman and degrading. Judgement therefore required a decision which determined the degree of state responsibility, the proper use of state resources, and an appropriate standard for human dignity in contemporary society. These matters were not resolvable by the mechanical application of an established rule, or by reference to the words of the convention itself, but rather called into play the Cosmopolitan–National opposition outlined in Chapter 5.

While there was judicial agreement on the engagement of article 3, there were qualifying arguments that national resources should be taken into account in interpretation (T, EWCA), and that a spectrum of harm should be considered in determining the degree of protection to be provided (Limbuela, EWCA). However, these arguments were eventually rejected and it was the cosmopolitan paradigm which held sway both in a majority of opinions and in the culminating House of Lords (HoL) judgement. A number of the judgements, including the final HoL decision, made reference to 'the standards of civilised society' in determining the level of suffering which would trigger state intervention, but they were setting this standard as much as they were applying it. In so doing, the judges were guided by both the detailed accounts of the personal experience of claimants as well as generic evidence about the paucity of charitable provision. It was this evidence which informed a construction of what human dignity should look like, and of what is or is not acceptable in our society, thus bringing together what Beck (2006) has termed the philosophical and the empirical dimensions of cosmopolitanism.

The reasoning was as much from the particular to the general as vice versa; an instance of what Ferrara (2008) terms 'the force of the example'. By this he means an act of reflexive judgement which can replace the reading of norms from a general law or principle with the deduction of norms by close consideration of a particular case. From this perspective, normativity and universalism are present in a judgement but only by an act of persuasion, in anticipation of general consensus which remains to be cultivated (Ferrara, 2008). The argument contains an echo of Dworkin's sense that judgement is both backward and forward looking; an unfolding political narrative and expression of a moral and political community in the making. Similarly, in Beiner's (1983:138) view, 'all political judgments are ... about the form of collective life which it is desirable to pursue', while Sedley (1995:392) has stated:

> Argument about the content of a right cannot be conducted in purely or even principally legal terms, and the answers given by the constitutional court are inevitably and rightly a function of a larger debate.

This sentiment expresses, in different tone, the openness of human rights which Douzinas sees as their major strength. Deliberation about the content of absolute rights is also deliberation about the nature of the society we wish to construct; more than an expression of the society we are, it is best seen as deliberation about the society we aspire to be. Accordingly, the claims made on behalf of deliberative democracy are not that it satisfies democratic standards in a majoritarian sense, but rather that it offers a means of protecting a minority against the majority – and the courts are called on to provide this protection where it seems that parliament has failed.

Deliberation on such matters is not confined to courtroom exchanges, however, and we saw in Chapter 3 that the delivery of a judgement can itself be a part of political dialogue. While the main body of a judgement is a justification of the decision in legal terms, in the cases at issue here we have seen that judgement can also contain a message aimed implicitly, or sometime explicitly, at the government. In fact, since the HRA does not permit the courts to strike down legislation but only to issue a statement of incompatibility (with Convention rights), the Act could be held to encourage this broader aspect of judgement. While incompatibility is not at issue in the present cases, given the incorporation of human rights concerns into S55 itself, the judgements nevertheless stand as a medium for dialogue with the government. Such a role has been actively embraced by some commentators to argue that:

> Successful challenges in the courts are not an affront to constitutional arrangements but are being worked out in a spirit of co-operation.
>
> (Lord Irvine, 2003:325)

'Co-operation' has been readily apparent in the past, and we have noted the conservative approach traditionally taken by the judiciary on immigration matters, such that before the passing of the HRA, Griffith (1997:342) was able to write:

> Judges are concerned to preserve and to protect the existing order ... Their view of the public interest, when it has gone beyond the interest of governments, has not been wide enough to embrace the interests of political, ethnic, social or other minorities.

Yet in the present cases we have an unfolding history which protects the human rights of a group marginalised in all of these ways, and contains some strong messages to the government to this effect. We can now reflect on the various component parts of judgement which contributed to this outcome.

What makes a judgement

In the course of this discussion the idea of judgement has arisen in different ways; the political judgement underpinning policy decisions, the judgement of 'ordinary citizens' in supporting or demanding political measures, and the judgement required in response to legal challenges. The first two areas of judgement are clearly interconnected, with politicians often introducing measures with an eye to securing electoral support, while legal judgement seems, at first sight, more narrowly technical. However, in the present history such judgement has functioned both as a constraint on the actions of government, and as a response to challenges initiated by civil society bodies, and therefore has a close relation to a more overtly political terrain of judgement. In fact, political objectives and the civil society response provide both the context of, and the need for, legal judgement in the present cases.

The preamble to the ECHR states that fundamental freedoms are best maintained by an effective political democracy and by the observance of the human rights on which those freedoms depend. Furthermore, the ECtHR has rejected a majoritarian approach to democracy (McHarg, 1999:671), and in this context has emphasised the fair and proper treatment of minorities as against any abuse of a dominant majority position. However, as the link between state and nation unravels then the extension of fundamental rights to all on national territory may become a critical question. The need for legal judgement can therefore be glimpsed in political concern about immigration control and public resources, as weighed against cosmopolitan conceptions of a reconfigured society. The starting point for a sociological understanding is therefore political debate asserting national interests in the context of alleged abuse of the asylum system, and the broader implications of such debate for a commitment to human rights.

There is a contrast between the early and the later cases in this history, the former considering the withdrawal of support in the context of domestic statutes and the Common Law, and the later judgements addressing human rights issues more directly. Once the entitlement of late claimers to support under domestic law had been removed, then human rights guarantees provided their only means of redress – and the possibility of a conflict between the policy and guarantees of fundamental rights was already apparent in the framing of S55. Recourse to human rights law in the later cases was set in motion by the action and support of civil society groups, in the absence of significant public opposition to the policy. Key advocacy groups were therefore central in calling the judgements into being and to some degree in framing their terms. The legal decision itself unfolded in an incremental manner over a series of judgements which demonstrated the existence of disagreement among the judiciary, both within and between cases.

The course of judicial deliberation revealed the two differing orientations sketched in Chapter 5 – the national and the cosmopolitan, and can be understood in terms of Habermas's notion of a regulated competition between paradigms. Given the tradition of judicial conservatism in the area of immigration, the positive outcome to this history perhaps throws some light on the way paradigms change, or new paradigms come into being. The beginnings of such change are likely to be found in the concrete features of social life. While a significant presence of asylum seekers is one such feature, so too is the enhanced awareness and institutionalisation of human rights. The scene was therefore set for deliberation in the courts about the content of fundamental rights, conducted against a background of political and public concern over the defence of national interests.

Once engagement of article 3 had been accepted the question of whether the treatment at issue was inhuman and degrading came to the fore. The 'cosmopolitan' nature of the resolution to this question was in part shaped by the role of civil society groups in bringing before the courts the misery and suffering of the disentitled asylum seekers. Thus, a critical stage of judgement required a reflexive consideration of the significance of such evidence, which given the indeterminacy of basic human rights principles, such as dignity and equal worth, amounted to an instance of argument from the particular to the general. This may be seen as a response to the invitation to judges to make an imaginative identification with the suffering of claimants, but also begged the broader question of the standards of protection required in a 'civilised society'. The outcome was an interpretation conceivably at odds with public opinion, and certainly in opposition to the application of the policy at issue; it constituted a statement about the limits of 'less eligibility' in relation to the treatment of a vulnerable group who were attempting to pursue a fundamental right.

This chapter has therefore offered a layered approach to understanding judgement in these cases, which moves from the political context, through civil society intervention, to resolution of a paradigm struggle via reflexive consideration of the individual circumstances of claimants. There is also implicit and explicit dialogue with the government in the delivery of the judgements. However, to complete the picture we need to consider one additional stage – the implications and effects of this history. Of course the most immediate effect was to prompt a suspension of S55 for most cases, and while the legislation still exists it has been made all but inoperable. One further possible effect could be a change in public perceptions – while the policy itself is based on an assumed public hostility to immigration and asylum, a judgement which asserts the basic rights and humanity of claimants offers a counterweight to these views. Thus, in addition to the legal, moral and political role, we see the scope for a social/educational role (Fredman, 2000), contributing to change in public values and perceptions as the legal system itself adjusts to the cosmopolitan reconfiguration of society. The overall success of the challenges perhaps approximates Honneth's suggested drive for recognition bred of the experience of dis-respect, and Alexander's hopes for a 'civil sphere' which can generate instances of civil repair, but still requires a shift in public sentiment for its full realisation.

Chapter 8

Conclusion

A sociology of rights

This closing chapter provides an opportunity to reflect on the study documented thus far and to consider the contribution it can make to a developing sociology of rights. We opened this volume with a reference to Arendt's (1979) discussion of 'the right to have rights', and her recognition of the paradox whereby those in most need of access to fundamental human rights were least able to realise them in practice. In the aftermath of the First World War, and unpersuaded by the promise of the universal rights of man, Arendt argued that displaced persons, once deprived of national citizenship, had no reliable means of securing the most basic of rights. Today, asylum seekers in flight from their country of origin or habitual residence, and in search of protection elsewhere, stand as one contemporary equivalent of this group. However, since the time of Arendt's writing a variety of international conventions has emerged which serve in different ways to secure the rights of non-citizens outside of their home country. We have noted a related literature which speaks – with differing degrees of speculation, in terms of post-national society (Soysal, 1994), world society (Meyer et al., 1997), global citizenship (Habermas, 2001) and cosmopolitan society (Beck, 2006). However, citizenship of a nation-state remains the most certain and secure means of access to many of the fundamental rights which we now regard as universal, at least in principle.

Universal human rights as expressed in established international conventions, are variously designated as qualified, limited or absolute, and thus carry differing degrees of certainty, with even absolute right amenable to conflicting interpretations. The experience of asylum seekers therefore provides an interesting test case of how far 'the right to have rights' has now been extended to incorporate groups outside of national belonging and in search of some protection. The ostensible right at issue in the present study has been that of access to basic maintenance, but this issue touches on two higher level, absolute rights – the right to seek asylum, and freedom from inhuman and degrading treatment. The early cases in our history preceded the Human Rights Act (HRA) but raised the question of whether the right to seek asylum could be meaningfully pursued without the means of survival, while in subsequent (post-HRA) cases the right to protection from inhuman and degrading treatment was brought into play. The uncertain content of this absolute right and its resolution is one of the key aspects of the present case history and raises a number of issues of wider sociological interest.

We have seen how rights may function as a marker of social belonging, as a means of social exclusion, as a system of status recognition, and as a mechanism of governance. These sometimes conflicting features are what led Habermas (1998:115) to write of the janus-faced nature of the nation-state, which in ideal–typical terms, functions as a system of egalitarian universals from within, and as a system of particularist privilege from without. They are also apparent when Fine (2007:127) counterposes the social norms of a national community with those of a more distant world community, a distinction which reflects two contrasting approaches to rights and entitlement. While a 'communitarian' approach emphasises proximity and affinity (eg Walzer, 1983), a 'cosmopolitan' approach emphasises obligations to different or distant others (Beck, 2006). Both have featured in attempts to theorise the development of asylum law and policy, yet we have seen that in practice some degree of compromise between the two has been necessary. The nature and scope of this compromise has provided a focal point for the present study.

While legal judgement has been central to the history presented here, and can usefully be analysed in terms of contrasting national and cosmopolitan paradigms of interpretation, for a full understanding of the cases at issue we must look beyond the courtroom. This study has therefore sought to place the legal cases in their social and political context, to explore the nature and import of civil society engagement, and to consider the broader implications and effects of legal decisions. The result has been a layered approach to judgement, which views judges as actors in a social and political process beginning outside the courtroom, and with ramifications that extend far beyond. Our account therefore opened by outlining a policy approach to asylum which, in the face of rising numbers, evaded issues of principle to rely instead on devices of deterrence and control. This 'governmentality' approach has provided a means of living with the liberal dilemma posed by universal obligations in the context of self-determining sovereignty, and one interesting aspect of policy in this context is the way in which rights and controls have been co-implicated.

Central to this process is the designation of different legal entitlements accorded to different migrant statuses to yield a system of civic stratification – a system of inequality by virtue of the rights which are granted or denied by the state.[1] Although non-citizens can make significant claims to rights from their host countries, trans-national obligations do not preclude the differentiation of migrant groups into categories designating differing degrees of legal entitlement. The nation-state thus retains considerable power over who gets what in terms of rights, and we have seen here how the civic stratification of non-citizens occupies a shifting terrain which changes in concert with global and national circumstances. In Britain from the 1980s onwards, welfare rights have played a central role in this process, especially in relation to concern about national resource protection and attendant allegations that bogus asylum claimants were being attracted by the availability of benefits. Debate about these and related issues marked the emergence of a 'culture of disbelief' (Cohen, 2002:xix) in relation to asylum seekers, and seemed as much concerned with the 'social steering' (Rodger, 2003) of public sentiment, as with any realistic prospect of enhancing control. To gain some understanding of the way such social steering might be achieved, we can look back to Marshall's classic essay on citizenship.

The idea that the granting or withdrawal of rights can act as a means of shaping public sentiment may be traced to Marshall's insight into the functioning of citizenship as a statement of equal social worth. His observations signal a distinction between the formal and informal dimensions of rights – the formal referring to entitlements conferred by a legal status, and the informal referring to associated judgements of moral worth. A likely association between the two suggests that rights can act as a form of social recognition which is linked to public perceptions of the standing of the recipient. It is in this connection that we have seen some scope for a dynamic understanding of rights, a possibility more explicitly developed in Lockwood's (1996) work. Lockwood's account of civic stratification shows how moral or material resources can contribute to the expansion of rights, an idea which is also present in Schneider and Ingram's (1993) discussion of 'contenders'. Where legitimate expectations with respect to rights are frustrated, especially for a group which has accrued a degree of social standing or moral worth, the result might be a drive for fuller recognition and entitlement. Thus, in Honneth's (1995) terms, the experience of disrespect or mis-recognition may fuel a movement for the fuller realisation of rights. Conversely, however, the removal of a right might serve to erode the position of a group by conferring a negative status which could undermine any capacity to resist.

In the case history documented here we have seen how asylum seekers were subject to a process of public discrediting as a prelude to the erosion of their rights, while the absence of significant or overt public sympathy, coupled with feelings of humiliation and despair, made self-organised resistance unlikely. However, one aspect of Lockwood's (1996:542) argument is his recognition of 'civic activism' as a possible source for the expansion of rights; 'the vocation of a small minority' who may promote the cause of the underprivileged, often by recourse to judicial review proceedings. Such recourse to legal measures as a corrective for those otherwise powerless in society is noted by a number of writers (eg Schneider and Ingram, 1993; Griffith, 1997; Alexander, 2006) and raises the interesting possibility that a judgement restoring the formal rights of a dispossessed group could also effect a repair to their informal standing. The history recounted in this volume reconstructs one attempt to achieve this end by the actions of a small group of lawyers and non-governmental organisations (NGOs) acting through the courts in pursuit of the fundamental rights of an outsider group. It provides an instance of civil society engagement in calling government action to account, and holds a further relevance in spanning a period of transition from the common law to the implementation of the HRA.

The early cases in our history stemmed from challenges to the withdrawal of support from late claimers which were rooted in domestic law, albeit supported by wider ranging references to the law of humanity and the European Convention on Human Rights (ECHR). The legal foundation of these early cases (*JCWI* and *M*) was, respectively, based on a finding of inconsistency with existing statute law, and on a ruling that dis-benefited asylum seekers were eligible for support under the National Assistance Act (NAA). However, once these anomalies had been rectified, in the first instance by confirming secondary regulations in primary legislation, and in the second by eliminating asylum seekers from entitlement under the NAA, there remained no further basis for challenge through the national courts. However, the subsequent passing of the HRA preceded a third attempt to remove support from late claimers, and marked a major development in Britain by the incorporation of an international rights convention into domestic law. Such a development has been seen by some as a reconfiguration of national sovereignty (Levy and Sznaider, 2006) achieved by writing the trans-national into the national to produce the both/and effect seen by Beck (2006) as a feature of cosmopolitanism. It was at this point, however, that the uncertain content of even an absolute universal rights became apparent.

Much of the litigation that followed turned on the interpretation of inhuman and degrading treatment, prohibited by article 3 of the ECHR and the HRA, and raising an issue at the 'cutting edge of human rights jurisprudence' (*Q*, EWCA, para 52). The task of interpretation had particular salience, given its significance for new and expanding areas of law (Dworkin, 1986), and our history demonstrates the attendant role of judgement in drawing the social and moral boundaries of rights, and therefore of society. While there has been much academic debate about the capacity of international law to reconfigure legal communities from the outside, here we see a corresponding scope for reconfiguring community from within. Hence, in the history documented above, narrow conceptions of the national interest and national resource protection were pitted against the ideals of a 'civilised society' and the universal principle of human dignity.

The cases under consideration were novel in testing out how far social rights could be read into a convention designed with civil and political rights in mind, and whether a positive obligation to provide basic maintenance could be drawn from a negative prohibition to refrain from imposing harm. The question was in principle disposed of fairly early in the history when the Court of Appeal (CA) confirmed that the withdrawal of support in the context of a prohibition on employment constituted treatment. However, it took much longer to establish concrete indicators for the finding of an imminent breach of article 3, such that the issue was resolved in incremental stages through a dialogue between judges. This dialogue also included deliberation over the logic and acceptability of S55, and the appropriate role of judges when resource constraints and deterrent intent ran up against the assertion of fundamental rights.

The nature and delivery of the judgements thus reveals the social and political import of the judge's role, but for a full understanding of legal interventions in the present history we have also looked to the contribution of civil society actors in bringing the cases to court and in fashioning the challenge to S55. The initiative was taken by a small network of lawyers and NGOs, often working in collaboration, rather than a more broadly based public sphere mobilisation of the sort envisaged by Habermas (1996). The difficulties of recruiting public sympathy for a group discredited by government allegations of abuse of the asylum system and a related drain on public resources, militated against such a development. Indeed, erosion of the credibility and status of asylum seekers in the eyes of the public shows the fragility of an over-reliance on the critical judgement of a public of citizens (Habermas, 1996:364). It serves as an illustration of the relationship between rights and status, whereby an attack on the social standing of a group can help undermine their claim to rights, while an erosion of rights can in turn confirm the negative status of those targeted for such treatment.

In the face of a hostile or apathetic public the courts may provide an alternative forum for the expansion and radicalisation of rights, and a substitute for the broader public sphere engagement in which Habermas (1996) seeks a deliberative space for the cause of the underprivileged. While Habermas recognises a potential role for the courts, this argument is not developed in his work, though we do find a recognition of the restorative power of the courts in Alexander's (2006) concept of 'civil repair'. He recognises the symbolic force of the law, and its double-edged nature – as a means of dividing and excluding, but also as a channel for the unmet aspirations to substantive equality. However, given the possibly disabling effects of stigma or disrespect, we find a role for Lockwood's 'civic activists', and his recognition that legal recourse is increasingly a route to civic expansion. The passing of the HRA in Britain has significantly enhanced this possibility.

Under the HRA the courts are charged with delineating the boundary of rights and a high level of scrutiny is required where these fundamental rights are at issue. This opens up the courts to legitimate debate about the content and reach of rights which require substantive interpretation. We therefore see a role for the courts as a participatory space whereby the lived experience of those denied more direct forms of representation can find expression, and it is here that civil society input comes to the fore. Indeed, in liberal democratic societies civil society is itself constituted by the guarantee of basic rights, most notably the freedoms of speech and assembly, and equality before the law, but also the capacity to challenge the actions of governments should they infringe on these or other fundamental rights. The coming together of interested NGOs and lawyers in this space is therefore an almost inevitable outcome when the rights of a powerless group are threatened or undermined.

The NGOs involved in this history serve the asylum population both directly – through the delivery of services with respect to welfare and legal advice, and indirectly – through an interest in monitoring and sustaining a rights-based society. These functions are manifest in the character and input of the various NGOs involved in the present cases; the Refugee Council, Liberty, Justice, Joint Council for the Welfare of Immigrants, Shelter, Migrant Helpline, Refugee Action, Community Law centres, and a number of smaller community-based organisations. Their initiating role lay in indentifying the possibility of a challenge to the withdrawal of welfare support from late claimers, in identifying cases for Judicial Review, in orchestrating the collection and presentation of evidence, and in the submission of critical interventions. The impact of these actions was in part linked to their role in dramatically revealing the scale of the problem unleashed by S55 through a strategy of bombarding the courts with cases. This strategy unfolded naturally from events as large numbers of asylum seekers found themselves destitute and scavenging for survival on the streets. However, the heart of the civil society contribution lay in providing the substance for deliberative debate on the meaning of 'inhuman and degrading'.

The evidence collected by NGOs and presented in the courts underpinned a translation of the physical and psychological suffering of their clients into the principles of human dignity and the standards of civilised society which the HRA is committed to protecting and upholding. Litigation thus provided the participatory space to inform and enrich an understanding of rights on the basis of the mundane suffering of asylum seekers forced into destitution; in other words, it enabled the meshing of individual experience and universal norms. The background of the S55 measure was bred of political concern about control of immigration, an ostensible desire to assuage, and possible hidden intent to cultivate, public hostility to asylum seekers. The cases at issue therefore brought a broadly defined public interest in the protection and pursuit of fundamental rights into conflict with a more parochial public concern with controlling and limiting asylum. In effect they represented a collision between public interest and public opinion, and harnessed the force of human rights in defending a powerless minority in the face of a seemingly hostile majority. In this process we can therefore see an instance of Dworkin's (2005:205) majority promise to minorities, of Alexander's (2006) civil repair through legal recourse, and of Honneth's (1995) recognition through rights.

While political concerns provided the backdrop to these cases, and civil society their enabling force, the critical task of judgement fell to the courts. They had to determine what fundamental rights, if any, were engaged by the treatment of asylum seekers, and whether a breach was imminent. In practice, this meant that national constraints were confronted in the courtroom by universal norms of protection, such that the cases under consideration offered a test of how far the cosmopolitan ideal could be translated into practical effect. A consideration of the case history from this perspective is particularly fitting, given that the original cosmopolitan right as expressed by Kant was a guarantee that foreigners should not be turned away if to do so would entail their destruction. This comes very close to the contemporary guarantee of *non-refoulement*, which is the basis of modern refugee law. Although our case history does not address the status determination process which underpins the granting of refugee status, it has been concerned with the right to hospitality while an asylum claim is being considered; a right which arguably underpins the higher level right to seek asylum.

The ideals of cosmopolitanism have a wider resonance, and have prompted a rethinking of the social sciences to take account of the porous nature of national boundaries, the emergence of multicultural societies, and the institutionalisation of trans-national rights. There is a question, however, as to how far the concrete recognition of these ideals is reflected in the functioning of society, and how far they have been met with both political and popular resistance at the national level. The realisation of universal rights is one possible litmus test, and the very fact of the passing of the HRA, which incorporated the ECHR into domestic legislation, is hugely significant. In writing universal principles into national law the global becomes rooted in the local, but as we have seen, much then rests upon the interpretation and application of those principles. We have noted that some writers see a certain openness in the content of human rights to be a positive feature, which allows their flexible application to create new worlds through the re-imagining of society. However, there is also the possibility of a restrictive rather than an expansive interpretation, such that national and cosmopolitan orientations come into conflict. While there should in theory be no question of balancing or qualifying those rights which are absolute and universal in nature (as, for example, through consideration of the national interest, concerns of proportionality, or deference to the executive) we see from the cases at issue here that some degree of tension is inescapable.

This then raises the question of what judges do when they judge, how the particular case history under consideration here was brought to a conclusion, and why so many cases were necessary for a final determination. Conflicting theoretical arguments in this field, respectively, suggest that judges seek to render the law coherent in principle and hence to arrive at one right answer (Dworkin, 1986; 2005), or conversely, that judges are necessarily influenced by ideological factors, while the law itself is riven with conflict (Unger, 1986). Though each of these positions represents some aspect of the judicial process, what has been more telling in the present cases is the emergence of two competing paradigms in the course of judicial deliberation. I have termed these paradigms the 'national' and the 'cosmopolitan'; the former being characterised by a restrictive approach to rights shaped by resource constraints and legitimate government concern to control immigration; the

latter by a more expansive approach to rights and a prioritising of fundamental protections over policy interests. Deliberation over these contrasting
orientations can be viewed in terms of Habermas's (1996) procedural
approach to judgement, whereby competing paradigms provoke a contest
between differing interpretations of the law which is resolved in the course of
the judicial process.

While such competition might seem to support a critical approach to the
law, in which judges are swayed by their own ideological preferences, the
paradigms themselves take shape in the course of an organic process of judicial
exchange. Though this exchange is at times conflictual, the cumulative effect of
the judgements can equally be viewed as a collaborative search for a just outcome. In practice the process is best understood not in terms of the opinion of
any single judge, but rather through a broader proceduralist approach to
understanding. This process in the present history had its origins in a political
attempt to address a social issue, contested by civil society action, and yielding
conflicting paradigms of judgement which were both tested and developed
through deliberation in the courts. The idea of a competition between paradigms, however, renders only a partial account of the judicial process and
leaves us with the question of how a resolution is finally reached, other than
by reference to one of the contested paradigms.

A 'narrative' approach to judgement (Jackson, 1991) suggests that an outcome will depend on identifying the 'best fit' from a pre-existing stock of
interpretations, but this does not readily address a developing area of law in
which no dominant narrative has been established. We have therefore considered the epistemological role played by evidence in this history, whereby
accounts of the lived experience of destitute asylum seekers invite an imaginative identification with their suffering, and claim the courts as a participatory
space for the reflexive interpretation of the law. This process was achieved less
through the application of general rules for the operation of human rights,
than through a reading of the universal out of the particular (cf Ferrara, 2008).
It remained, however, to place this exploration of the process of judgement
back in its social and political context, and to assess the broader implications
of a case history in which the normative features of cosmopolitanism are
played out in empirical application.

While immigration, asylum and trans-national, universal rights have all been
seen as features of an emergent cosmopolitan society, they occur in the context
of a state sovereignty which, though arguably reconfigured (Levy and Sznaider,
2006), retains considerable power to shape the designation and delivery of
rights for non-citizens. The conceptual device we have adopted as a means to
explore this process and its outcomes has been civic stratification – the
elaboration of hierarchical system of legal statuses, each with different rights
attached. The analytical application of this concept has been given a dynamic
quality by its pairing with the identification of 'target groups' in the
policy-making process, and the related recognition that rights are open to

manipulation by the state, are closely related to controls, and are linked to the evaluation and conferral of social status.

We have seen how the division of asylum seekers into at-port in-country claimants was a prelude to the discrediting of the latter group by a set of related and unsubstantiated assumptions; that the late claimers enter the country by deceit, are attracted by benefits, and are 'bogus' asylum seekers. These assumptions served to reduce their public standing, to justify the sub-sequent removal of their support, to substantiate claims of effective action against non-genuine applications, and to act as a deterrent to all asylum seekers. The inability of the policy design to address the ostensible concern of reducing 'bogus' asylum claims signalled an irrationality in terms of the stated objective, but was also indicative of a hidden purpose. It had the effect of moving late claimers for asylum from 'dependant' to 'deviant' in terms of both policy objectives and public perceptions, and stands as an example of Honneth's (1995) notion of disrespect. This raises the question of whether the judicial process could offer redress, not simply by restoring the right to support, but by providing a corrective to the stigmatising nature of this treatment and its effects.

The courts have provided a public forum in which the irrational design of the policy, the punitive nature of National Asylum Support System (NASS) decision-making, and the improper use of the courts by the government, have all had an airing. The effect of the judgements in rendering S55 virtually inoperable serves in some respects as an instance of 'civil repair', but a broader corrective to the negative standing of asylum seekers is unlikely without some fuller engagement of the public imagination. Adherents of the cosmopolitan perspective have in this context argued for the development of a cosmopolitan citizenry (Habermas, 2001; Beck, 2006; Isin and Turner, 2007) which could play a role in calling elected representatives to account and in making 'the right to have rights' meaningful beyond the bounds of citizenship. However, while cosmopolitanism imagines new forms of belonging, and universal human rights constrain the actions of states with respect to citizens and non-citizens alike, these developments can be met by resistance at the national level. We may find that in practice 'banal cosmopolitanism' (Beck, 2006) lags some way behind the cosmopolitan ideal.

It is against this background that legal judgement, in determining the uncertain content of rights, may be seen as part of a struggle over the structure of social existence and as offering some scope for redrawing the boundaries of community. This role, in the context of the HRA, has drawn judges more firmly into the political arena and attached enormous significance to the interpretation of the law in the light of fundamental principles, such as human dignity. By requiring greater scrutiny of the law where fundamental rights are involved the HRA has at times required a challenge to executive power, and has even been viewed as an 'assault on democracy'.[2] However, democracy is grounded in a freely functioning civil society, made up of rights bearing individuals and constituted by a guarantee of certain fundamentals of a social existence. It depends, therefore, not simply on a system of electoral representation but also on the rule of law and on a system for the protection of rights which, among other things, defends the vulnerable minority. More specifically, the courts assume a role in securing the participation of those who are allowed no voice in the parliamentary system, and in providing a forum for deliberation about the content of rights.

It is through this deliberation that we see the importance of different paradigms of interpretation, and their anchoring in the shifting contours of the social world. This raises the questions of where new paradigms have their origin, and it is here that a sociological approach comes into its own, in the understanding of how new claims can emerge from changes in circumstance. In the present study, the features of what Beck (2006) terms banal cosmopolitanism – notably the presence of foreigners on national territory, and the incorporation of universal norms into domestic law, have forced a change in governance. The treatment of an outsider group, contested by interested parties in the context of a freely functioning civil society, and given expression in the courts, fed a newly emergent cosmopolitan paradigm of interpretation. This in turn acts back on systems of governance and – at least in potential – on public understanding. The whole process, incorporating as it does the identification of a problem, the mobilisation of support, the formulation of a claim, its articulation through evidence, and its interrogation in the courts, can be viewed as an instance of the social construction of a right.

This is not to say that rights have no existence outside of this process, but that it is a social engagement which gives rights their full meaning, and this cannot be determined by a mechanical application of the law. Indeed, there is a constant process of interaction between politicians, civil society actors, and the courts, in response to changing social circumstances. Part of that change relates to the position of the judiciary itself, and we have noted the conservative tradition which prevailed among the judiciary in the 1970s and 1980s in the area of immigration. A reconfiguration of the law with respect to fundamental rights via the HRA, coinciding as it did with an aggressive politics of deterrence and control with respect to immigration, seems in the present cases to have turned conservatism into activism via the defence of universal rights. However, where the content of those rights is not self-evident, then judges must engage in a process of reflexivity and persuasion – the former to determine for themselves the meaning of a right, and the latter to convince others that their determination can be justified. It is here that the dialogic element of judgement comes to the fore.

Part of that dialogue is what in Habermasian terms we have called the participatory aspect of judgement, whereby the lived experience of claimants is given expression in the courts. A second element of dialogue takes place between the judges themselves, but must also be accompanied by an internal dialogue – Jackson's (1991) 'private moment' of judgement, to which we have no direct access. A further aspect of dialogue assumes both a direct and indirect form, and engages with the government on the acceptability or otherwise of policy and its implementation. This shades into the final element of dialogue, which lies in the delivery of the judgement and its justificatory purpose, and which is aimed at multiple audiences. The final delivery of a judgement must seek to persuade all parties to a dispute – who constitute the immediate audience, but a judgement will also speak to an unidentified and imagined public, which exists as much in the future as in the present. It is in this context that one might think of the educational role of judgement, which we have suggested in the present study may be part of a linkage between rights and social standing, or rights and recognition.

Though the account rendered here reads as a success story in contesting the punitive treatment of a powerless group, we have cautioned against too optimistic a view of its more general significance. We have noted the continuing use of destitution as a deterrent control for failed asylum seekers, and campaigns are currently being waged against the practice of holding the families of asylum seekers, including dependent children, in detention. Nevertheless, the history documented above stands as testimony to the effect which can be achieved by a small number of dedicated people, exercising the right to contest government action, and armed with the guarantee of fundamental human rights for all. We can at this point reflect on the study as a whole and extract from it what can be said with respect to a developing sociology of rights.

1. The conferral of a right can act as an expression of the boundaries of moral obligation for a given society. It demonstrates an acceptance of responsibility on the part of the state and therefore constitutes a statement of connectivity between the granter and the holder of the right.
2. The obligation thus expressed by a right may be on the basis of proximity and reciprocity – as in communitarianism; or of common humanity – as in cosmopolitanism/universalism. In practice different categories of rights will correspond to these different orientations towards obligation.
3. The spirit informing universal human rights is that certain rights are owed to individuals by virtue of their humanity, and as an expression and defence of human dignity. Through this spirit, human rights have come to be closely associated with a cosmopolitan outlook.
4. Rights expressed in established human rights instruments may in practice be subject to qualification and interpretation. A qualified right may be granted only subject to certain conditions, while the precise content of a right may be amenable to differing interpretations. Both qualifications and interpretations will reflect judgements about the degree of connectivity and therefore of moral obligation between the granter and the holder of a right.

5. Degrees of proximity and commonality may be deliberated and contested, while conversely the recognition of obligation between parties is amenable to cultivation. As a result, rights are themselves open to manipulation for political advantage, but can also be a focus for expansive social action.

6. The conferral or denial of a right both shape and reflect the social and moral standing of the holder of that right, and can, respectively, be seen as an expression of recognition or of disrespect. The latter may be stigmatising.

7. The allocation of rights at any given moment in any given society will constitute a hierarchy of formal legal statuses which also carry informal social implications, while this designation of different legal statuses with different associated rights is a key aspect of governance. It provides the opportunity both to determine (formal) entitlement and to steer (informal) social perceptions.

8. The designation of legal statuses and the classification of individuals will change with circumstances, such that the number and nature of statuses may expand, while individuals may move up or down the hierarchy over time. Thus, there may be movement in the constitution of the legal statuses themselves, and/or across these statuses over time.

9. Movement across legal statuses will accompany changes in the moral standing of incumbents, such that an improvement in legal status will often also entail an improvement in social standing, while a deterioration of that status will undermine public standing. Correspondingly, the conferral of additional rights on a social group is often linked to an improvement of social standing, and an erosion of rights to its diminution.

10. The spirit of human rights may be harnessed to campaign for an expansion of actual entitlement, or to contest too restrictive an interpretation of an established legal right. The process by which this happens is a social process entailing mobilisation, contestation, recognition and obligation.

11. In this process, the courts provide a participatory space for deliberation about the content and conferral of rights. Individuals or groups may avail themselves of this space in the process of claiming a right, using the courts as a forum in which the social effects of denials and exclusions are displayed and challenged.

12. In rendering legal decisions judges act as arbiters in this process, but their opinions have a wider bearing on the contours of rights in society, and therefore potentially on the social and moral standing of the groups affected.

13. Differing interpretations of the content and application of a right may coalesce into different paradigms of judgement. These paradigms emerge from deliberative exchange between judges over time, while the decisions

of judges are both a reflection of, and an influence on, the direction of change in society.

14. The points enumerated above combine to yield an expression of what is meant by the claim that rights are socially constructed but also act as a social force.

Notes

1 For a fuller elaboration and application of this concept in relation to migration, see Morris (2002).

2 Blunkett, as quoted in Guardian Unlimited, 2003.

Bibliography

Agamben, G. (1998) *Homo Sacer: Sovereign Power and Bare Life*, Stanford, California: Stanford University Press.

Alexander, J.C. (2006) *The Civil Sphere*, Oxford: Oxford University Press.

Altman, A. (1986) 'Legal Realism, Critical Legal Studies and Dworkin', *Philosophy and Public Affairs*, 15: 205–35.

Arendt, H. (1978) *Life of the Mind Vol 2 Willing*, London: Secker & Warburg.

——(1979) *The Origins of Totalitarianism*, New York: Harcourt Brace.

Arshi, M. and O'Cinneide, C. (2004) 'Third Party Interventions: the public interest reaffirmed', *Public Law*, pp. 69–77.

Beck, U. (2006) *Cosmopolitan Vision*, Cambridge: Polity Press.

Beck, U. and Sznaider, N. (2006) 'Unpacking Cosmopolitanism for the Social Sciences', *British Journal of Sociology*, 57: 1–23.

Beiner, R. (1983) *Political Judgment*, London: Methuen.

Benhabib, S. (2004) *The Rights of Others*, Cambridge: Cambridge University Press.

Billings, B. and Edwards, R.A. (2004) 'Safeguarding Asylum Seekers Dignity', *Journal of Social Security Law*, 11: 83–111.

——(2006) 'A Case of Mountainish Inhumanity', *Journal of Social Security Law*, 13: 169–80.

Bloch, A. and Schuster, L. (2002) 'Asylum and Welfare: contemporary debates', *Critical Social Policy*, 22: 393–413.

——(2005) 'Asylum Policy under New Labour', *Benefits*, 43: 115–18.

Bobbio, N. (1996) *The Age of Rights*, Cambridge: Polity Press.

Bolderstone, H. and Roberts, S. (1995) 'New Restrictions on Benefits for Migrants', *Benefits*, 33: 11–15.

Boswell, C. (2000) 'European Values and the Asylum Crisis', *International Affairs*, 76: 537–57.

Bottomore, T. (1992) 'Citizenship and Social Class: forty years on', in T.H. Marshall and T. Bottomore (eds) *Citizenship and Social Class*, London: Pluto Press, pp. 55–93.

Bradley, A. (2003) 'Judicial Independence under Attack', *Public Law*, pp. 397–407.

Browne-Wilkinson, Lord (1998) 'The Impact of Judicial Reasoning', in B.S. Markesinis (ed.) *The Impact of the Human Rights Bill on English Law*, Oxford: Oxford University Press, pp. 21–23.

Brubaker, W.R. (ed.) (1989) *Immigration and the Politics of Citizenship in Europe and America*, Lanham, Maryland: University Press of America.

Burchell, G., Gordon, P. and Miller, P. (1991) *The Foucault Effect*, Hemel Hempstead: Harvester Wheatsheaf.

Campbell, T. (1998) 'Legal Positivism and Deliberative Democracy', *Current Legal Problems*, 51: 66–92.

Cane, P. (1995) 'Standing Up for the Public', *Public Law*, pp. 276–87.

Carens, T. (1992) 'Migration and Morality: a liberal egalitarian perspective', in B. Barry and R. Goodwin (eds) *Free Movement: Ethical Issues in the Transnational Migration of People and Money*, London: Harvester Wheatsheaf, pp. 25–47.

Cassese, A. (1991) 'Can the Notion of Inhuman and Degrading Treatment be Applied to Socio-economic Conditions?', *European Journal of International Law*, 2: 141–45.

Clayton, R. (2004) 'Judicial Deference and Democratic Dialogue', *Public Law*, pp. 33–47.

Cohen, R. (1994) *Frontiers of Identity*, London: Longman.

Cohen, S. (2001) *States of Denial*, Cambridge: Polity Press.

——(2002) *Folk Devils and Moral Panics: the Creation of Mods and Rockers*, 3rd ed., London: Routledge.

Cohen, S., Humphries, B. and Mynott, E. (2002) *From Immigration Controls to Welfare Controls*, London: Routledge.

Cruz, A. (1995) *Shifting Responsibility*, Stoke-on-Trent: Trentham Books.

Daly, M. (2003) 'Governance and Social Policy', *Journal of Social Policy*, 32: 113–28.

Dean, H. (1998) 'Popular Paradigms and Welfare Values', *Critical Social Policy*, 18: 131–56.

Donnelly, J. (2003) *Universal Human Rights in Theory and Practice*, New York: Cornell University Press.

Douzinas, C. (2000) *The End of Human Rights*, Oxford: Hart.

Douzinas, C. and Warrington, R. (with McVeigh, S.) (1991) *Postmodern Jurisprudence*, London: Routledge.

Duvell, F. and Jordan, B. (2002) 'Immigration, Asylum and Welfare: the European context', *Critical Social Policy*, 22: 498–517.

——(2003) 'Immigration Control and the Management of Economic Migration in the UK', *Journal of Ethnic and Migration Studies*, 29: 299–336.

Dworkin, R. (1986) *Law's Empire*, Oxford: Hart.

——(2005) *Taking Rights Seriously*, London: Duckworth.

Dwyer, P. (2004) 'Creeping Conditionality in the UK: from welfare rights to conditional entitlements', *Canadian Journal of Sociology*, 29: 265–87.

——(2005) 'Governance, Forced Migration and Welfare', *Social Policy and Administration*, 39: 622–39.

Feria, M. (1996) 'Commentaries on the Social Security (Persons from Abroad) (Miscellaneous Amendments) Regulations 1996', *Immigration and Nationality Law and Practice*, 10: 91–101.

Ferrara, A. (2008) *The Force of the Example: Explorations in the Paradigm of Judgment*, New York: Columbia University Press.

Fine, R. (1997) 'Civil Society, Enlightenment and Critique', in R. Fine and S. Rai (eds) *Civil Society, Democratic Perspectives*, London: Frank Cass, pp. 7–28.

——(2006) 'Cosmopolitanism and Violence', *British Journal of Sociology*, 57: 49–67.

——(2007) *Cosmopolitanism*, London: Routledge.

——(2009) 'Cosmopolitanism and Human Rights: radicalism for a global age', *Metaphilosophy*, 40: 8–23.

Flynn, D. (2003) *Tough as Old Boots?* London: JCWI.

Fordham, M. (2007) 'Public Interest Intervention: a practitioner's perspective', *Public Law*, pp. 410–13.

Foucault, M. (1991) 'Governmentality', in G. Burchell, P. Gordon and P. Miller (eds), *The Foucault Effect*, Hemel Hempstead: Harvester Wheatsheaf, pp. 85–104.

Fredman, S. (2000) 'Judging Democracy: the role of the judiciary under the HRA', *Current Legal Problems*, 53: 99–129.

Freeman, G.P. (1986) 'Migration and the Political Economy of the Welfare State', *Annals of the American Academy of Political and Social Science*, 485: 51–63.

Geddes, A. (2003) 'International Migration and State Sovereignty in an Integrating Europe', in S. Spencer, (ed.) *The Politics of Migration*, London: Blackwell, pp. 150–62.

Gibney, M. (2004) *The Ethics and Politics of Asylum: Liberal Democracy and the Response to Refugees*, Cambridge: Cambridge University Press.

Gillespie, J. (1996) 'Asylum and Immigration Act 1996', *Immigration and Nationality Law and Practice*, 10: 86–90.

Glidewell Panel (1996) *The Asylum and Immigration Bill*, London: Justice.

Goodwin-Gill, G.S. (2001) 'Asylum 2001 – A Convention and a Purpose', *International Journal of Refugee Law*, 13: 1–15.

Gordon, P. (1991) 'Governmental Rationality', in G. Burchell, P. Gordon and P. Miller (eds) *The Foucault Effect*, Hemel Hempstead: Harvester Wheatsheaf, pp. 1–51.

Gordon, P. and Newnham, A. (1985) *Passport to Benefits?*, London: Child Poverty Action Group.

Grande, E. (2006) 'Cosmopolitan Political Science', *British Journal of Sociology*, 57: 87–111.

Greater London Authority (2005) *Into the Labyrinth*, London: GLA.

Griffith, J.A.G. (1997) *The Politics of the Judiciary*, London: Fontana Press.

Habermas, J. (1996) *Between Facts and Norms*, Cambridge: Polity Press.

——(1998) *Inclusion of the Other*, Cambridge: Polity Press.

——(2001) *The Post-national Constellation*, Cambridge: Polity Press.

——(2006) *The Divided West*, Cambridge: Polity Press.

Hailbronner, K. (1990) 'The Right to Asylum and the Future of Asylum Procedures in the European Community', *International Journal of Refugee Law*, 2: 341–60.

Hale, S. (2004) *Community by Contract*, paper presented at Political Studies Association Conference.

Hannett, S. (2003) 'Third Party Intervention: in the public interest?', *Public Law*, pp. 128–50.

Harlow, C. (2002) 'Public Law and Popular Justice', *Modern Law Review*, 65: 1–18.

Harlow, C. and Rawlings, R. (1984) *Law and Administration*, London: Weidenfeld & Nicolson.

——(1992) *Pressure Through Law*, London: Routledge.

Hart, H.L.A. (1961) *The Concept of Law*, Oxford: Oxford University Press.

Hathaway, J. (1990) 'A Reconsideration of the Underlying Premise of Refugee Law', *Harvard International Law Journal*, 31: 129–83.

Held, D. (2004) *Global Covenant*, Cambridge: Polity Press.

Hollifield, J.E. (1992) *Immigrants Markets and States*, Cambridge, Massachusetts: Harvard University Press.

Honneth, A. (1995) *The Struggle for Recognition*, Cambridge: Polity Press.

Inter-agency Partnership (2004) *The Impact of Section 55*, London: Inter-agency Partnership.

Irvine, D. (2003) 'The Impact of the HRA: parl, the courts and the executive', *Public Law*, pp. 308–25.

Irvine of Lairg, Lord (2003) 'The Impact of the HRA', *Public Law*, pp. 308–25.

Isin, E.F. and Turner, B.S. (2007) 'Investigating Citizenship: an agenda for citizenship studies', *Citizenship Studies*, 11: 5–17.

Jackson, B.S. (1991) *Law, Fact and Narrative Coherence*, Liverpool: Deborah Charles Publications.

Jacobson, D. (1996) *Rights Across Borders: Immigration and the Decline of Citizenship*, Baltimore, Maryland: Johns Hopkins University Press.

Jessop, B. (1999) 'The Changing Governance of Welfare', *Social Policy and Administration*, 33: 348–59.

Joint Council for the Welfare of Immigrants (1997) *Immigration Nationality and Refugee Law Handbook*, London: JCWI.

——(1998) *Fairer Faster Firmer? Response to the White Paper*, London: JCWI.

Joppke, C. (1998) 'Asylum and State Sovereignty', in C. Joppke (ed.) *Challenge to the Nation State*, Oxford: Oxford University Press, pp. 109–52.

Juss, S. (1997) *Discretion and Deviation in the Administration of Immigration Control*, London: Sweet & Maxwell.

Kant, I. [1797] (1994) 'Perpetual Peace: A Philosophical Sketch', in H. Reiss (ed.) *Kant: Political Writings*, Cambridge: Cambridge University Press.

Kaye, R. (1994) 'Defining the Agenda', *Journal of Refugee Studies*, 7: 144–59.

Kennedy, D. (1997) *A Critique of Adjudication*, Cambridge, Massachusetts: Harvard University Press.

Legomsky, S.H. (1987) *Immigration and the Judiciary*, Oxford: Clarendon Press.

Levy, D. and Sznaider, N. (2006) 'Sovereignty Transformed: a sociology of human rights', *British Journal of Sociology*, 57: 657–76.

Lister, R. (2003) *Citizenship: Feminist Perspectives*, London: Palgrave.

Lockwood, D. (1996) 'Civic Integration and Class Formation', *British Journal of Sociology*, 47: 531–50.

Marshall, T.H. (1950) *Citizenship and Social Class and Other Essays*, Cambridge: Cambridge University Press.

Mayor of London (2004) *Destitution by Design*, London: GLA.

McHarg, A. (1999) 'Reconciling Human Rights and the Public Interest', *Modern Law Review*, pp. 671–96.

McLaren, L. and Johnson, M. (2004) 'Understanding the Rising Tide of Anti-immigrant Sentiment', in *British Social Attitudes*, 21st Report, London: Sage, pp. 169–200.

Meyer, J., Boli, J., Thomas, G.M. and Ramirez, F.W. (1997) 'World Society and the Nation States', *American Journal of Sociology*, 103: 144–81.

Michelman, F. (1986) 'The Supreme Court 1985 Term – foreword: traces of self-government', *Harvard Law Review*, 100: 4–77.

——(1996) 'Parsing "A Right to Have Rights"', *Constellations*, 3: 200–09.

Migrant Rights Network (2008) *Papers Please*, London: MRN.

Migration News Sheet (various) Brussels: Churches Commission for Migrants in Europe.

Morris, L.D. (1994) *Dangerous Classes*, London: Routledge.

——(1997) 'A Cluster of Contradictions: the politics of migration in the EU', *Sociology*, 31: 241–59.

——(1998) 'Governing at a Distance', *International Migration Review*, 32: 949–73.

——(2002) *Managing Migration: Civic Stratification and Migrants Rights*, London: Routledge.

——(2004) *Control of Rights*, London: JCWI.

——(2006) *Rights: Sociological Perspectives*, London: Routledge.

——(2007) 'New Labour's Community of Rights', *Journal of Social Policy*, 36: 39–57.

——(2009a) 'Welfare, Asylum and Civil Society: a case study in civil repair', *Citizenship Studies*, 13: 365–79.

——(2009b) 'An Emergent Cosmopolitan Paradigm? – asylum, welfare and human rights', *British Journal of Sociology*, 60: 215–315.

——(2009c) 'Civic Stratification and the Cosmopolitan Ideal: the case of welfare and asylum', *European Societies*, 11: 603–24.

——(2010) 'Asylum Welfare and the Politics of Judgment', *Journal of Social Policy*, 39: 1–20.

Nash, K. (2007) 'The Pinochet Case: cosmopolitanism and intermestic human rights', *British Journal of Sociology*, 58: 418–35.

Norrie, A. (1993) *Crime Reason and History*, London: Weidenfeld & Nicolson.

Palmer, E. (2007) *Judicial Review, Socio-economic Rights, and the Human Rights Act*, Oxford: Hart.

Parekh, B. (2006) *Rethinking Multiculturalism*, London: Palgrave.

Philips, A. (1992) 'Universalist Pretensions in Political Thought', in M. Barrett and A. Phillips (eds) *Destabilising Theory*, Cambridge: Polity Press.

Plender, R. (1999) *Basic Documents on International Migration Law*, The Hague: Kluwer Law International.

Plummer, K. (2006) 'Rights Work: constructing lesbian, gay and sexual rights in late modern times', in L. Morris (ed.) *Rights: Sociological Perspectives*, London: Routledge, pp. 152–67.

Prosser, T. (1983) *Test Cases for the Poor*, Policy Pamphlet 60, London: CPAG.

Refugee Council (2004) *Hungry and Homeless*, London: Refugee Council.

Rodger, J. (2003) 'Social Solidarity, Welfare and Post-emotionalism', *Journal of Social Policy*, 32: 403–21.

Rose, N. and Miller, P. (1992) 'Political Power Beyond the State: problematics of government', *British Journal of Sociology*, 43: 173–205.

Sales, R. (2002) 'The Deserving and the Undeserving? Refugees, asylum seekers and welfare in Britain', *Critical Social Policy*, 22: 456–78.

Sassen, S. (1998) *Globalisation and its Discontents*, New York: The New Press.

Schneider, A. and Ingram, H. (1993) 'Social Construction of Target Populations', *American Political Science Review*, 87: 334–46.

Schuster, L. (2003) *The Use and Abuse of Political Asylum in Britain and Germany*, London: Frank Cass.

Schuster, L. and Solomos, J. (2004) 'Race, Immigration and Asylum: New Labour's agenda and its consequences', *Ethnicities*, 4: 267–300.

Scoular, J. (1997) 'Case Analysis', *Journal of Social Security Law*, 4: 86–90.

Sedley, S. (1995) 'Human Rights: a twenty-first century agenda', *Public Law*, pp. 386–400.

Shutter, S. (1995) *Immigration and Nationality Handbook*, London: JCWI.

Simpson, A.W.B. (2004) *Human Rights and the End of Empire*, Oxford: Oxford University Press.

Skinner, Q. (1978) *The Foundations of Modern Political Thought*, Cambridge: Cambridge University Press.

Smith, A. (1995) *Nations and Nationalism in a Global Era*, Cambridge: Polity Press.

Soysal, Y. (1994) *Limits of Citizenship*, Chicago: University of Chicago Press.

Spencer, S. (1995) *Identity Cards Revisited*, London: IPPR.

Stevens, D. (2004) *UK Asylum Law and Policy*, London: Sweet & Maxwell.

Stevens, R. (2005) *The English Judges*, Oxford: Hart.

Storey, H. (1994) 'United Kingdom Controls and the Immigration Welfare State', *Journal of Social Welfare and Family Law*, 6: 14–28.

Taylor, C. (1994) *Multiculturalism*, Princeton, New Jersey: Princeton University Press.

Tazreiter, C. (2004) *Asylum Seekers and the State*, Aldershot: Ashgate.

Thomas, R. (2003) 'Asylum Seeker Support', *Journal of Social Security Law*, 10: 163–73.

Turner, B. (1990) 'Outline of a Theory of Citizenship', *Sociology*, 24: 189–214.

Turner, B.S. (1988) *Status*, Milton Keynes: Open University Press.

——(1993) 'Outline of a Theory of Human Rights', *Sociology*, 27: 485–512.

Unger, R.M. (1986) *The Critical Legal Studies Movement*, Cambridge, Massachusetts: Harvard University Press.

Walzer, M. (1983) *Spheres of Justice*, New York: Basic Books.

Webber, F. (2004) 'Asylum – from deterrence to destitution', *Race and Class*, 45: 77–85.

Weiler, J. (1992) 'Thou Shalt not Oppress a Stranger', *European Journal of International Law*, 3: 65–91.

Willman, S. (2003) 'The Will of Parliament', *New Law Journal*, 153: 281.

Woodhouse, D. (1998) 'The Judiciary in the 1990's', *Policy and Politics*, 26: 458–70.

Woolf, H. (1998) 'Judicial Review – the tensions between the executive and the judiciary', *Law Quarterly Review*, 114: 579–93.

Zolberg, A.R. (1989) 'The Next Waves: migration theory for a changing world', *International Migration Review*, 23: 403–30.

Zolberg, A.R., Suhrke, A. and Aguayo, S. (1989) *Escape from Violence: Conflict and the Refugee Crisis in the Developing World*, Oxford: Oxford University Press.

Official publications

Department of Social Security (1995) *Explanatory Memorandum to the Social Security Advisory Committee*, London: DSS.

——(1996) *Social Security (Persons from Abroad) (Miscellaneous Amendments) 1996*, London: HMSO.

Home Office (1998a) *Fairer, Faster and Firmer*, CM 4018, London: HMSO.

——(1998b) *Rights Brought Home: The Human Rights Bill*, CM 3782, London: HMSO.

——(2002a) *Control of Immigration: Statistics, United Kingdom 2002*, London: HMSO.

——(2002b) *Secure Borders, Safe Haven*, CM 5387, London: HMSO.

——(2004) *Control of Immigration Statistics UK 2003*, Cm 6363, London: Government Statistical Service.

——(2005) *The Five Year Strategy for Asylum and Immigration*, Cm 6472, London: HMSO.

House of Commons (2006) *Judicial Review: A Short Guide to Claims in the Administrative Court*, Research Paper 06/44, London: House of Commons Library.

——(various) *Hansard*.

House of Lords (various) *Hansard*.

Immigration and Nationality Department (1995) *Annual Report*, London: Home Office.

Joint Committee on Human Rights (2002) *Nationality Immigration and Asylum Bill: Further Report*, Twenty-third Report of Session 2001–2, HL 176, HC 1255.

——(2004) *The Children Bill: Nineteenth Report of Session 2003–4*, HL161/HC537, London: HMSO.

——(2007) *Tenth Report of Session 2006–7*, HL 81–1, HC 60–61.

Select Committee on European Legislation (1992) HC97-xiii, London: House of Commons.

——(1995) HC70-xxvi, London: House of Commons.

Social Security Advisory Committee (1994a) *The Housing Benefit and Council Tax Benefit (Amendment) Regulations*, Cm 2483, London: HMSO.

——(1994b) *The Income Related Benefits Schemes (Miscellaneous Amendments) (No. 3) Regulation*, Cm2609, London: HMSO.

——(1996a) *The Social Security (Persons from Abroad) Miscellaneous Amendments Regulations*, Cm 3062, London: HMSO.

——(1996b) *Benefits for Asylum Seekers*, HC81 Session 1995/6, London: HMSO.

Acts of Parliament

Department of Health and Social Security (1948) *National Assistance Act*.

Department for Children Schools and Families (1989) *The Children Act*.

Department of Health (1990) *The National Health Service and Community Care Act*.

Home Office (1971) *Immigration Act*.

——(1993) *Asylum and Immigration Appeals Act*.

——(1996) *Asylum and Immigration Act*.

——(1998) *Human Rights Act*.

——(1999) *Immigration and Asylum Act*.

——(2002) *Nationality Immigration and Asylum Act*.

Speeches

Blair, T. (1999) Beveridge Lecture, in R. Walker, (1999) *Ending Child Poverty*, Bristol: Policy Press, 18 March.

——(2000) 'Values and the Power of the Community', Global Ethics Foundation, Tübingen University, Germany, 30 June.

Blunkett, D. (2003) 'Managing Migration in the 21st Century', Royal Institute for International Affairs, 12 November.

Roche, B. (2000) 'Fight against Clandestine Entry Networks', Paris, 21 July.

Straw, J. (2000) 'Towards a Common Asylum Procedure', European Conference on Asylum, Lisbon, 16 June.

News sources

Guardian Unlimited (2003) 'Blunkett Hits Out at Power of Courts', 21 February.

Guardian (2004) 'Fear Infects Flexible Workplaces', 2 September.

——(2005a) 'Blunkett Plans Clamp on Benefits for Disabled', 15 May.

——(2005b) 'Migrants may be Forced to Send Cash Home', 20 July.

——(2005c) 'Asylum Centres Plagued by Racism and Abuse', 22 July.

——(2006) 'Immigration Shakeup', 8 March.

——(2008a) 'Land of No Return', 13 June.

——(2008b) 'Labour's Handling of Legal Aid Makes a Mockery of Rhetoric on Fairness', 10 March.

Independent (2003) 'Blunkett Forced to Soften Law on Asylum', 19 March.

News.bbc.co.uk (2003) 'UK Discussing UN Asylum Obligations' accessed 24 March 2009.

Cases (in chronological order)

R v Eastbourne [1803] 4 East 103, 102 ER 769 – cited as *Eastbourne*, 1803.

R v Secretary of State for Social Security (SSSS) ex parte *JCWI*, QBD – cited as *JCWI*, QBD.

R V SSSS ex parte *JCWI* [1996] 4 All ER 385 – cited as *JCWI*, 4 All ER 385.

R v Westminster Council ex parte *M* [1997] 1 CCLR 69 – cited as *M* 1 CCLR 69.

R v Westminster Council ex parte *M* [1997] 1 CCLR 85, CA – cited as *M* 1 CCLR 85.

O'Rourke v UK application [2001] ECtHR – cited as *O'Rourke*.

Pretty v UK [2002] 2 FCR 97 ECtHR – cited as *Pretty*.

R v Secretary of State for the Home Department ex parte Q [2003] EWHC 195 (Admin) – cited as *Q*, EWHC.

R v SSHD ex parte Q [2003] EWCA Civ 364 – cited as *Q*, EWCA.

R v SSHD ex parte Q, D, H and others [2003] EWHC 2507 (Admin) – cited as *Q, D, H and others*.

R v SSHD ex parte S, D and T [2003] EWHC 1941 (Admin) – cited as *S, D and T*, EWHC.

R v SSHD ex parte T [2003] EWCA Civ 1285 – cited as *T*, EWCA.

Runa Begum v Tower Hamlets LBC [2003] 1 ALL ER 731 – cited as *Runa Begum*.

Matthews v Ministry of Defence [2003] UKHL 4 – cited as *Matthews*.

R v SSHD ex parte Gezer [2004] EWCA Civ 1730 – cited as *Gezer*.

R v SSHD ex parte Zardasht [2004] EWHC 91 (Admin) – cited as *Zardasht*.

R v SSHD ex parte Limbuela [2004] EWHC 219 (Admin) – cited as *Limbuela*, EWHC.

R v SSHD ex parte Tesema [2004] EWHC 295 (Admin) – cited as *Tesema*.

R v SSHD ex parte Adam [2004] EWHC 354 (Admin) – cited as *Adam*, EWHC.

R v SSHD ex parte Adam, Tesema and Limbuela [2004] EWCA Civ 540 – cited as *Limbuela*, EWCA.

R v SSHD ex parte Adam, Limbuela and Tesema [2005] UKHL 66 – cited as *Adam*, UKHL.

Index

absolute rights: existence 17–18, 145; legal judgements 62–64
'abstract nakedness of being human': concept 3
access to rights: barriers 7–8; citizenship, and 128; 'civic expansion', and 113; control *see* control; differentiated rights 11–12; esteem, and 87–88; naturalised citizens 2; non-citizens 7; sovereignty, and 152–53; stateless persons 2
activism within legal judgements 135–37
Adam case 61–66, 81–83, 84, 99–101
advantaged as target population 112
aliens, naturalised citizens as 2
Arendt, Hannah, right to have rights, on 1–21, 145
Arendt's paradox: meaning 2; overview 1–5, 145
'art of government' *see* 'governmentality'
'as soon as reasonably practicable' requirement (NIAA 2002): evidence against 79; Parliamentary debate on 71–72
asylum: control by nation state 29–30, 91; cosmopolitanism 90; ECHR right to 2; Geneva Convention, and 23, 29; government policy, and 23–43; judicial review applications 70; legal judgements, and 45–67; politicisation 28–30; UK commitment 28–29
asylum seekers: 'bogus' 114–15, 153; changes of status 112–16, 153; contenders, as 118–20; dependants, as 115–16, 153; deviants, as 115–16, 118–20, 153; refugee status 23; source countries 28; target population, as 113–15; welfare rights *see* welfare rights

'asylum shopping', prevention 32–33
axes for plotting: inequality 110–11

'bare life', concept 3
'blitz' campaign against NIAA (section 55) 76–78
'bogus' asylum claims 114–15, 153
book: main themes 1; outline 19–21; propositions 155–57

'citizen', relationship to 'man' 1–2, 3
citizenship *see also* membership rights: access to rights, and 128; basis of 13; basis of inequality, as 109–11; beyond membership rights 7; equality, and 5–7; gender issues 9; human rights, and 3; inclusion and exclusion 7–9; inequality, and 10; models 10; residence, and 7, 10–11; right to have rights, and 3; social class, and 5–7; social integration, and 118; status, and 5–7, 14, 147
civic deficit and protest 14
'civic disabilities' 14
'civic exclusion' and conflict 14
'civic expansion' of rights: judicial review, and 113, 118–19; support for 138
'civic gain' 14
civic stratification: civil repair, and 119; operation of 32; overview 10–12, 13–15, 146–47; UK and 32–36
civic stratification and cosmopolitanism: chapter summary 21, 107, 109; conflict 91–92
civil stratification and target populations: asylum seekers 113–15; overview 109–11; policy design 111–13

civil repair: access to rights, status issues 87–88; civic stratification, and 119; cosmopolitanism, and 87–88; legal judgements, and 68–70

civil repair and role of: courts 85–88; legal profession 76

civil society 72–73; attitudes to asylum 117–18; cosmopolitanism, and 15–17, 125–26; relationship to law 137

civil society and challenges to government policy see also civil repair: chapter summary 20, 68, 86; models 68–70; overview 68–88, 133, 134–35, 137–39, 147–48

claims to rights: role in institutionalisation of rights 131–33; status, and 13

collective identity and entitlement 24–25

'common sense' approach in legal judgements 101–4

communitariansm and cosmopolitanism 4, 24–26

conservatism of legal judgements 135–37

contenders: asylum seekers as 118–20; target populations, as 112

contextualised universalism, concept 9

contraction of rights 116–18

control: access to rights, of 4, 23, 113–14; asylum, of 29–31, 91; civil society challenges see civil society; cosmopolitanism perspective 91–92; welfare rights, of 33–36

cosmopolitan paradigms, interpretation of legal judgements 97

cosmopolitan right: claim 7; hospitality, as 2, 8–9, 151

cosmopolitanisation: characteristics 107–8; distinction from cosmopolitanism 107, 122–23, 127; extent of 107–23; universal rights, and 108, 151

cosmopolitanism: asylum, and 90; civic stratification see civic stratification; civil repair, and 87–88; civil society, and 15–17, 125–26; communitariansm, and 4, 24–26; critique 8–9; dimensions of 125; distinction from cosmopolitanisation 107, 122–23, 127; ECHR as embodiment 95; HRA, and 105; human rights, and 127–29; impact on legal judgements 104–6; migration, and 90; nationalism, and 89; NIAA section 55,

as 105; overview 15–17; perspective on control 91–92; sociological analysis 90–91; theories 107–9; UK policy 95–96

cosmopolitanism and legal judgements: chapter summary 20–21, 21, 89, 105–6, 125, 143–44; overview 89–106, 130

courts see judiciary

Declaration of the Rights of Man and Citizen: focus of rights 2; role of 1

dependants: asylum seekers as 115–16, 153; target population, as 112

deviants: asylum seekers as 115–16, 118–20, 153; target population, as 112

difference, awareness of 9

differentiated rights, overview 9–12

discontent and civic stratification 14

discrimination, experience of 9

'dissatisfaction' and inequality 6–7

Dublin Convention 1990, adoption 32–33

entitlement: awareness of 9; collective identity, and 24–25; plotted against status 110–11; social recognition of 12–15

equality of citizenship 5–7

esteem: access to rights, and 87–88; citizenship, and 13

European Convention of Human Rights (ECHR): adoption 2; asylum right 2; commitment to 29, 95; conceptions 139–40; cosmopolitanism, and 95; embodiment of cosmopolitanism, as 95

European Convention of Human Rights (ECHR) and Article 3: interpretation 148–49; interpretive role of courts 86; NIAA section 55, as to 78–85, 95–96; paradigms of legal judgements 96–98

European Convention of Human Rights (ECHR) and Article 3 legal judgements: application, on 50–67, 140; decisive moments 99–101; role of of judges 131

European Convention of Human Rights (ECHR and: Article 3 threshold: destitution 116; evidence 81–83

European Union (EU): freedom of movement within 4; UK entry 32–33

evidence: against NIAA (section 55) 78–83; from NGOs see non-governmental

organisations (NGOs); role in legal
judgements 101–4; threshold for breach
of Article 3 81–85
exclusion from citizenship 7–9

freedom of movement within EU 4

gender issues and citizenship 9
Geneva Convention: adoption 2; asylum,
and 23, 29; definition of refugee 24;
'illegal' entry 31–32; *non-refoulement*
see *non-refoulement*; operation of
27–28; sovereignty 25; UK policy 28,
29, 39, 95
globalisation: cosmopolitanism, and 15;
within nation state 89–90, 125
government and asylum, overview 23–43
'governmentality': overview 30–32;
process of 11

hospitality: cosmopolitan right, as 2, 8–9,
151; refuge, as 2
Housing and Immigration Group (HIG),
case brought by 74
human rights: citizenship, and 3;
conflicting features 146;
cosmopolitanism, and 15–17, 127–29;
gap between theory and application
17–18; hierarchy 17; indeterminacy 128;
institutionalisation 17, 127–28, 131;
legal judgements, and 18–19, 129–31;
social and political role 129;
sovereignty, and 17–19, 90–91; theories
131–33; trans-nationalism, and 5; wider
principles, and 130
Human Rights Acts (HRA):
cosmopolitanism and 105; impact of
71–72, 135–37, 153–54; legal
judgements prior to 47–50; legal
judgements under 50–67
human rights treaties, adoption 2
humanity as guarantee of rights 2

'illegal' entry: Geneva Convention 31–32;
UK policy 31–32
'imagining' of rights 12
Immigration Act 1971 controls 31–32
Immigration Law Practitioners
Association (ILPA), campaign against
NIAA (section 55) 74
'inalienable rights' of stateless persons 2
inclusion in citizenship 7–9

inequality: axes for plotting 110–11;
citizenship, and 10, 109–11; civic
stratification 10; 'dissatisfaction', and
6–7
inhuman and degrading treatment (IDT):
decisive moments in decision making in
legal judgements 99–101; interpretation,
overview 148–49; judgement whether
140; NGOs evidence 80–81
inhuman and degrading treatment (IDT),
threshold of: decisive moments 100–
101; evidence 84–85
International Committee of Refugees, role
of 27

Janus-face nature of nation state 4, 146
Joint Council for the Welfare of
Immigrants (JCWI), case brought
by 72–73
judicial review (JR): applications for 70;
'civic expansion' of rights, and 113,
118–19; NASS 75–76; NIAA (section 55)
72–85; political process, as 70–71;
procedure 70; role in liberal democracy
70–72; spending on 70
judiciary: conflict with executive 134; role
in democracy 134; role of 85–88, 131,
139, 149, 150–51

Law of Humanity: legal judgements
47–49; principles 95
legal judgements *see also* judicial review
(JR): absolute rights 62–64; activism
within 135–37; *Adam* case 61–66, 81–
83, 84, 99–101; areas of 142–44;
argumentation 139–42; background 45–
47; background legal principles, and
132; chapter summary 19–20, 45–46;
civil repair, and 68–70; civil society
input, and *see* civil society; 'common
sense' approach 101–4; conservatism of
135–37; cosmopolitanism, and *see*
cosmopolitanism; decisive moments in
decision making 99–101; evidence, role
of *see* evidence; HRA, impact of 135–
37; HRA, under 50–67; human rights,
and 18–19, 129–31; influences on 151–
52; justification of 101–4; Law of
Humanity, and 47–49; legal foundation,
overview 148; *Limbuela* case 59–60, 81–
83, 84, 99–101; moral reasonings, and
132; NAA, and 49–50; negative rights

62–64; NIAA (section 55), application of 50–67, 153; overview 45–67; paradigms of interpretation 96–98, 132, 138–39, 146; political context 133–35; politics of 66–67, 130; positive rights 62–64; pre-HRA 47–50; social process, as 131–33; sociological analysis 92–96; status, and 120–22; *Tesema* case 60–61, 81–83, 84, 99–101; third party interventions 83–85; 'wait and see' approach 101–4; welfare rights, and 34–36; *Zardasht* case 59, 81–83, 99–101

legal judgements and application of ECHR:Article 3 50–67, 86; role of of judges 131, 139

legal profession: campaign against NIAA (section 55) 73–85; role of civil repair 76, 147–48, 149–50

liberal democracy: constraints on nation state 27; judicial review, role of 70–72; judiciary, role of 134

Liberty, third party interventions 85

Limbuela case 59–60, 81–83, 84, 99–101

limited rights 17, 145

'man', relationship to 'citizen' 1–2, 3

media and public opinion 117–18

membership, basis of 13

membership rights *see also* citizenship: beyond citizenship 7; citizenship, and 24–25; non-citizens, and 3; operation by nation state 4; status, and 5–7; universal rights, and 4–5

migrants and differentiated rights 11

migration: consolidation of universal rights, and 91–92, 107; cosmopolitanism, and 90; nationalism, and 107

monitoring and rights provision 12

moral reasonings in legal judgements 132, 138–39

nation state: control *see* control; globalisation within 89–90, 125; Janus-face nature 4, 146; liberal democracy constraints on 27; obligations to non-citizens 25–27; operation of membership rights 4; right to have rights, and 25; trans-nationalism, and 8

National Assistance Act (NAA), legal judgements 49–50, 73

National Asylum Support System (NASS): judicial review (JR) 75–76; legal judgements 50–67; operation of 36, 40, 75; third party interventions in legal judgements 85

national paradigm for interpreting legal judgements 97–98

nationalism: concept 133; cosmopolitanism, and 89; migration, and 107

Nationality Immigration and Asylum Act (NIAA), 2002 section 55; ASRP requirement *see* 'as soon as reasonably practicable' requirement (NIAA 2002); 'blitz' campaign 76–78; campaign against 72–85; cosmopolitanism 105; ECHR 78–85, 95–96; evidence against 78–83; judicial review (JR) 72–85; legal judgements 50–67, 153; operation of 115–16; test cases 76–78

naturalised citizens, status as aliens 2

negative rights, legal judgements 62–64

New Labour: asylum policy 36–42, 115–16; policy documents 37–38; safe haven policy 39–40

non-citizens: access to rights 7; membership rights, and 3; nation state obligations to 25–27

non-governmental organisations (NGOs): advocacy role of 137, 139, 147–48, 149–50; campaign against NIAA (section 55) 73–85

non-governmental organisations (NGOs) case brought by: HIG 74; ILPA 74; JCWI 72–73

non-governmental organisations (NGOs) evidence against: ASRP requirement 79; brought by Refugee Action 79, 80; brought by Refugee Council 103; inhuman and degrading treatment 80–81; (section 55) 78–83; role of 102–3, 150

non-governmental organisations (NGOs) third party interventions: legal judgements, in 83–85; Liberty 85; Shelter 84–85, 102–3

non-refoulement: commitment to 2, 23, 28, 29; concept 151; legal judgements 73

'norm entrepreneurs' 12–13

paradigms of interpretation of legal judgements 96–98, 132, 138–39, 146

perpetual peace model (Kant) 2, 8
policy: contraction of rights 116–18; design
   and civic stratification 110–11; design
   and types of target population 112
politics of legal judgements 66–67, 130
positive rights, legal judgements 62–64
post-nationalism, claim of 7–8
protest: civic deficit, and 14; role of 13;
   social shame, against 13
provision of rights, monitoring and
   surveillance, and 12
public opinion and media 117–18

qualified rights 17, 145

recognition: rights as social rights, of
   12–15; social honour, and 13–14;
   struggle for 13
refuge, hospitality as 2
refugee, Geneva Convention definition 24
Refugee Action, evidence: ASRP
   requirement, against 79; inhuman and
   degrading treatment, against 80
Refugee Council, evidence 103
refugee law, development 27–28
refugee status: asylum seekers, and 23;
   otherness of 91, 128
residence and citizenship 7, 10–11
resistance: role of 13; social shame, to 13
right to have rights (Arendt): nation state,
   and 25; overview 1–21

safe haven policy, New Labour's 39–40
Shelter, third party interventions 84–85,
   102–3
'skilled workers', preferential treatment
   11, 37–38
social class and citizenship 5–7
social construction of rights 12–15
social honour and recognition 13–14
social integration and citizenship 118
social shame, resistance to 13
sociological analysis: cosmopolitanism,
   of 90–91; legal judgements, of 92–96
sociological analysis of rights: overview
   145–57; propositions 155–57
sovereign self-determination and universal
   rights 3, 23–24
sovereignty: access to rights 152–53;
   Geneva Convention, and 25; human
   rights, and 17–19, 90–91
stateless persons, access to rights 2

status: access to rights, and 87–88;
   changes to asylum seekers' 112–16;
   citizenship, and 5–7, 14, 147; civic
   stratification, and 32; legal judgements,
   and 120–22; membership rights, and 5–7;
   plotted against entitlement 110–11;
   rights, and 7, 9–10, 13
surveillance: 'governmentality', and 30;
   rights provision, and 12

target populations of policy
   design 112
Tesema case 60–61, 81–83, 84, 99–101
test cases as to NIAA (section 55)
   76–78
third party interventions in legal
   judgements 83–85
trans-nationalism: basis for asylum claim,
   as 25; concept 7; human rights, and 5;
   nation state, and 8

United Kingdom: civic stratification, and
   32–36; civil society challenges to policy see
   civil society; commitment to asylum
   28–29; ECHR, and see European
   Convention of Human Rights (ECHR)
   1953; entry into EU 32–33; 'external
   controls' 31; Geneva Convention, policy
   on 28, 29, 39, 95; HRA see Human Rights
   Acts (HRA); 'illegal' entry, policy on 31–
   32; Immigration Act 1971 controls 31–32;
   legal judgements 45–67; legal judgements
   as to welfare rights 34–36; NASS see
   National Asylum Support System (NASS);
   policy asylum, chapter summary 19;
   policy and cosmopolitanism 95–96; visas,
   use of 31
Universal Declaration of Human Rights
   (UDHR), adoption 2
universal personhood 7
universal rights: claim 7; classification
   145; consolidation, conflict with
   migration 91–92, 107;
   cosmopolitanisation, and 108, 151;
   membership rights, and 4–5; origin of
   concept 1; sovereign
   self-determination, and 3, 23–24
universalism: application of principles 25;
   world government, and 4

variable rights and civic stratification 32
visas, UK use of 31

'wait and see' approach in legal
    judgements 101–4
welfare rights: asylum seekers 11; control
    of 34–36; New Labour policy 36–42;
    theory of governance 37

'world citizen', concept 125
'world culture', concept 25
world government and universalism 4

Zardasht case 59, 81–83, 99–101